PIANO LESSONS

ACKNOWLEDGEMENTS

Thank you to Noel Sanders, University of Technology, Sydney, for suggesting this book. Thank you also to Jodi Brooks, Toby Miller, New York University, Roger Horricks, Auckland University, New Zealand, Susan Dermody who gave us the title, Belinda Hilton at Village Roadshow, Jan Chapman Productions, Peter Galvin, Judy Robinson at Buena Vista for her help with the stills, John Libbey, and to Raymond X. Devitt for his encouragement. Thanks also to those people at UTS and Auckland University who supported the early stages of this book, and to the numerous people at US and UK universities who helped us.

We are grateful to our contributors for remaining helpful and enthusiastic to the end.

Felicity Coombs and Suzanne Gemmell

PIANO LESSONS

APPROACHES TO THE PIANO

FELICITY COOMBS AND SUZANNE GEMMELL

SOUTHERN SCREEN CLASSICS: 1
SERIES EDITOR: NOEL KING

John Libbey
LONDON · PARIS · ROME · SYDNEY

Cataloguing in Publication Data

Piano Lessons: approaches to *The Piano*

1. Piano (Motion picture). I. Coombes, Felicity. II. Gemmell, Suzanne.
(Southern screen classics; 1)

791.4372

ISBN: 1 86462 035 8 (Paperback)

Published by

John Libbey & Company Pty Ltd, Level 10, 15–17 Young Street, Sydney,
NSW 2000, Australia.
Telephone: +61 (0)2 9251 4099 Fax: +61 (0)2 9251 4428
e-mail: jlsydney@mpx.com.au

John Libbey & Company Ltd, 13 Smiths Yard, Summerley Street,
London SW18 4HR, England
John Libbey Eurotext Ltd, 127 avenue de la République,
92120 Montrouge, France.
John Libbey at C.I.C. Edizioni s.r.l., via Lazzaro Spallanzani 11, 00161 Rome, Italy.

Printed in Malaysia by Kum-Vivar Printing Sdn. Bhd., 48000 Rawang, Selangor Darul Ehsan

CONTENTS

PREFACE

ane Campion's *The Piano* arrived at a time of renewed interest in the Australian film industry and in fact did much to further it. The critical acclaim received by *The Piano* at Cannes and its world-wide box office success was followed up by winning three Academy Awards. Global interest was assured for the Australian film industry. *Strictly Ballroom* and *Romper Stomper* had already been recognised for bringing a brash new personality to Australian film. *Priscilla* was to follow shortly after. It was certainly a time of change in the style of contemporary Australian film.

Our view of ourselves was changing from a past of historical remembrance films which had attempted to identify our national heritage or compensate for a lack thereof. Films such as *Gallipoli*, *The Lighthorsemen* and *Breaker Morant* told of wars we had fought, *We of the Never, Never* showed us settlement in the outback of Australia, and *My Brilliant Career* all subdued us with the trope of colonialism. *The Piano* was an attempt to view colonialism but informed by post-colonialism.

This book is designed to explore the reception of the film in the areas of film and cultural studies. As *The Piano* quickly became a topic of hot debate, critics and movie-goers adored and deplored it, but discussed it none the less. Whether viewed as a psychoanalytic, post-colonial, romance or feminist analysis, everyone seemed to articulate differing interpretations. So, we have gathered these essays together from a broad field of perspectives, and rich in analysis, for further study.

The film departs from the realist traditions of colonial film through Jane Campion's quirky camera direction. She gives us images of a teacup and a wedding veil that became representative of a transported imperial culture and a piano that shifts from 'monstrous beauty to an emblem of death'. Stuart Dryburgh, the director of photography, was filming in pockets and filming a piano in the oddest of circumstances, with as much time given to the piano as to any central character. The period films of Merchant-Ivory were never like this.

Perhaps it is the contemporary mix of genres and narrative deviations that causes all the fuss around this film. The audience has expectations of the genre they engage with and *The Piano* clearly falls into several categories. It is a romance, it is historically placed, and it has a great deal of cultural significance. The style of the film indicates both an historical romance and a contemporary romance in an historical setting.

The strained moral codes of the subjects disrupt the sensitive narrative norms of cinema. Frequently, writers found its haunting attributes more befitting the areas of melodrama particularly the gothic melodrama with its workings of pity and fear and its obvious connection through the mute heroine. Emotion and expressive outbursts supported by symbolism are melodramatic codifications on which the film relies heavily. Strangely, within different segments of the film, audience identification of the villain and the persecuted becomes interchangeable between Baines, Stewart, and Ada. This has created many dynamic interpretations of the text.

The film also invokes a broad range of post-colonial discourses. We understand post-colonialism to encompass the period from the first moment of colonisation up to the present day, and we position the film as a post-colonial text because of its many referents to New Zealand's colonial past and also its contemporary debates over both national identity and the indigenous culture's pursuit of self determination. The contributors examine both the film's resonances of imperialist discourse that speak through the representation of New Zealand's colonial history and its bold reworking of the dominant subject positions afforded to the central characters – in particular Ada McGrath. Almost every essay discusses the relationship between the oppressor and the oppressed, each with a different approach to uncovering the ideology that informs the film.

Post-colonial themes are represented both in the narrative development and in the representation of the 1850s settler colony. The story relies on the imperial version of New Zealand's settler history, tracing the process of transportation, acquisition and transformation of the land; reliant from the outset on the possibility of displacing the heroine half way across the world to take her position in the pioneering project. This colonial narrative is established only to be disrupted via the narrative machinations of romance, whereby desire transcends the unequal relations of power and, albeit violently, the colony releases the heroine to pursue her fortunes with her lover. Such an ending is a testament to the problematic terrain that the film must negotiate in order to resolve the converging post-colonial themes it employs en route.

Response to the film included reaction to the film's portrayal of New Zealand's colonial history. Much of the excitement centred on the notion of national myth making at a time when white New Zealanders were re-evaluating their national identity in the context of renewed Maori claims for social justice. The film's characterisation of the colonisers and the absence of a strong voice for the colonised came under scrutiny. Of equal concern was the film's failure to represent New Zealand's race history, relegating it to the mystical sphere of a sacred time in pre-history.

Images of the land also featured prominently as a vehicle with which to explore the re-presentation of New Zealand's cultural history. *The Piano* certainly challenges the myth making of the preceding body of Australian films that retold the foundation stories of pioneer settlement and expansion. It engages with this colonial tale with the clear intention to rewrite it and, despite its many successes, comes under close scrutiny for its failures

An essay by Laurence Simmons was included for its sheer breadth of understanding of the role that images of the land have played in the formation of New Zealand's national identity and the particular role that the land played in *The Piano*. Simmons explores the ambiguities of the word landscape itself, tracing the history of the conventions of representation of the land to argue that Campion's vision of colonial New Zealand falls squarely within the ambit of colonialist modes. Simmons touches on the film's referents to the literary genres of the Western and the Romance, a point that is taken up in earnest by Bridget Orr. Orr's essay concentrates on the film genres of the Western and the Romance, recalling the implication of the film in the production of national identity. Using such cinematic origin myths as Griffith's "Birth of a Nation" as a point of departure, she compares *The Piano* to a range of Australian and New Zealand films that narrate the nation. Central to this investigation is the role of the male pioneering subject in these films and *The Piano*'s feminist de-centring of the Pakeha male pioneering subject.

Though the film is heralded as a powerful feminist exploration of nineteenth century sexuality, it has come under intense examination for its ambivalent treatment of race and race history, issues relating to the peculiar inflection afforded to the national character of New Zealand in Miramax's packaging of the film, and the conflation of nationalism and colonialism encountered in the process. The colonial narrative of origin is exposed as the appropriation and enclosure of landscape as the first and only expression of civilisation.

The many minds unsettled by this haunting film were fuelled again by the director as the stories arising from the film continued to grow. Following the publication of the scripts, a novel co-authored by Jane Campion and Kate Pullinger was published to give further insight to an audience that still had many questions. *Piano Lessons* differs by questioning and interrogating the film as a text, relying on the articulation of the many different voices of the contributors to assert an overview of the film as both a cinematic achievement and a cultural product.

We have been keenly aware of the position that this book itself occupies, as yet another text that has been produced about *The Piano* and we have deliberately sought contributors from Australia and New Zealand, and expatriate New Zealanders, in order to draw criticism from the same cultural map that the film hails from. In doing so we have managed to capture the local particularities of the colonial tropes at work in the film.

The contributors convey a mixture of sentiments regarding the film, some critical of the politics of representation employed in the film and some enamoured by its visual and musical tropes. An entire volume could have been devoted to this one film – a testament to the film's power to inspire debate. Though much more has been written about *The Piano*, herein lies an authoritative collection of what we consider to be the film's most compelling elements – how the film stakes its claim as a melodrama, its post-colonial biases, feminist ploys, psychoanalytic themes and modes of self-representation.

Felicity Coombs and Suzanne Gemmell

CONTRIBUTIONS

An essay received from **Ruth Barcan** and **Madeleine Fogarty** during the early stages of gathering together this collection developed a lively argument around the many voices which have been generated by the film. Different voices played an important role in the preparation of this book and they were never more apparent than in the case of feminist readings of the film. A great divide in those feminist readings produced multiple and divergent views emerging from the film's audience. That no one voice can articulate these feminist concerns is illustrated in this account. The sheer volume of comment circulated around this film is exemplified by Ruth Barcan and Madeleine Fogarty addressing various reading and speaking positions available to articulate reactions to the film. From a self conscious feminist position, they style the various models of reading the film as constituting a range of performances – each with their own social, institutional and discursive register and each with its own emotional and intellectual tensions and effects. Specific models which come under consideration include *The Piano* as a Feminist and feminine film, the erotics of violence, the film as failed narrative or as myth, and its uneasy positioning within the genre of the Romance.

Neil Robinson writes of two films, *The Piano* and *Letter From an Unknown Woman* (Max Ophuls, 1948). As a point of departure he uses figurations of women writing in the two films mapping their understandings of and relationships to women writers and women's writings in order to argue for a reconsideration of how melodramatic structures operate within the woman's film genre. Arguing against Mary Ann Doane, his ultimate claim is that woman's films do not follow melodramatic conventions to conservative ends. Whereas melodramas usually enact violent ejections of characters to threaten the stability of the social order in order to restore its stability, *The Piano* and *Letter* side with the ejected characters (both male and female) in order to criticise both the repressiveness of social orders and the violent means they use to maintain their stabilities. A main point of analysis, the relationship between women's bodies and their efforts to write and speak, argues that a trade-off economy operates in the films in which the women are made to sacrifice their bodies in order to productively articulate. The narrational strategies of the film are examined for the degree of control the women assert over the storytelling. In *The Piano*, music, like letter-writing in *Letter*, is a force which alternatively motivates and exceeds the narration – it is one among the competing narrational forces. In both films, the efforts of the women to write may be violently interrupted, but ultimately have a supernatural charge which lingers eerily – like a ghost of the sacrificed woman – in the minds of the viewers. For Robinson, that supernatural power of women's writing in the films points to a need to reject a formulation of the woman's film as a genre which endorses the melodramatic expulsion of disruptive figures.

Another author from NYU is **Richard Allen**, whose paper offers a close psychoanalytic reading of the representation of the heroine and more specifically her muteness, examining how her character operates in the film. Allen identifies ways in which various subject positions are constructed in the narrative, addressing themes such as the conception of the self, the conflict between love and power, and the unconscious. In an informed analysis of the film, Richard Allen provides a comprehensive rationale for the 'elective mutism' of Ada McGrath. He introduces the relation of muteness to the Gothic melodrama and explains how Jane Campion subverts and transforms the conventions of melodrama in her subject positioning of Ada.

Kirsten Moana Thompson, based at New York University, focuses on the soundtrack and how the narrative movement between the three central melodies emblematises the conflicts and struggles between different parts of Ada's interiority. Thompson investigates how the thematic importance of these melodies functions as aural emblems evoking the physical and psychological confinements in which Ada is placed. Ada, who had no voice, produced a strong representation of her self through her piano. The audience engages with both the sight of the musician and the sound of the music through the melodies used on the film soundtrack and played by Ada. Thompson builds on the idea that the music, sound and silence are riddled with allegorical resonances.

A different approach to the representation of Ada is **Felicity Coombs**' essay, which reads the narrative framing of Ada through a relationship formed by feminine and colonial representations imbued in the physical body of her piano. Here, the distinct prominence of the piano uncovers the social positioning not only of women in the nineteenth century, but also its social role: how the piano functions in the context of this film 'as a vehicle for the symbolic representation of the close link between women and the Victorian domestic culture'. The essay also points to the sonoric connection of their bodies teasing out an aural world of interaction between Ada, the piano, and Baines.

Stella Bruzzi writes of the complex sensual and sexual relationship of both costume and body in *The Piano*. Under Campion's direction, the camera subverts the scopophilic gaze from the male subject creating instead an interrelationship between an active female subject and the feminine sense of touch. Bruzzi evaluates the unconventional portrayal of the female heroine, Ada, as instating a female subjectivity. This chapter was previously published in Screen36:3, Autumn 1995.

Lynda Dyson skilfully argues that the film is so preoccupied with upholding Ada's bourgeois femininity and securing her fate in the colonial culture that it glosses over the history of Maori resistance. She locates her argument in the contemporary post-colonial anxieties over New Zealand's past, teasing out the primitivist discourse in the film that positions the Maori collectively outside of culture and history. This chapter previously appeared in Screen 36:3, Autumn 1995.

Historical uses of landscape to construct a vision of nation are the theme of a paper by Laurence Simmons. By exploring the landscape of the film, Simmons traces the history of New Zealand landscape, weaving 'a network of textual invocations' in colonial art and literature traditions of both the European and colonial environment. Analysis of these images provides a departure point for an examination of themes of cultural nationalism in the earlier stages of his argument. He interrogates colonialism's discursive practices through moments of irony, the fractures and occlusions of its formal syntax, and the psychoanalytic paradigms of its discourses of the body in opposition to a patriarchal order. He argues that ultimately *The Piano* re-narrativises the strategies of previous attitudes to the land where only the post-contact European possesses the ability to enunciate and represent the 'other'.

Anna Neill argues that the film gives a voice to a national identity untroubled by Maori claims for sovereignty, as the Maori do not exist in the historical space of the colonising culture but rather are frozen in a sacred time prior to colonisation. She draws on other texts that attempt to write difference out of the modern myths of nation and to replace it with the notion of a shared relationship to the past, one that mourns the loss of an unrecoverable Maori history. In doing so, she exposes the selective version of post contact history that *The Piano* portrays.

Another exacting account of the formation of nationhood in *The Piano* comes from **Bridget Orr** in her essay 'Birth of a Nation: From Utu to The Piano'. A common inclusion of the colonialist genre, the Western is placed alongside the Romance to explore the production and reception of *The Piano* as a revisionist reworking of the two genres – just as current Hollywood films often rework established generic codes. Bridget Orr recalls the implication of film in the construction of national identities. Taking the role of such cinematic origin myths as Griffith's *Birth of a Nation* as a starting point, she compares several films to explore the parody of these generic conventions in *The Piano*. Central to this investigation is the apparent decentring of the (Pakeha) male pioneering subject.

Claire Corbett offers a richly personal account of working as second assistant editor on *The Piano*. Her story unfolds both as a look behind the scenes at the unfamiliar world of the feature film cutting room, the technical processes and work practices, and also the rigid structures at play in the hierarchy of a film crew. Her paper reveals much about the nature of lower echelons of film work, as well as film lore – well understood by crew members but rarely made explicit.

AUTHORS

Madeleine Fogarty is a Ph.D candidate at Melbourne University. She completed her Masters thesis on The Phallus in Psychoanalysis and Hard-Core Pornography in 1994 at Berkeley and Melbourne University.

Ruth Barcan teaches in the School of Humanities at the University of Western Sydney, Hawkesbury. She is currently researching a cultural study of Nudity in Australia.

Kirsten Moana Thompson, B.A., M.A.(Hons) Auckland University, (English) Ph.D New York University, (Cinema Studies), Co-editor with Terri Ginsberg of *Perspectives on German Cinema*, G.K. Hall, 1997. Author of "Ah Love!; Pepé le Pew, Narcissism and Cats in the Casbah" in *Reading The Rabbit; Explorations in Warner Bros. Animation*, New Jersey: Rutgers, 1998.

Richard Allen is Associate Professor and Chair of Cinema Studies at New York University. He is author of *Projecting Illusion: Film Spectatorship and the Impression of Reality*, New York: Cambridge University Press, 1995, and co-editor (with Murray Smith) of *Film, Theory, and Philosophy*, Oxford: The Clarendon Press, 1997. An earlier version of this essay was presented at Washington Square Institute for Psychotherapy and Mental Health, New York and published in their in-house journal *Issues in Psychoanalytic Psychotherapy*, 17:2, 1995.

Neil Robinson is a Ph.D. candidate in English at the University of Chicago and a graduate of Rice University.

Felicity Coombs is an Honours graduate of the University of Technology, Sydney. She is currently directing a one hour television documentary.

Stella Bruzzi is a lecturer in film at Royal Holloway, University of London. She has published widely in the areas of cultural studies and film and is a regular contributor to the film journal *Sight and Sound*. Her book, *Undressing Cinema: Clothing and Identity in the Movies* was published by Routledge in 1997.

Laurence Simmons is a lecturer in Film and Television studies at the University of Auckland. He has written various critical articles on New Zealand film and the visual arts and is currently television columnist for the popular culture magazine 'Pavement'. His most recent publications are: "Broken Barrier: Mimesis and Mimicry" and "Livin' and Lovin; in New Zealand's First Film Musical", both on the work of pioneer filmmaker John O'Shea. At present he is co-writing a book that examines New Zealand film in its historical and social context.

Bridget Orr is an Assistant Professor in the Department of English at Fordham University, New York. She has published essays on post-colonial literature and culture and is currently completing a book on Restoration drama.

Anna Neill is an Assistant Professor in the English Department at the University of Kansas. She is the author of several articles on eighteenth-century literature and political culture, and is currently writing a book on representations of national sovereignty in eighteenth-century discovery literature.

Lynda Dyson teaches Media and Cultural Studies at Middlesex University, London, UK. She has recently completed a Ph.D called 'Traces of Identity: Constructions of white ethnicity in settler colonies'.

Claire Corbett is a Sydney writer currently working on her first novel. 'Cutting it Fine: Notes on The Piano' was first published in Re:Publica, Issue 1. She has also published "Fixating" in Picador New Writing 3, "When We Had Wings" in Re:Publica Issue 4 (which was also broadcast on radio), "Inferno in Civic" published in Splash, a Penguin anthology.

1

GENDER, PSYCHOANALYSIS, MELODRAMA

CHAPTER 1

PERFORMING THE PIANO

RUTH BARCAN AND MADELEINE FOGARTY

The Piano was remarkable for the quantity and quality of debate that it sparked, both in public and in private. While all major release films arouse a healthy level of discussion, the lively debate that surrounded the release of *The Piano* was quite unusual – and itself worthy of discussion. Very particular and striking 'Piano discourses' came into circulation; the film seemed both to crystallise and problematise established generic categories of public reception. We both clearly remember having conversations that followed remarkably similar lines; indeed, these conversations often seemed to be having us.

We regarded these conversations as comprising a series of performances of *The Piano*, many of which could be considered feminist. Thinking of these conversations in this way became a way of examining our own anxieties about the film itself and about the kinds of reading and speaking positions that were available to articulate our ambiguous reactions to the film. We are not going to do a performance of *The Piano* here, if a performance means a single coherent 'interpretation'. Rather, we will pursue the *series*, floating between media publicity and reviews of the film, and our own academically situated and produced reading frameworks. The different performances overlap and overlay each other, and we are interested in their intersections as well as in the gaps between and within them. In other words, each of the following performances of *The Piano* allows certain 'truths' to be told about the film, while simultaneously foreclosing other possibilities. We are 'playing *The Piano*,' as a multitude of overlapping, yet conflicting, interpretations. We choose the term 'performance' to describe the various acts of speaking about *The Piano*, not merely as a play on words that describes our experiences of animated conversation about the film, but also to situate our anxieties within debates about the performativity of language.

For us, one of the key performances of *The Piano* was at a dinner party with other (female) feminists. It was a heated debate about the merits of the film, in particular about the notorious 'bargain' struck by Ada and Baines, by which she is to earn her beloved piano back through a series of erotic transactions. The argument was animated, passionate even, but curiously stifling, as the terms of the debate seemed to be set out in advance. In brief, it kept structuring itself as a false polarity between those who admired the film and those whose reactions were more ambivalent. Ambivalence was interpreted as opposition – it seemed one was either for the film or against it. Our own reservations seemed performable only as a 'set piece,' especially the kind of performance we will deliver below as a *con forza* rendition. To try and escape this false polarity, we could only endlessly repeat the tale of our own seduction, another set piece.

We recall this debate as simultaneously engaging and painful: engaging, because we felt the pull of different reading positions; painful, because we felt the tension between them, and furthermore because our feminist concerns were articulable only in this rather stock way – a performance that one could choose either to indulge in or, increasingly, to avoid. We risked becoming types, even to ourselves. These anxieties were subtended by doubts about the possibility, and increasingly the desirability, of discovering any one reading position able to subsume or transcend the set performances. What was most unsettling was our will to silence, which seemed to be related to the performative aspect of the whole argument. On many occasions we remained as silent as Ada on realising that our concerns would be received with hostility.

These issues resonate for us with a problematic discussed by Tania Modleski in her book *Feminism Without Women* – appropriately enough, in the chapter titled 'The Scandal of the Mute Body'. In this chapter, Modleski argues that 'a fully politicised feminist criticism' has always been performative, in the sense that it has aimed not merely to ascertain or explain already constituted meanings or subjectivities, but to bring new ones into being.[1] Feminism, then, aims not merely to participate in already existing communities but also to transform them. Modleski draws on Sartre's concept of 'committed' or 'engaged' writing[2] in order to argue that feminist writing is not merely performative but committed. Committed writing, in Sartre's sense, presupposes and has confidence in the freedom of the reader. Since feminist writing both assumes a degree of freedom in its readers (otherwise they would not be able to engage with it) and also promises freedom as the goal for them, it is, suggests Modleski, both performative and utopian.[3] Modleski remains hostile to poststructuralism, considering it to preclude Sartrean-style commitment. Her utopian project is to save the possibility of referential language for a feminist future when the traditionally mute body, the mother, will be given the same access to the names – language and speech – that men have enjoyed.[4]

Although we cannot concur with Modleski's analysis, insofar as she posits the possibility of a rhetoric that guarantees a particular future, we are sympathetic to the drive behind her analysis, and we find her arguments useful for articulating a difficulty that we faced when speaking about *The Piano*. In our performances of various set pieces about *The Piano*, we came to feel like Don Juan, whom Modleski also discusses, when we wanted to feel a little more like her version of Sartre, transmitting a dream or a vision to others,[5] or at least allowing a dream to be envisaged. To clarify, it was not that we wanted to convince others of the truth of our reading(s). Indeed, we remain unconvinced that we *have* any one reading of the film, for readings are things one does rather than has, and doing is always contextual. Rather, we wanted to be able to perform our ambivalence without being positioned as speaking within what Meaghan Morris has termed the "awesome genre" of nagging.[6] In the context of everyday social interchange, we felt the lack of some readily available discursive paradigm that would grant us *some* confidence that the terms of debate, if not our opinions, which were themselves quite labile, might be shared.

This piece represents our attempt to articulate a position on *The Piano*, or rather, to execute an academic performance of *The Piano*. In choosing to execute multiple readings, we are not wanting to fall into an uncommitted pluralism. For we not only acknowledge our inevitable complicity with any readings we might problematise or reject, but also recognise their attractions. In our final *rubato* performance, we try to bring the series to a close with foreclosure, recognising that this performance has been shaped, inspired and constrained by all those that precede it.

1. MYSTERIOSO: THE PIANO AS 'FEMININE' FILM

An obvious rendition of *The Piano* is as a 'feminine' film, the expression of an essentialised, romanticised femininity. For this reading we draw on the film's visual imagery and its key tropes, as well as on the mythologies surrounding Campion herself. It is possible to see *The Piano* as a woman's film – seductive, fantastic and mysteriously erotic. First, the film concentrates on a woman and her daughter, placing them in alien landscapes that academic feminism has long been taught to read as 'feminised' – the antipodes, the beach, the dark forest, even underwater. These hostile landscapes function as prisons or as obstacles to be crossed, in a way that Teresa de Lauretis, for example, considers to be paradigmatic: the feminine position is seen as a mythical obstacle, or simply, as the space in which the movement of narrative discourse occurs.[7] The visual motif of the entwined branches of the dark forest, reiterated in the cage of Ada's hooped petticoat, or the memorable scenes of the struggle through thick, sucking mud, with shoes and dresses gradually succumbing, can certainly be read in this way. Many reviewers likened the film's effective creation of a striking emotional and physical landscape to the casting of a spell. Campion herself employed this image:

> ". . . for me, the film does weave a magic, it does have a spell. But every screening is very different".[8]

The weaver of this spell is a goddess, an angel, with the power gently and lovingly to manipulate her cast, softening even that hardened tough guy, Harvey Keitel:

> "Jane is a goddess," says Harvey Keitel, making the compliment seem less extravagant, more reasoned, than it might from other lips.[9]

This became quite a common trope.[10] Many commentators, including Campion herself, saw the film as the descendent of a line of turbulent Romantic and post-Romantic female writers, especially the Brontës and Emily Dickinson. Kerryn Goldsworthy, for example, detected resonances with *Jane Eyre*, especially in Ada's almost sacrificial wounding.[11] In many reviews, speculation about aesthetic genesis was linked discursively to a mythologising of motherhood. Images of gestation and birth abounded in discourse surrounding the film, aided by the well-publicised details of Campion's own life, occasionally spilling over into excess:

> Over its gestation period of a number of years (since 1986) Campion's script like good wine or cheese has matured and fermented into a richly layered, immaculately detailed blueprint.[12]

Some of the most touching visual images forming part of the epiphenomena around the film were the scenes of both Campion's and Hunter's obvious affection for the young Anna Paquin. It seems fitting, then, that it was by and large the female participants who received recognition at the Academy awards.

2. CON SPIRITO: THE PIANO AS FEMINIST FILM

The Piano can also be read as a feminist film; indeed, many reviews articulated an overlap between the categories 'feminine' and 'feminist.' Deborah Mandie, for example, immediately followed her evocation of Campion's auratic feminine presence with the assertion that "Campion is also a guru for feminist film makers".[13] The production team comprised an unusually high number of women in key roles, who assumed financial and managerial roles in addition to 'artistic' ones – producer, director, screenwriter, editor, costume designer.[14] It was also the first film directed by a woman to win at Cannes.[15] Of course, *The Piano* can also be considered feminist on thematic grounds, since it focuses on a strong heroine who scorns the marriage arranged for her, and who demonstrates a "steadfast refusal to submit to her husband's will."[16] Her muteness can be read as a strategy of protest, and it can be argued that the bargain with Baines is an act of her own will, a stubborn determination to win back her rights.

Likewise, *The Piano* is an unusual mainstream film in that it focuses on a woman without objectifying her. Moreover, it works hard to be aesthetically beautiful, and focuses on female sexual desire. Many women have argued that the film gives female viewers opportunities for erotic identification that are rare in contemporary mainstream cinema. Indeed, in our heated discussions about the film, in order to prove that we were not immune to these possibilities, and in order to avoid stereotypically feminist (self)constructions, we commonly found ourselves protesting too much – vigorously asserting that Yes, we had found the film erotic. But the false polarity of erotic enjoyment and critical displeasure was difficult to dismantle.

3. CON FORZA: THE PIANO AND AN EROTICS OF VIOLENCE

In August, 1993, the Coalition Against Sexual Violence Propaganda newsletter carried a two paragraph review of *The Piano*, with the first paragraph condemning it as sexist and the second declaring it to be racist. The writer lamented what she saw as the film's shift away from a depiction of two strong women towards a focus on an aggressive and coercive male sexuality. Even more bluntly, Lisa Sarmas replied to a review by Kerryn Goldsworthy that had highlighted the ambiguity of the transaction, by contending that the relationship between Baines and Ada constituted, quite simply, rape.[17] Few interpretations of the film were as direct as this one, but nonetheless, many critiques of the film focused on the bargain as an eroticised and glamorised sexual harassment. Clearly, since the piano functions not only as Ada's sole means of self-expression – a replacement for the voice she has chosen to forswear – but also metonymically as an extension of herself, the bargain with Baines is a compromise made to win back her own speaking voice. Campion herself made it clear that Ada's muteness functioned as a device for increasing the importance of the piano and therefore for rendering the sexual compromise more significant. That is, the importance of the piano necessitated the muteness and not the other way around:

> "I wanted to create a strong relationship with the piano – she compromises herself so much for it, it would have to be something really big to make her do that. So I felt if she couldn't speak, the piano would mean so much more to her; it would be her voice. And it did have useful repercussions throughout the movie....Makes it sexier, too: if you can't talk things out, you have to do it in other ways..."[18]

Ada is sexier because she can't talk, a sexiness which Campion expressed in terms of traditionally gendered polarities of thinking and feeling, human and animal, male and female:

> "The film is also very much about love and sex. . . her not talking is more animally, you know. It takes you back into a feeling world rather than a thinking world'.[19]

Although some critics did find that "sound and silence [were in] perfect harmony",[20] others were disturbed by the models of desire at work here. Interestingly, the same device, Ada's muteness, was able to be read both as fashionably feminist, for example, by Neil Jillett, and as alarmingly conservative. In terms of the feminist reading positions we are concerned with here, though, one of the most troubling things about the combination of erotics and coercion was that it opened up dichotomies that we would want to see as false. Either politics had to yield to erotics and aesthetics or one had to acknowledge that the powerful eroticism of these scenes depended on asymmetrical power relations, and repudiate pleasure as a result.

The question of eroticised violence is even more interesting in terms of the meta-discourse surrounding the film. For it is not only Ada who cannot speak that complex desire. The discursive conventions of reviewing require that the richly ambiguous emotional and erotic experience of a film, with all the complex regimes of desires that it enacts, be translated into a concise linear narrative summary. So how can the nature of the relationship between Ada and Baines be articulated? In almost every review we saw,[21] language fails at this crucial moment. The bargain was a pressure point under which language either all too clearly named its object, freezing it corpse-like into one deathly meaning or else cracked under the strain and resisted naming names.

The CASVP review is an example of the first case. In this account, the bargain is an act performed by men upon passive women; the syntax mirrors this as it leaves the women behind:

> "Initially the characters of Ada and Flora are representative of strong

women and a wonderful relationship exists between the two. As it progresses they are pushed aside and the film becomes one, not about them, but rather male sexuality which, for a change(?), equals manipulation, control, competition, jealousy, power inequity and violence. Ada's husband (Stewart) and his neighbour (Baines), who subsequent to his sexually violent 'bargains' becomes her lover and rescuer, share the 'spotlight' of manipulator, controller and aggressor at different times."[22]

Conversely, the *Farrago* reviewer, intent on reading the film as a feminine/feminist artwork, concentrates on "the unique secrecy of the bond between women"; her only mention of the arrangement that forms the basis of the plot is to note that,

"Eventually love and the strings of Ada's passions intrude into the silent world of music and mother and daughter".[23]

Another reviewer was more candid about the nature of the transaction, but strained the plot in order to read the arrangement as initiated by Ada:

"Disabled and disempowered Ada initiates the first of a series of bargains when she asks their neighbour, well travelled but ill-educated seaman George Baines (Harvey Keitel), to transport the piano up to the house; in a typical economically rationalist move Stewart asserts his will once more, exchanging the piano with Baines for a tract of land. These economic transactions take a different turn when Baines suggests that Ada can earn her piano back in exchange for 'lessons' (each has a different kind in mind). This idea of sexual barter is hardly novel....but Campion's richly layered script is steeped in psychological, erotic and poetic dimensions; how effective is the omission of dialogue in these powerfully erotic scenes."[24]

Given that most critical interest or contention revolved around the question of Ada's agency, we find it interesting that many reviewers had recourse to the passive mood to recount the details of the bargain. Moreover, many of the descriptions of the arrangement slipped into a telling ambiguity. For Lynden Barber, Baines

"*is allowed* to take the piano back to his cabin in exchange for some land. Under the guise of giving him 'piano lessons', Ada sets about winning it back via a deal Baines will later abjure for turning her into a 'whore'. (our emphasis)"[25]

Just who instigates the arrangement and just who or what is "turning her into a whore" remains an interesting grammatical ambiguity. A similar slippage occurred in Neil Jillett's account of the deal. Jillett, one of the few newspaper reviewers to be quite hostile to the film, describes the arrangement as follows:

> "Stewart points out to his wife that she can still use the piano by giving Baines music lessons. Baines agrees to this and soon offers to return the piano if Ada will submit to a rising scale of sexual demands. Her agreement leads to a rather unsettled atmosphere in the fledgling settlement, then to an act of betrayal and some violence."[26]

In the logical ellipsis between the first and second sentences, the author of the plot remains ambiguous. The final sentence is also elliptical – partly, of course, to protect crucial plot details in accordance with the review form. But the preponderance of nouns also obviates the need to clarify actants, action and agency. In only one case that we saw was the refusal to specify these things self-conscious – when Kerryn Goldsworthy wrote,

> "....land is offered for a piano; and a piano is offered in instalments, for something that doesn't really have a name".[27]

In most of the reviews, though, the intricacies of Ada's and Baines' relationship were unselfconsciously unspeakable.

Clearly, our purpose here is not to suggest that one or other of these readings is correct but to indicate that the review narrative and, by extension, any such renarrativising process, requires certain emphases, omissions and decisions to make it cohere within the terms of any one interpretive schema. Equally clearly, much is at stake every time any one of us performs such an operation. If it is true that women have learnt to read cultural products in a kind of oscillation between a masculine and feminine subject position – to use Mulvey's slightly different metaphor, in a kind of psychological transvestism[28] – then executing a feminist critique may involve both pain and pleasure. But psychological structures of desire and pleasure are also a question of disciplinary and discursive formations, what Janice Radway has called an "interpretive community".[29] For example, when viewing the film, and when discussing it with friends, we both wished that we had been able simply not to notice the issue of coercion, since it intruded into one kind of viewing pleasure, but our disciplinary trainings rendered this unlikely. In this instance, the analytical tropes and methodological training associated with a certain kind of academic feminism served to foreground certain textual features above others.

While belonging to such a community may sometimes mean that one's reading(s) take on an oppositional resonance, this is not always the case. To execute a feminist critique may certainly be a matter of reading against a textual grain, but it may also well mean reading *with* the grain of an academic interpretive community. Just what is at stake in situating oneself in this reading community depends on any number of things, including questions of formations within certain disciplinary and institutional contexts. For one of us, critiquing models of desire such as those arguably at work in *The Piano* meant critiquing the reading positions through which she had learnt to enjoy and analyse artistic products – a new critical framework still powerful, if no longer dominant, in many Australian institutions. Such a resistive reading thus necessarily involves both pain and pleasure. Pleasure, in "mak[ing] public our otherwise private discontents",[30] and finding them to be shared by others; pain, in repudiating part of one's own internalised interpretive schemas which have, ironically, been gained themselves through political struggle. Since women have historically had to fight to gain access to tertiary education, learning to read the text 'properly' constitutes one kind of feminist victory.[31] It is theoretically true for Annette Kolodny to say that:

> "To question the source of the aesthetic pleasures we've gained from reading Spenser, Shakespeare, Milton, and so on [or, we might add, from Gothic romance], does not imply that we must deny those pleasures."[32]

It is also true to say that the strategic process of bracketing off these pleasures, or maintaining a kind of split reading identity, although not always theoretically tenable, requires some energy, and may detract from the pleasure of an unself-conscious reaction.

So to return to *The Piano*, what is the name that is not one? Sarmas suggests that it does have a name and "that name is rape".[33] For others, that name was more delicate: romance.

4. ROMANZA: THE PIANO AS ROMANCE

Marxist or early feminist critics of the romance have often seen it as a working through of the kinds of ideological complexities outlined above. That is, romance can be considered a popular cultural form in which patriarchal capitalist ideologies are masked or reworked as female pleasure. Such an analysis sees the ideology of romantic love celebrated in romance as a way of negotiating the fraught relationship between the economic and emotional bases of marriage. Feminist work on the romance, especially in the '80s, tended to concentrate on formalist or structuralist analysis of the conventions of the genre. Such analysis showed romance to be a highly formulaic genre, with quite rigorously observed conventions of narrative and characterisation.

These were usually outlined as follows: the narrative focuses on the courtship of a heroine – a spirited, though inexperienced, young woman who at the start of the narrative is at a moment of transition. She is in some way alone in the world (orphaned, estranged from her family, away from home), and out of her familiar environment. She meets the hero, whom she generally dislikes or distrusts on account of his arrogance, surliness, or even veiled brutality. Despite her distrust, she falls prey to a passion for him that is reciprocated, but clouded in misunderstandings and discord. She has a rival in her passion, usually in the form of a more sexual woman (the female foil); there may often be a counterpart male foil. The misunderstandings are cleared away (usually in a 'revelation scene'), but the passion is rarely consummated until the hero has been in some way 'feminised.' This involves the almost obligatory declaration of love, whereby the hero's sexual passion is brought within the compass of the ideology of romantic love. The declaration is followed by the proposal and the narrative closes soon afterwards.

Despite repeated praise for the originality of *The Piano*, it is clear that the film closely follows romance conventions. Only minor deviations occur, such as the absence of a conventional female foil figure.[34] Most relevant here is romance's cloudy economy of desire, in which the lines of courtship and coercion, agency and victimage, are blurry. Ada's hostility to Baines gradually melts as he shows himself to be vulnerable, sensitive to music and increasingly unhappy with the sexually coercive nature of their arrangement. Although there is no spoken declaration of love, it is Baines' refusal to continue to 'whore' Ada that seems to be the turning point in her feelings towards him. In generic terms, this represents the classic shift from lust to love, although the film is arguably more subtle and ambiguous than this reduction would suggest.

As in all romances, the affective economy in *The Piano* is subtended by an economic one.[35] Three different models of white[36] heterosexual contracts are implied with *The Piano*. The film presents the purely ecomonic arrangement of Ada's arranged marriage to Stewart as sterile and unworthy of her. It also hints back to an implied earlier relationship of unrestrained passion – an intense love that left Ada with her daughter Flora – an emotional solace but also an economic liability. But of course the film's focus is on the third kind of contract – the one that teeters unstably between the economic and the erotic, before reaching a closure that reconciles these oppositions. Ada's and Baines' relationship is that kind of economic/erotic arrangement whose slippery terrain it has traditionally been romance's function to constitute, whose contradictions, repressions and coercions romance has masked, and whose pleasures and desires it has celebrated.

5. PROGRAMME MUSIC: THE PIANO AS FAILED NARRATIVE OR AS MYTH

To perform *The Piano* as romance is to focus on the familiarity of its narrative patterning rather than on the originality of its plot. But the narrative of *The Piano* has also been criticised as grossly flawed, principally in terms of plausibility. Lynden Barber commented on the unlikeliness of many plot elements, but considered that this was submerged in the experience of viewing the film. He recognised that film viewing is a temporal practice in which emotional response may often be heightened, rather than the exercise of the critical faculties on a text grasped as a whole.[37] Far less approvingly, *The Age*'s reviewer Neil Jillett posed a series of questions begged but unanswered by the plot. After the film's success at the Oscars, *The Age* ran two more features on *The Piano*, including an article by Carmel Bird, in which she accused the film of being a collection of images rather than a story:

> "I don't dispute Jane Campion's brilliance as a maker of images. But I think that as a story-teller she leaves a lot to be desired. This film claims to tell a story ... It looks like a bad dream, works on your mind like a bad dream, but it also reckons it's telling a story. It isn't."[38]

After listing, like Jillett, a series of questions that the plot doesn't answer, Bird concluded:

> "I suggest the real answers to these questions are never going to be found in plot or character. There's one answer – Jane Campion wanted to create photo-opportunities for a series of powerful pictures and ideas that haunt her imagination. She succeeded, but at the expense of story."[39]

Such observations resonate curiously with Jillett's denigration of Ada's muteness as a "feminist" device:

> "The fashionably 'feminist' symbolism does not seem to grow naturally out of the story. It is as if Ada's muteness – which means the film has to be slowed by many bursts of sign language – is being used as a symbol around which everything else is laboriously assembled."[40]

Compare this with Bird's assertion that "the inconsistencies in the story keep getting in the way of the dream."[41] In Jillett's account, a symbolic device gets in the way of narrative; in Bird's, visual imagery is the culprit. These criticisms were refuted, two days later, by yet another article in *The Age*, in which Ian Robinson argued that the plot recounts a mythic journey, and that its structure is "the oldest and greatest story of them all."[42]

This seeming polarity can be reframed a little by reading this debate through the kinds of frameworks opened up by feminist narratology and film criticism. Bird's and Jillett's criticisms, for example, rely implicitly on the kind of model famously proposed by Laura Mulvey, who saw mainstream film as structured around "the split between spectacle and narrative."[43] Mulvey's famous contention was that in narrative cinema the female, as bearer of the scopophilic male gaze, functions as a spectacle, and that spectacle is an obstacle to the narrative thrust:

> "The presence of woman is an indispensable element of spectacle in normal narrative film, yet her visual presence tends to work against the development of a story line, to freeze the flow of action in moments of erotic contemplation. This alien presence then has to be integrated into cohesion with the narrative."[44]

Now, quite clearly, *The Piano* is not the kind of classic Hollywood narrative of which Mulvey wrote – for one thing, as we have seen, Ada is not at all the stereotypical "erotic object for the spectator within the auditorium".[45] And yet, in more abstract terms, the deep structural patterns, the gendered opposition between stability and motion, home and away, may still be considered to operate here. Some feminist theorists[46] have contended that the archetypal narrative structure (of which Robinson speaks) relies on a gendered pattern of departure-obstacles-return, where the desire that impels the narrative onwards can be read as 'masculine' in terms of deeply entrenched metaphorical codings that replicate an Oedipal logic.

The romance genre itself can be read in terms of this archetypal patterning – as a version of the quest narrative. The male protagonist's goal, and consequently, the narrative telos, is a cluster of feminised signifiers – home, family, security – and a feminine principle both obstructs and completes his journey. But, as we will see below, Teresa de Lauretis has problematised the notion of the female as obstacle to the narrative. It may perhaps be, then, that Robinson's claim that *The Piano* does tell a story may be reconcilable with Bird's and Jillett's doubts about the split between spectacle and narrative. Perhaps *The Piano* can be considered programme music – music that is both representation and narrative – but in order to arrive at such a formulation we need to consider the role of the spectator.

6. CONCLUSION: RUBATO – AT THE PERFORMER'S PLEASURE

If all the often contradictory renditions above can be considered in some way feminist, as we have claimed, then clearly, they represent different performances of feminism. These can be caricatured as pro-woman, pro-art, pro-myth, anti-art, anti-eroticism, pro-politics – all of which are predicated on the kinds of false oppositions we found so constraining in many of our conversations about the film: eroticism versus ethics, art versus politics etc. What we want to pose here, then, is a kind of cipher for these various readings that might begin to dismantle such polarities and unpack the complex ways in which pleasure is constituted and deployed.

Cultural Studies has at moments proven to be rather drab in its repeated insistence that pleasure itself provides a site of resistance to dominant culture. The shift away from Frankfurt School style denunciations of popular forms has involved sophisticated re-theorisations of the processes of consumption, but can occasionally tip over into reifications of pleasure. In such cases, an argument for pleasure is only weakly constitutive of a programme for political action. We do not want to argue against formulations of pleasure as resistance; rather, we want to shift focus slightly by suggesting that the private practice(s) of pleasure constitute an important, if fraught, site for feminist speculation. A politics of pleasure is difficult theoretical and ethical terrain, because it is easy, in both popular and academic common sense, to equate critique with non-pleasure. We simply want to signal a relationship between pleasure and performance, noting that the scope and availability of pleasures in performance are dependent on the interpretive communities to which one 'belongs'.

As we found ourselves both inside and outside of the many readings of *The Piano* detailed above, we felt precluded from a coherent position of pleasure. But we also feel a certain amount of anxiety in the Don Juan like position of the purely performative, that is, in simply displaying the kinds of performances above as equally valuable and equally available responses to the film. In our early conversations with others about the film, we detected a resistance to articulations of ambivalence. Media reviews also often presented the film as either a series of images or a story, a romance or a rape, rather than a rich imbrication of these singularities. Mulvey's separation of spectacle and narrative can be seen as another set of oppositions, which, though it allows us to say that we loved the cinematography and felt hesitant about the narrative, fails to account for the ways in which these aspects of *The Piano*, and cinema in general, are overlaid.

This brings us, as a kind of finale, to one more musical metaphor – the *rubato* that lends its name to this section. *Rubato* – traditionally translated in music texts as 'at the performer's pleasure' – is a moment of authorised license within performance. It is an instruction or permission from the composer to the performer allowing the latter to interpret a certain passage (or sometimes an entire piece) according to his or her own will. To play a piece *rubato* is to take license with the speed, style or tone – to invest it with one's own interpretation – usually in a romantic or emotional manner. What might it mean to perform *The Piano rubato*? We suggest that every performance is a *rubato* one – since it involves one's own personal and shared emotional and intellectual investments, one's own licensed interpretation of a set of textual codes, in such a way as to bring pleasure to the performer. Indeed, drawing on Richard Dyer's model of theorising stars,[47] we might even consider *The Piano* itself, as cultural event, as a large-scale performance of anxieties about femininity and female desire. In its richness and ambiguity, its crystallisation of contemporary cultural anxieties, it made available all kinds of *rubato* renditions by individuals and reading communities.

Our rubato rendition is the presentation of these various performances. This interrelationship allows us to theorise our reluctance to subscribe to the polarities within which we were positioned and which drove many of our conversations about the film. Deconstructing them enables us to articulate our ambivalent responses to *The Piano* without recourse to set pieces. Thus it is that we cannot limit ourselves to any *one* interpretation of *The Piano*; rather, we want to signal our pleasure in a meta-performance, not as a demonstration of academic hermeneutic dexterity, but in order to acknowledge the overdetermination of our viewing experience. Furthermore, the term *rubato* signals a passion that might be equatable with a moment of commitment which, if not exactly Sartrean, allows us to express political investment without reifying it. We hope to have suggested that the performances above are not mutually exclusive 'choices' — that they frequently intersect and overlay each other, even while they may contradict each other. To conclude, we suggest that *all* interpretation involves pleasure and pain, binds viewing subjects into interpretive or discursive communities, or is produced by these communities, and renders a final interpretation unperformable.

NOTES

1. Tania Modleski, "Some Functions of Feminist Criticism; or, The Scandal of the Mute Body" in *Feminism Without Women: Culture and Criticism in a "Postfeminist" Age,* New York: Routledge, 1991. p51.

2. Outlined in *L'Existentialisme est un humanisme* (1946).

3. Op. cit. Modleski,'91. p48.

4. Ibid. Modleski, '91. p48.

5. Qtd. in Modleski, '91. p48.

6. Introduction to *The Pirate's Fiancée: Feminism, Reading, Postmodernism*, London: Verso, 1988. p15.

7. Jacques Derrida. 'Structure, Sign and Play in the Discourse of the Human Sciences' in *Writing and Difference*, (trans.) Alan Bass, Chicago: Univ. of Chicago Press, 1978: "... the ethnologist accepts into his [sic] discourse the premises of ethnocentrism at the very moment when he denounces them. This necessity is irreducible: it is not historically contingent. We ought to consider all its implications very carefully". p 282. Though this comment is directed at ethnographers it can be generalised to cultural critique at large.

8. Teresa de Lauretis, "Desire in Narrative," in *Alice Doesn't: Feminism, Semiotics, Cinema*, Bloomington: Indiana University Press, 1984. p143.

9. Andrew L. Urban, "Campion Keyed up for Home-Town Premiere," *The Australian,* 3 Aug 1993. p1.

10. Deborah Jones, "Piano's Good Companions," *The Australian,* 6 Aug. 1993. p10.

11. See, for example, Deborah Mandie, Review of *The Piano, Farrago,* Sept. 1993. p26.

12. Kerryn Goldsworthy, "What Music Is," *Arena Magazine*, 7, Oct./Nov. 1993. p47.

13. Mary Colbert, Review of *The Piano, Filmnews*, 23.6 Aug 1993. p14.

14. Op. cit. Mandie, Sep. 1993. p26.

15. Jan Chapman, Jane Campion, Veronica Jenet and Janet Patterson respectively. The writer of "the book of the film" is also female.

16. Lynden Barber, "Playing it Low-key," *Sydney Morning Herald*, 3 Aug. 1993. p24.

17. Simon Keizer, Review of *The Piano, Honi Soit*, 16, 2 Aug. 1993. p24.

18. "What Rape is," Letter to the editor, *Arena Magazine*, 8, Dec./Jan. 1993. p14.

19. Andrew L. Urban, "Piano's Good Companions," *The Australian*, 6 Aug. 1993. p11.

20. Jane Campion, qtd. in op. cit. Barber, 13 Aug. 1993. p24.

21. Evan Williams, "Sound and Silence in Perfect Harmony," *The Weekend Australian,* Review 7–8 Aug. 1993. p12.

22. Lynden Barber's interview with Jane Campion would count as an exception; he says simply: "She agrees to trade sexual favours for [the piano's] return." in op. cit. Barber, 3 Aug. 1993. p24. His review of the film, though, will be discussed below.

23. Marnie, *"The Piano,"* CASVP Newsletter, August 1993.

24. Op. cit. Mandie, Sep. 1993. p26.

25. Op. cit. Colbert, 6 Aug 1993. p14.

26. Lynden Barber, "An Undeniable Masterpiece," *Sydney Morning Herald*, 5 Aug. 1993. p24.

27. Neil Jillett, "Keys Missing from The Piano," *The Age*, 5 Aug. 1993, p20.

28. Op. cit. Goldsworthy, Oct./Nov. 1993. p47.

29. "Afterthoughts on 'Visual Pleasure and Narrative Cinema' Inspired by *Duel in the Sun,"Popular Fiction: Technology, Ideology, Production, Reading*, (Ed.) Tony Bennett, London: Routledge, 1990. p151.

30. Janice Radway, "Interpretive Communities and Variable Literacies: The Functions of Romance Reading," in *Rethinking Popular Culture: Contemporary Perspectives in Culture*, (Ed.) Chandra Mukerji and Michael Schudson, Berkeley: University of California Press, 1991. pp465-86.

31. Annette Kolodny, "Dancing through the Minefield: Practice and Politics of a Feminist Literary Criticism," *Feminist Studies*, 6.1, Spring 1980. p1.

32. Ibid. Kolodny, '80. p12.

33. Ibid. Kolodny, '80. p16.

34. Lisa Sarmas, "What Rape is," Letter to the editor, *Arena Magazine*, 8, Dec./Jan. 1993. p14.

35. Note, though, that the Maori women can be read as fulfilling this structural function, since their open and contentedly sexual nature is stressed throughout the film. We will take this moment to note that much could be said about the representation of the Maoris – particularly their rather Romanticised association with the land and with 'natural' sexuality, as well as the 'cross-dressing' that Campion employed consciously as a metaphor for colonisation (see Lop. cit. Barber, 3 Aug. 1993. p24.). Clearly, it is beyond the scope of this paper to address such issues; we simply signal them here.

36.   For more on this, see, for example, Jan Cohn, *Romance and the Erotics of Property: Mass-Market Fiction for Women*, Durham: Duke University Press, 1988.

37.   Cf. the film's Romanticised depictions of sexual relations *outside* such contracts i.e. in the Maoris' comments about sex.

38.   Lynden Barber, "An Undeniable Masterpiece," *Sydney Morning Herald*, 5 Aug. 1993. p24.

39.   Carmel Bird, "Mysteries of a Tale Left Lacking," *The Age,* 22 Mar. 1994. p15.

40.   Ibid. Bird, 22 Mar. 1994, 15.®

42.   Carmel Bird, "Mysteries of a Tale Left Lacking," *The Age* 22 Mar. 1994. p15.

43.   Ian Robinson, "Campion's Champion says that Myth is The Piano's Forte," *The Age,* 25 Mar. 1994. p13.

44.   Laura Mulvey, "Visual Pleasure and Narrative Cinema," *Screen* 16.3 (1975) p12.

45.   Ibid. Mulvey, '75. p11.

46.   Ibid. Mulvey, '75. p11.

47.   See, for example, Meaghan Morris, "At Henry Parkes Motel," *Cultural Studies* 2.1, Jan. 1988.: pp1-47.

48.   See, for example, Richard Dyer, *Stars,* London: BFI, 1982 and *Heavenly Bodies: Film Stars and Society*, London: BFI, 1986.

CHAPTER 2

WITH CHOICES LIKE THESE, WHO NEEDS ENEMIES?

THE PIANO, WOMEN'S ARTICULATIONS, MELODRAMA, AND THE WOMAN'S FILM

NEIL ROBINSON

The Piano is both a contemporary woman's film and a contemporary melodrama. Like women's films from the classical Hollywood cinema, it addresses a female spectator and tells the story of a woman who attempts to resolve the tensions between her own subjectivity and erotic desire, and the patriarchal world in which she lives. Like melodramas, the film deploys characters who define the contours of their community in order to point toward – because it is difficult to explicitly state – the ways that the community is achieved and maintained. However, The Piano does not simply replicate the melodramatic structures of the classical woman's film; it deploys and alters those structures in an effort to successfully represent what the classical woman's film fails to produce: a tenable position of female subjectivity and desire.

This essay begins with Peter Brooks' description of melodrama and argues that figurations of storytelling in *The Piano* demonstrate the film's allegiances with melodrama because they indicate the difficulty of expressing emotions or articulating society's core values. Rather than utilise direct expressions, the film offers ongoing negotiations around stories, which therein raises a question whether the story the film tells is itself under negotiation.

Often analyses of women's films describe a staged struggle in which the female protagonist attempts to control the filmic narration and thereby assert her subjectivity, but fails when the masculine narration subordinates or silences her. A comparison of *The Piano* with *Letter from an Unknown Woman* (Max Ophuls, 1948, US) shows that *The Piano* departs from the classical woman's film because Ada's music, the primary means of representing her 'voice,' is not recuperated by the narrative in order to subdue her articulative power. However, like *Letter from an Unknown Woman*, *The Piano* represents a world in which women only articulate their subjectivities and desires at the cost of their bodies; patriarchy demands that women's bodies be violently sacrificed to their articulative processes.

At its end, *The Piano* deploys a traditionally melodramatic ending in which the community expels the character whom it deems the villain, but the film does so not to affirm the social order, as in traditional melodrama, but instead to critique the false either/or choices which patriarchy offers to both women and men. My argument affirms Mary Ann Doane's claim about the classical woman's film that patriarchy suppresses female subjectivity and narrational authority; however, Doane fails to account for the ways that the woman's film may use melodrama in order to produce a critique of patriarchal oppression.

This essay concludes when it argues that although *The Piano* offers a more complete representation of female subjectivity and desire than does the classical woman's film, it fails to escape the pressure which patriarchy places on the female body to sacrifice itself in order to give the woman's expressions enduring presence. This analysis of the ways that *The Piano* deploys and revises conventions of the melodrama and the classical woman's film not only better accounts for the progressive potential of the classical woman's film, it also demonstrates the need for feminism to refuse patriarchy's demand to sacrifice the female body in order to produce meaningful female articulations and to retain the woman's corporeality when representing her subjectivity.

The Piano contains a number of icons which, according to Peter Brooks in his study of melodrama, we associate with melodrama: hyperbolic gesture, music (the *melos* of 'melodrama'), and a mute protagonist.[1] Brooks argues that these icons are common to melodrama because they reflect and express the ineffability of melodrama's main subject. That is, melodrama "in large measure exists to locate and to articulate the moral occult," which he describes as "the domain of operative spiritual values which is both indicated within and masked by the surface of reality."[2] But because the moral occult resists articulation in language, melodrama utilises gesture, music and mutes, which attempt to articulate without appealing to language. This does not deny possible languages of gestures (Ada, for example, has one), or of notes, rather than of words; but when faced with the task of signifying the compelling moral and spiritual structures which undergird a social system, melodrama operates around the inadequacies of such languages – no matter what their building blocks:

> "The articulation of melodrama's messages in this kind of sign language ... suggests the extent to which melodrama not only employs but is centrally about repeated obfuscations and refusals of the message and about the need for repeated clarifications and acknowledgments of the message."[3]

When I think about *The Piano* as a melodrama, I want to first focus on attempts to articulate in various modes – writing, sign language, playing music, and (perhaps) telepathy – and the ensuing networks of miscommunication and re-communication which these articulations set in motion. As Brooks argues, no one articulation is sufficient to convey a message; instead, an articulation spawns a number of iterations which circulate through the community. In *The Piano*, acts of articulation never stand alone but instead are always subject to negotiation and demands for re-iteration.

A good example of communication which is subsequently altered and confused by other iterations is a mystery which the film never solves, the story of Flora's father. The audience certainly notices his absence early in the film, but when we first hear Flora's description of him, his absence gains a mysterious charge because the story which she tells feels like a fiction and not a history or memory. Later, when Flora requests that Ada tell the story of her father, she entreats that she wants to hear it *again*, as if it were a bedtime story which no longer conveys information but instead now calms and pleases the child. When Ada tells the story of Flora's father, the audience sees the full expressive range of Ada's body as it not only employs sign language but nearly resembles a dance. The content of the story seems less important to Ada than her delight in telling it.

When Flora explains her father's absence to Morag, she has clearly learned from her mother not to convey the facts of the story as simply and clearly as possible, but instead to perform a story that will affect her audience and please herself as she tells it. While the content of Flora's version of the story has little similarity to Ada's, Flora's face registers the same thrill of producing a story which enchants her audience. She learns quickly to back away from a narrative which her audience resists:

AUNT MORAG (*Frowning.*): And where did they get married?

FLORA (*Her Scottish accent becoming thick and expressive.*): In an enormous forest, with real fairies as bridesmaids each holding a little elf's hand.

AUNT MORAG *sits back, regarding* FLORA *with obvious disapproval and disappointment.* She smooths back her hair.

FLORA: No, I tell a lie, it was a small country church, near the mountains ...

AUNT MORAG *is becoming involved again. She leans forward.*[4]

Despite Flora's unreliability, Morag believes the outrageous story that she tells, as long as it is not ridiculously fantastic. What we learn from Flora's story is not the truth about her father – we know that Ada has not spoken since she was six years old, and so never could have been the opera singer of Flora's story; instead we learn that Flora, like Ada, gains pleasure from telling an enchanting story with great expressiveness. The film one-ups the outrageousness of the story when it deploys an animation shot of Flora's father burning after he has been struck by lightning. While we know that we are being lied to, like Morag we forgive that fact as long as the storytelling pleases us. The multiple iterations of the story render murky its content, and suggest that the teller and audience negotiate the story in order to find a telling which pleases both. Brooks' claim that melodrama is about saying and re-saying the message until it is clarified and heard takes form in *The Piano* as a set of dialogues between senders and recipients of messages who decide the form and style of the messages.

Additionally, Ada, Flora and Morag negotiate not only the style of the story but also its content. What these stories point toward in the moral occult, although they never precisely express it, is that an unmarried mother and a fatherless child cannot simply exist, but must always be explained. That is, the society that the film depicts (and, almost as surely, that in which the film is shown) does not offer the subject positions 'unmarried mother' and 'fatherless child,' and therefore some story must be told about those who seem to inhabit those positions in order to properly place them – in this case, as 'widow' and 'orphan' (and not, for example, as 'whore' and 'bastard'). Affirming Brooks' description of melodrama, *The Piano* does not expressly articulate this feature of its moral occult, but instead offers expressive articulations whose passion suggests the importance of this implied meaning.

When the negotiations around a story are not satisfactorily completed, the audience may interrupt the storytelling. The production of the Bluebeard story represents an audience which suddenly ends the storytelling because it has not been satisfactorily involved in the negotiations which precede the performance. Before the performance at the school, the Reverend shows a segment of the community – and the film's audience – how the effect of the axe attack will be created for the play's audience by the use of shadows.[5] Nessie must be coaxed to participate in the rehearsal – she pulls her hand back the first time the Reverend brings his cardboard axe down – and when she sees the shadow of the axe chop her hand's shadow, she shrieks despite knowing that it is an illusion. For those present and for the film's audience, the trick of the shadow play is revealed in order to assure us that the violence which we see on the play screen is not real; in order to enjoy the thrill of watching the performance, one must know with certainty that the violence is illusory.[6]

However, the Maoris in the audience have been excluded from this pre-perform-ance negotiation, and when the performance is finally staged, they mistakenly interpret the shadow play as reality. As a result, they move to defend Nessie against Bluebeard's attack, tear through the screen during the performance, and thereby (and nearly violently) disrupt the storytelling. Only when the performers provide visual verification that each of Bluebeard's wives' heads is in fact connected to the body of a living actress can they defuse the violent defence of the women that the Maoris intend to make. Despite the difference in scale between this disruption and Morag's disbelief at the outrageousness of Flora's description of her parents' fairy wedding, both demonstrate the fragility of the moment when the storytelling both engages the storyteller's passions and sparks the audience's imagination.

The negotiations over stories take place not only between the characters, but also between the characters and the story the film tells. When we see the nearly violent way that the Maoris express their dissatisfaction with the Bluebeard story, we understand that 'negotiation' may be an inappropriately civil name for a response to a narration and its storyteller, and indeed criticism of the woman's film has described female characters who *struggle* to assert some narrational control over a film in order to ascertain the degree to which women's films meaningfully represent female subjectivity.[7] Often such criticism will examine the use of voice-overs.[8] In order to describe the negotiations over narration in *The Piano*, I offer as a point of comparison an analysis of narration and voice-over in a classical woman's film, *Letter from an Unknown Woman*. This comparison demonstrates that although on one hand *The Piano*, unlike *Letter from an Unknown Woman*, mostly eschews voice-over narration and lacks a struggle for narration in which the woman's voice-over participates, on the other hand the enduring power of the woman's letter to speak beyond her presence and life in *Letter from an Unknown Woman* finds a rhyme in the music of *The Piano*. Music in *The Piano* functions as Ada's entrée and continuing presence in the negotiation about how her story is told, and therefore demarcates some space of female subjectivity.

The frametale of *Letter from an Unknown Woman* centers on Stefan Brand (Louis Jourdan), a pianist who arrives at his home late one evening and prepares to leave Vienna to avoid fighting a duel. He finds a letter waiting for him from Lisa Berndle (Joan Fontaine), which tells the story of her enduring love for Stefan despite his obliviousness to her existence. Having been just another notch on Stefan's bedpost, Lisa describes in her letter the relationship he could never remember, the son he never knew existed, and the life he claimed to want but never had. And never can have, because he learns (from an attached note) that Lisa died of typhus just as she completed her letter. His life view altered by the contents of the letter, Stefan changes his mind about duelling Lisa's husband (Marcel Journet), and the film ends as he rides off, presumably to be killed.

The letter of the film's title can refer to a number of texts: the diegetic letter that Stefan reads; the framed story that the letter tells, presented as flashbacks dotted with Lisa's voice-over readings of parts of the letter; and/or the entire film, if the title describes the film and not merely its contents. The difficulty of identifying a single titular letter reminds us that in melodrama, no single articulation is sufficient, and that its messages must be multiply transmitted and received in order to be understood. The question I raise here is what comes *from* Lisa, the unknown woman – which parts of the film are her articulations?[9]

The letter of the title only *may* refer to the written text which Stefan reads. The postal route the letter travels to reach Stefan makes it a transaction not only between Lisa the writer and Stefan the reader. Lisa doubts whether she will send the letter – "Will I ever send it? I don't know" – and indeed, it is not Lisa but Mary Theresa, the Sister in charge of St. Catherine's hospital, who mails the letter.[10] Mary Theresa's attached note registers uncertainty that Stefan is the letter's intended recipient ("We believe it was meant for you as she spoke your name just before she died"), indicates that the nuns have read and judged Lisa's letter ("May God be merciful to you both"), and establishes Mary Theresa as the only signer of the letter.[11] The packaged letter which Stefan receives, then, looks like a judgment of Stefan and Lisa, sent by their judge, Mary Theresa, who offers Lisa's letter as evidence against them. The letter alone does not declare itself to be from Lisa and intended for Stefan. Instead, the events and remembrances sparked by Lisa's letter – Lisa's voice-overs, the flashbacks, John's (Stefan's butler's) writing Lisa's name on a pad of paper – confirm the author and addressee. The letter is not bound to its physical manifestation: Lisa's act of writing generates a written text which is neither the only nor the most important effect of her act.

The second of the possible texts to which the title may refer – the framed story told by flashbacks and voice-overs – also does not conclusively establish Lisa's subjectivity. Although the letter-writer controls what words are put on her pages, the film subordinates her version of the story when it silences her voice-over and departs from her optical point of view.[12] Karen Hollinger, in her study of the woman's voice-over in both women's films and *film noir*, observes that in between voice-overs, flashbacks tend to stray freely from the narrating subject; the voice-over "establishes within the film a fight for narrative power as the narrator struggles to gain control of the narrative events recounted ... [I]t creates an extreme tension between word and image."[13] The flashbacks in *Letter from an Unknown Woman* generate this sort of tension. The camera adopts optical points of view that are not Lisa's when it follows Stefan as he pays the fares for the train ride in the park, and when it turns to the conversation among the members of the all-woman band. Robin Wood argues that the independence of the film's narration generates a critical perspective: "The tendency of the film to draw us into [Lisa's] vision is balanced and counterpointed throughout by a conflicting tendency to detach us from the 'dream' and comment on it ironically, hinting at a prosaic reality that Lisa excludes, exposing some of the very unromantic mechanisms on which the dream depends."[14] When they refuse Lisa's version of her own story, the flashbacks establish a different author-audience relationship; the film addresses its audience, overwrites Lisa's address to Stefan, and thereby antagonises her self-articulation.

When Lisa's voice-over does guide the image track, it seldom wrests narrative control from the camera, but instead usually only lasts long enough to affect transitions between places and times. In such cases, the film uses Lisa's voice-over to maintain narrative intelligibility, but the deferrals of the image track to Lisa's voice suggest that linearity restricts the narrative in a way that does not bind Lisa, who can skip over large passages of time and space. Following Laura Mulvey, Mary Ann Doane gives a clearer sense of this opposition between woman and narrative: "the figure of the woman is aligned with spectacle, space, or the image, often in opposition to the linear flow of the plot. From this point of view, there is something about the representation of the woman which is resistant to narrative or narrativisation."[15] The narration of *Letter from an Unknown Woman* tends toward a linearity that is unfettered by Lisa's narration and her position outside that linear timeline (because she is both a woman and dead), but utilises her narrator position outside linear time and contiguous space in order to tell its story efficiently. When Lisa's voice merely explains a gap in time or place, her narrating agency becomes a tool of the linear narrative, and her independent subjectivity is ignored.

However, Lisa's voice-over occasionally breaks into the diegesis to accomplish more than just a shifting of scene. When Lisa sees Stefan bring another woman home and resigns herself to moving to Linz with her family, the scene does not immediately dissolve to Linz; a short dissolve to Stefan reading Lisa's letter gives her the opportunity to attack him on the sound track: "You who have always lived so freely, have you any idea what life is like in a little garrison town?"[16] Given a small space in which her voice can control the flow of the narrative, Lisa forces a brief return to the frametale where her narrating voice directly addresses Stefan. Where the flashbacks usually address their narrative to the viewer, these disruptions switch the route of address back to originating with Lisa and directed toward Stefan. At the point that she tells Stefan of their son, her voice-over detaches itself from the text he reads and continues to speak to him even while he examines pictures of their son which accompany the letter. The sound track presents a voice detached from the letter which seems to spawn it, a voice not limited by a reader who turns his eye away from the written text. Despite the efforts of the film to constrain and narrativise Lisa's voice, something of it remains to suggest that she transcends not only time, space and the limits of the handwritten pages, but also her death, to give her a haunting, ghostly power.

Although *The Piano* begins and ends with Ada's voice-over, that voice-over, unlike Lisa's, does not compete with the film for narrative control. In between the first and last segments, we do not hear Ada's voice, and the camera moves freely among and outside the characters' points of view. However, while Ada's mind's voice does not struggle for narrative control, the music of the piano operates like Lisa's voice-over in a number of ways. The opening voice-over ends just before she plays the first notes of her piano; the closing voice-over begins only after the piano has been thrown overboard, its reverberations upon hitting the water have ended and it is finally silent. The sound from the piano fills exactly the space created by Ada's silence: "I don't think myself silent, that is, because of my piano."[17] The music helps to motivate and smooth over narrative transitions between places and times. Sometimes, it provides Ada with a means to control the progress of the narrative: when Baines starts to rub his arms on her neck, she changes the song she plays from a slow piece to a lively, almost comical Chopin, and thereby ruins the mood for Baines, who backs away. At other times, other narrative actors interrupt the music: the maid startles Ada's first performance, and Stewart's presence stops Ada from playing the 'keys' she etched into the table.

The longer the film lasts, the more the music exceeds the diegesis. When Ada looks down at the piano left on the beach, the camera adopts her point of view and the sound track fills with internal diegetic music – the music in Ada's mind.[18] But the full orchestration which accompanies the piano has no onscreen referent; it calls attention to its production in (and Ada's awareness of) the larger world beyond the local setting (perhaps she reaches out through her music to address the viewer/listener). In sound bridges, the music of the piano transcends, in addition to diegetic space, the linear time of the narrative and boundaries between the characters. As Ada and Flora stare at Baines to try to convince him to take them to the beach and the piano, we hear the piano; a cut to the beach reveals that this music is Ada's playing on the beach. This revelation forces us to reconsider our initial impression that the sound is nondiegetic, but we cannot simply account for it in diegetic terms, because initially it accompanies an image from a long-past time and far-distant place; the warping of time in this moment refuses linear understanding. Music, like the figure of the woman Doane describes, here resists narrativisation, and therefore reflects Ada's non-linear subjectivity. A later shot of Ada playing for Baines precedes a reverse shot of Baines lying on the bed, listening; when he pulls the curtain away to look at her, we see from his point of view that Ada no longer sits at the piano, even though her playing lingers in Baines' mind and continues to affect him. Ada's music provides a trace of her presence despite her absence. These sound bridges blur distinctions not only between times (that of the playing and that of remembering) and between exterior and interior (whether the sound's source is the piano or a character's mind), but also between characters, since both Ada and Baines seem to author the music.

As the film progresses, the sounds of the piano free themselves from the diegesis more completely. In the climactic scene, piano music swells when Stewart reads the key Ada intends for Baines; the written-on key carries a sufficient trace of Ada to initiate her music, and that music is no longer housed in the piano: despite the claim of the Maori who retrieves the key – "It's lost its voice – it can't sing" – the missing key does not create a gap in the sound track.[19] When Stewart strikes the piano with an axe, the resultant diegetic noise fades but the non-diegetic music continues to increase in volume and pace, becoming nearly frenetic. The music stops only when he severs Ada's finger, and then only momentarily: as Ada gets up, the piano music reasserts itself. Ada's playing spawns an extension of herself that reacts to and influences its surrounding environment; her text exists beyond the moment of its writing and continues to articulate for its silent author.

Although my description of Ada's music recalls my earlier argument that Lisa's voice exceeds its initial iteration and provides an enduring presence, the treatments of these articulations in the two films differ because *Letter from an Unknown Woman* allows Lisa's voice to speak only when it is narratively expedient, after which the film usually silences her, whereas *The Piano*'s music bridges spaces and places but is not then silenced. Doane claims that the classical woman's film exhibits a "generalized strategy whereby the films simultaneously grant the woman access to narration and withhold it from her". "Muteness, she argues, is "only an extreme instance" of this strategy, and that, like reticence, amnesia, or silence, it is used to justify "the framing of her discourse within a masculine narration."[20] However, because she does not speak, Ada seems to avoid the pitfall associated with voice-over narration which Lisa faces, that moments of non-linearity associated with the woman will be recuperated by a linear narrative in order to effectively muzzle the woman's articulations of subjectivity. Unlike the classical woman's film, *The Piano* does not silence its protagonist in order to maintain a tradition of masculine narration; instead, Ada chooses silence and articulates her emotions through music which linear narration cannot completely contain. When Brooks describes the expressive, non-linguistic gestures of melodrama, he mentions that Denis Diderot's "proposition of a dramaturgy of inarticulate cry and gesture" implies "a deep suspicion of the existing sociolinguistic code".[21] Melodrama expresses a suspicion that conventional language has become too mediated to adequately express true emotions. *The Piano* similarly suspects language, but in this case for gendered reasons: Ada's expressive gestures – in music and with her body – imply a suspicion of patriarchy's language and emotional repressions.

Ada's music and Lisa's voice are products of articulative acts which the authors do not fully control, nor which the narrative fully subordinates. There is cause for optimism about the existence of these 'voices' because they evince a space of female subjectivity which is absent from Doane's argument that those women's films which dare to render female desire "begin with a hypothesis of female subjectivity which is subsequently disproven by the textual product."[22] If we attend to these traces of articulation which outlast narrativisation and linger in the viewer's mind, we might argue against Doane. However, that optimism falters when faced with the circumstances which produce these enduring articulations. Both films record violent economies of exchange in which a woman's body is sacrificed to produce an enduring articulation. These films describe a danger for women, that in order to speak with an enduring voice, their bodies must be destroyed – they must (in Lisa's case, literally) become ghosts.

Whether *Letter from an Unknown Woman* endorses Lisa because she is a victim of Stefan's womanising and her letter because it powerfully refuses the anonymity his womanising demands, or indicts her because she is complicit in the failure of their relationship and her letter because it revengefully attacks Stefan and results in his death, the film in either case generates respect for and amazement at the letter's power. The letter's point of production helps to clarify the source of its power. Lisa writes from a hospital where her son has died of typhus and where she soon dies as well. Her disease progresses as her writing does, and so the price of writing is paid by her body. When she completes the letter, she has no body left with which to sign it. Lisa may not willingly participate in this sacrifice of her body, and her knowledge (or at least suspicion) that she is sick may empower her to write and thereby end her silence toward Stefan, but nonetheless her letter comes to substitute for her body and the writing process records that translation. The letter is the only trace of this exchange, and as a record of violence against the author's body, it demands its reader's attention. Critics debate whether Lisa intends to destroy Stefan or simply to force him to acknowledge her, but their discussion reveals that the letter successfully establishes Lisa's subjectivity because the readers of the letter (Stefan and the viewer) feel compelled to attend to Lisa and *her* desires, rather than only to Stefan's wishes and how his gaze subjects her body to his (and the viewer's) scopophilic pleasure.[23]

Lisa's body does not compel the same attention to her subjectivity, but is instead objectified. When she and Stefan are together, he sees her as just another in the long line of his sexual conquests. But Lisa believes they share a unique and meaningful experience which links her with the object of her fantasies and produces a son. Lisa's body becomes a register of their relationship; although Stefan can forget his relationship with Lisa, her pregnant body (and later the body of her son) constantly remind her. Lisa's body operates like a text that different people read differently. Stefan projects onto her body the image of the one-night lover he desires, while Lisa sees in her own body evidence of the lasting relationship she desires. As a text, her body is flexible and consequently inaccurate: rather than transmit to its readers an understanding of Lisa's desires, her body instead reflects the readers' own desires.

As her letter supplants her body, it registers more explicitly Lisa's desires, her value to Stefan as an 'unknown' woman, and marks their relationship as one of irrevocable loss. The letter conveys her value to him since her living, silent body could not. When Lisa demonstrates her uniqueness, she does so by *not* speaking: "I wanted to be one woman you had known who asked you for nothing."[24] Lisa believes her invisibility makes her valuable to Stefan, so if she were to speak she would no longer be unknown and therefore no longer valuable.[25] Because the letter arrives after her body has been destroyed and because Lisa does not send it, it speaks of her silent fidelity without betraying it. The letter marks in Stefan's memory that their relationship existed. Although that act of inscription summons a set of "death-dealing" images which result in the eventual obliteration of Stefan's memory, the film also marks Lisa's subjectivity in the viewers' memories; the letter finds its final audience in the viewer.[26] As in any act of translation or transubstantiation, the similarity between body and letter is tinged with a difference: where the body fails to indicate to Stefan Lisa's individuality, to speak her worth when she is silent, and to mark the fact of their relationship, the letter succeeds.

The violent self-sacrifice of Lisa's body required to generate her letter gives the traces of that writing an eerie power that eludes containment in any one location or time. The handwritten pages which Stefan reads, the voice-overs and flashbacks they spark, and the reels of film on which those images and sounds are captured all manifest traces of Lisa's writing and evidence the film's violent economy of writing. The letter seems something like the monster in a horror film: it transcends rules of logical time and space; each attempt to bury it may temporarily obscure it but, like any good incarnation of the repressed, it returns violently to reassert its enduring presence and to demand recognition;[27] and most importantly, the letter is not limited to one filmic incarnation.

The Piano repeats *Letter from an Unknown Woman*'s violent economy because Ada's body must also be horrifically sacrificed in order for her to become meaningfully articulate. Early in *The Piano*, Ada's body comes under two duelling male gazes that tend to ignore her subjectivity. When he first sees her on the beach, Stewart asks what she has brought with her. Ada points to labels which clearly indicate the contents of the trunks, but Stewart ignores both the labels and her gestures to them, and instead looks at her body, on which he reads his disappointments: "You're small. I never thought you'd be small ... She's stunted, that's one thing."[28]

Stewart is particularly callous toward Ada's ownership of the piano and the articulations she makes to express that ownership. He ignores her "The Piano?" note, her signs, and Flora's audible translations of those signs, which all express Ada's desire to bring the piano. Stewart tries to demonstrate his authority to make decisions ("Let's not discuss this any further"), and finally ends the discussion by switching topics ("Might I suggest that you prepare yourself for a difficult journey.")[29] Eventually Stewart trades the piano to Baines as if he owns it, and then rebukes Ada for making a claim on it:

> ADA's *breathing becomes heavy with anger, she writes furiously on her pad*: "The piano is mine. It's *mine*."

> STEWART *regards her note and her passion with suspicion and disdain*.
>
> STEWART: Can't go on like this. We're a family now, we all make sacrifices and so will you![30]

Stewart ignores both the text Ada writes and the individual subjectivity she claims through her note. Campion's stage directions demonstrate a clear link between Ada's articulations and her emotions, which both disturb Stewart. He willingly sacrifices Ada's ability to own property and the one object which contains traces of that ability – her name on the planks of the piano's crate mark it as hers – when he subjects her to a family structure which allocates space for only one owner, the patriarch.

Baines complies with this exclusion of Ada from economic exchanges when he barters with Stewart for the piano. Like Stewart, Baines wants Ada to sacrifice to him: he takes the piano to initiate an economic exchange whereby Ada must give Baines access to her body in order to regain ownership of her instrument and the rights and abilities – to own and to speak – for which it stands. Specifically, the exchange is measured by Ada's fingers and the black keys on the piano, which come to stand for one another: when Ada and Baines first make their bargain, she plays the lowest black key and holds up her right index finger (the one which Stewart will mutilate); when they set the last of the prices, Ada holds up ten fingers and Baines practically names them "ten keys".[31] The exchange operates under certain rules which organise both the piano and Ada's body for piece-by-piece consumption. Finally, the rules of this economy force Ada to lose: if she regains the piano which is rightfully hers, she will have given her body to Baines.

Because this oppressive economy suffocates Baines as well, he tries to end their exchange, and thereby reveals the unfulfilled desires which push the narrative toward its climax. Baines tells Ada, "I have given the piano back to you. I've had enough. The arrangement is making you a whore and me wretched. I want you to care for me, but you can't."[32] He reveals that the leverage over Ada's body which ownership of the piano gives him is insufficient to purchase his desires. The economy which offers Ada, like Lisa, subjectivity at the cost of a body through which to exert it also promises Baines bodily pleasure if he foregoes his desire to be loved. Like the women's choices, Baines' is a false one – he cannot enjoy his body or Ada's without an emotional attachment, so he refuses the choice. Ada also comes to reject the either/or economy. She realises that her desire to speak her identity through the piano has become eroticised: when she plays the piano in Stewart's cottage, she looks back over her left shoulder to the spot where she would find Baines if she were playing in his hut; she kneads the back of her hands into the keys of the piano, just as Baines rubbed his hands onto her skin. In short, she finds that bodily desire and articulation of an independent selfhood are inseparable; therefore, trading her body for the powers to own and speak is no trade at all – it is a sacrifice that sets her on a suicidal path.

Stewart represents the force which seeks to reassert the traditional rules of economic exchange, even when it threatens his own emotional interests. When he sees the piano leaving Baines' property, Stewart thinks it continues to mark the barter he and Baines make, and promises to "make sure that you are properly taught, with, you know, music written on sheets"[33] – a figuration of writing which would be produced by and contain the trace of an exchange. When Baines indicates that the piano is now a gift for Ada, Stewart again feels threatened by the piano. The very concept of a gift – a thing given without payment – threatens Stewart because it challenges the tenets of the exchange economy in which he believes; the uncompleted, unbalanced exchange is a void that nags Stewart. What most threatens Stewart is that the piano once again marks Ada's owner-ship and subjectivity in a way he cannot ignore or control. Pounding on the piano and ordering Flora to play anything, he attempts to bring his family's piano-play-ing under his control.

Stewart also believes that even though Ada made love with Baines, Stewart can shift her desire to him – first by trying to rape her, then by locking her in his house. Ada does direct her sexual energies toward Stewart, but she does not allow him to touch her; that is, she asserts the right to control her body and, unlike Lisa, to only allow it to register her own desire. Stewart misreads Ada as warming up to him because he ignores the distance which Ada puts between him and her body, selfishly interprets the meaning of her sexual advances and disregards the desires which Ada expresses.

But the wood-burned key, the *text* of Ada's desire – like the text of Lisa's desire and unlike the women's bodies – cannot be wilfully misread. It clearly articulates Ada's emotions – "Dear George you have my heart Ada McGrath" – and when we see her hand writing, she burns "my" into the wood; her act of writing names her desire as it names herself, and seeks to make both present for Baines, who feels her absence.[34] However, the key's words can only have meaning for Stewart: Baines cannot read them.[35] When this clear articulation of desire reaches Stewart, it alters his mood violently. Later, he demonstrates how difficult it is to express the threat the key poses to him: "You pushed me too hard. You cannot send love to him, you cannot do that. Just…even…even to think about it makes me very angry."[36] The finger-key metonymy which Baines and Ada established reminds us that the key inscribed with desire stands not just for the desiring woman, but also for her body, which Stewart previously misread. The inscription on the key leaves him without an option to ignore the key or an opportunity to misread its meanings. His response is to violently reformulate the finger-key equation: to destroy the source of writing and desire, he severs a finger from Ada's body in order to carve into her body a prohibition of her desire, and so reverses Ada's inscription, which severed a key (finger) from her piano (body) in order to express her desire. As Stewart drags her to the chopping block, he asks, "Why do you make me hurt you? ... You have made me angry. SPEAK! Speak to me! You will answer for this. Speak or not you will answer for this!"[37] Whereas Ada's piano playing avoids the pitfall of recuperation by masculine discourse, here her textual production provides patriarchy an entrée through which it violently attempts to force her to speak its language. In the process of mutilating Ada's body, Stewart enforces the demand of the violent economy that the woman's body pay for the articulation of her desire. Finally, he replaces Ada's finger for the key in the handkerchief-wrapped package, and co-opts Ada's postal agent when he steps between Flora and her mother to tell Flora, "You give this to Baines. Tell him if he ever tries to see her again I'll take off another and another and another."[38] The sacrifice of the body to textual production which articulates female desire is compelled as if it were mandated by the society's moral fabric ("the domain of operative spiritual values" or "moral occult" that Brooks de-scribes).

In the end, Ada extricates herself from Stewart's repressive social order only when she threatens retaliatory violence. Her threat takes a form that leaves no diegetic trace of its articulation; Ada seems to insert her thoughts directly into Stewart's mind. In a moment where Stewart attempts to join his sexual desires for Ada and his violent oppression of her by raping her as she recovers from his attack, she retaliates with a extra-linguistic threat which Stewart later names for Baines: "She said, 'I am afraid of my will, of what it might do, it is so strange and strong'."[39] Whether these words are Ada's or the voice of patriarchy's unspoken fear of women, the intimation that the patriarch might have to pay with his body for the desires he inscribes onto the woman's body is more than Stewart can stand, so he masquerades that *he* chooses to end the relationship ("I wish her gone. I wish you gone"), and gives into Ada's desire to be free from him.[40]

Even as Stewart functions to uphold the patriarchal order, the violent economy he helps to perpetuate victimises him. Clearly, Stewart is ill served by his social order. His efforts to subordinate Ada to his will invariably reduce his power. When the camera adopts Stewart's point of view to voyeuristically record Ada and Baines' sexual intercourse, the viewer feels that as desirable as the Ada-Baines relationship may be, it causes Stewart pain which he does not entirely deserve.

While he acts horribly toward Ada, Stewart is crippled by the societal norms around marriage which motivate him. As Sam Neill says, Campion

> "by no means saw Stewart as the villain of the piece – which I found extremely encouraging. Certainly he serves that function from time to time, but he is not the villain. I don't condone what he does, but I see it as entirely understandable because of the time he lives in: and he's a man of his time … What happens to him, I think, is that this shell – a carapace that Victorian men could assume – is cracked and disintegrated by the power of his feelings for Ada, leaving him very exposed. I think of him as being a man who has lost all his skin."[41]

Neill describes his character's failings as if they were bodily ills, and thereby reminds us that *The Piano* demonstrates that those who desire are subject to bodily discipline, even if they are the men who enforce that discipline. Like Ada, Flora and Baines, Stewart both suffers from and perpetrates the violence and misery which pervade the film.

Each of the main characters simultaneously occupies the positions of victim and attacker, and this leads us to the most important way in which *The Piano* modifies the parameters of melodrama that Brooks describes. According to Brooks, characters in melodrama exteriorise the tensions of the moral occult: their expressive, externalised gestures personalise "good" and "evil." Melodramas operate under "the logic of the excluded middle," in which no position other than good or evil is ultimately available to any character.[42] The violent economy of exchange in *The Piano* places characters into similarly manichaeistic positions, but rather than 'good' and 'evil' we might identify these positions with respect to violence: the film's logic allows for no non-violent position; one is never *neither* victim nor attacker, and is usually both. The victim and attacker positions available to the characters reveal an important divergence from the logic of the excluded middle and, therefore, traditional melodrama. According to Brooks, "The ritual of melodrama involves the confrontation of clearly defined antagonists [good and evil] and the expulsion of [the evil] one of them."[43] Melodrama ends with a "confirmation and restoration" of the social order which affirms good when it purges itself of evil.[44] When social order is restored in *The Piano*, it does indeed depend on expelling characters: Ada, Baines and Flora leave for Nelson. But the reasserted social order lacks the viewer's sympathies, because it is nearly devoid of protagonists – only Stewart remains, and his cruelty towards Ada and inextricability from patriarchy make him mostly unsympathetic – and because the community treats those whom it exiles so cruelly. The film ends without confirming the society, although that society is clearly restored, because the film avoids a traditionally melodramatic ending which would affirm the righteousness of the restoration and thereby justify its violent means. *The Piano* leaves Stewart's social order to confirm itself offscreen and follows Ada, Baines and Flora when they are expelled.[45]

The film refuses to generate characters who are *either* good *or* evil; therefore, just as Ada and Baines recognise and reject the falsity of the either/or choices which the violent economy demands, the film chooses to be expelled rather than endorse a wrongful villainisation of its characters. It rallies the viewer's sympathies around the expelled characters rather than the expelling order. Ultimately, *The Piano* enforces the melodramatic ritual of expulsion to reveal the violent 'evil' inherent within the restored, 'good' social order.[46] We may compare *The Piano* with other advanced melodramas which do not lodge good and evil in particular characters. Brooks writes of Henry James' *The Turn of the Screw*, "The logic here is that of the excluded middle, which we encountered repeatedly in melodrama....What has changed from the world of primary melodrama is that we no longer know how to choose because of our epistemological doubt: we no longer can or need to identify persons as innocence or evil; we must respond instead to the ratios of choice themselves."[47] The response which *The Piano* offers rejects these ratios of choice; it recognises the untenability of the subject positions which patriarchy makes available, and so refuses to choose among them.

The Piano then brings to an analysis of the woman's film the possibility that even a woman's film which constrains its characters and demonstrates the lack of a female subject position can still exist to critique – rather than to enforce – patriarchal repression. In this regard, *The Piano* helps me distinguish my feelings about the woman's film from those of Doane, who argues that "the woman's film does not provide us with an access to a pure and authentic female subjectivity, much as we might like it to do so."[48] She concludes with an account of the similarities among women's films which "suggests that even in its deep structure this type of film is ideologically complicit."[49] In Doane's reading, women's films represent the film industry's response to the crisis of female subjectivity centred around the reorganisation of gender roles during World War II.[50] They end with acts of patriarchal closure which crush the efforts of female characters to realise their desires, stylise femininity and resubmit the image of the woman to the male gaze. Her reading nicely fits the melodramatic ritual of expulsion: the woman, cast as 'evil', articulates desires that threaten the 'good' social order; therefore, her silence, suppression, and even death are necessary to its stability. The conclusion of *The Piano* certainly demonstrates the untenability of Ada's subjectivity within the community, but I would resist a reading which argued that the film finally endorses brutally violent patriarchal closure. Instead, the film demonstrates an allegiance with those whom patriarchy melodramatically expels.

From this position, the traces of a woman's writing which endure in the viewer's memory and which point toward her repressed subjectivity in a classical woman's film like *Letter from an Unknown Woman* seem to be not merely "something slip[ping] through,"[51] but rather the intended product of the film. Doane categorises *Letter from an Unknown Woman* as a love story,

> "one of the most vulnerable sites in a patriarchal discourse. Its flaw is to posit the very possibility of female desire. For this reason it often ends badly, frequently with the death of the female protagonist, its melodrama verging on tragedy....The woman associated with excessive sexuality resides outside the boundaries of language; she is unrepresentable and must die because, as Claire Johnston points out, death is the 'location of all impossible signs'."[52]

For Doane, the woman's film and specifically the love story endorse these endings which reassert the ideology of the patriarchy which produces the films. However, *Letter from an Unknown Woman* produces the voice and ghostly image of a woman whose body and life have been sacrificed for her untenable desire and for her articulation of that desire, not to affirm the propriety of that sacrifice but instead to generate in its audience a sense of dissatisfaction with a world which demands that sacrifice. At the end of the film, when Stefan leaves to fight the duel with Lisa's husband, the world of Vienna which the film depicts will, with Stefan's impending death, have rid itself of the last traces of Lisa's presence (indeed, her ghostly image fades from the frame) and, as a result, of the last traces of value to the film's audience. The film ends when Stefan's carriage drives off, not just because the melodrama has successfully restored the social order – as in Stewart's world – but because the world of that social order has been emptied of interest for the audience.

Therefore, I agree with Stanley Cavell when he writes that within the woman's film genre, it is possible for a film to pass judgment on the restored social order. He writes, "There is surely a sense of sacrifice in this group of films; they solicit our tears. But is it that the women in them are sacrificing themselves to the sad necessities of a world they are forced to accept? Or isn't it rather that the women are claiming the right to judge a world as second-rate that enforces this sacrifice; to refuse, transcend, its proposal of second-rate sadness?"[53] He articulates what I think would be Doane's response, "that the world the woman judges as second-rate is instead a hell on earth that finally extirpates her judgment altogether"[54] – in other words, that patriarchy successfully eliminates the space for even the woman's refusal. But a film which depicts the suppression of a woman's articulations and of her space in order to judge that suppression addresses an audience which keeps alive traces of the woman's articulations and can take up the critique of the suppressing patriarchy. *Letter from an Unknown Woman* may not represent a viable subject position for its heroine, but the film anticipates and, indeed, generates in its audience an affective response which criticises the lack of such a subjectivity.

The Piano does attempt to represent a viable female subjectivity, but Ada faces the death Doane describes: that which patriarchy ascribes to females who desire. Like *Letter from an Unknown Woman*, in which the black carriages which carry Stefan to the duel look like hearses, *The Piano* offers a symbolic burial at its end: when Ada's piano is tossed overboard – and nearly carries her to her death – it resembles a seaman's casket (a Maori oarsman says, "It's a coffin. Let the sea bury it.")[55] It is as if a woman must enter a second, otherworldly (after)life in order to articulate her desire without fearing retribution on her body. Oddly, the world of Nelson into which Ada enters seems like a more developed social order, with its bright lighting, proper houses (instead of huts), and manicured lawns (rather than endless mud), and Stewart's world seems other-worldly in retrospect.[56] Following Michael Booth and Eric Bentley, Brooks writes, "It is clear that the affective structure of melodrama brings us close to the experience of dreams." More particularly, he writes that the audience of the melodrama "accede[s] to the experience of nightmare."[57] While Stewart sees his marriage as a nightmare which shatters his own sense of order – "I want to wake and find it was a dream, that is what I want" – Ada, the woman whose desires patriarchy villainises, also experiences a nightmare.[58] Patriarchy is a nightmare from which Ada is trying to awake, and her near death demonstrates that only by the narrowest of margins does she escape its prohibitions against female desire.

The ending of the film cannot be read as a perfect dream or an ideal reality, however. While Ada becomes a piano teacher – a profession which would reward her ability to communicate through the piano rather than punish her for it – and chooses to learn how to speak again, we remember that Lisa has to resort to writing because her speech is ignored by Stefan; returning to that mode of articulation does not avoid the traps patriarchy sets. I wonder if Ada is being forced into another false either/or choice, in which she can be either a writer or a speaker, but neither can sufficiently articulate her desire. Furthermore, Ada substitutes blindness – draping a cloth over her head while she practices her sound – for her muteness; her body continues to be stifled during acts of articulation. Blindness may be a particularly important constraint if we attend to Doane's claim about flashback narration in the woman's film: "What is really at issue with respect to specifically filmic narration is not control of language but control of the image. For there is a sense in which vision becomes the signifier of speech in the cinema."[59] If Ada gains access to spoken language at the cost of her ability to see, she may lose any opportunity to exert control over her image. What is at stake in the control of the image is not only thorough access to signifying processes but – importantly for the purposes of this essay – a voice in the representation of the female body. A desirable space for female subjectivity would accommodate not merely voice and language but also image and the body – that which decidedly does not endure in *Letter from an Unknown Woman*.

To assess the degree to which *The Piano* achieves a representation of that space is extremely difficult. The final image of the film – even if it is only a dream or vision – gradually obliterates from sight Ada's drowned body. Any optimism we may have about the emergence and endurance of her voice must be tempered by a feeling that the female subject may again be pushed out of her body into ethereal forms. *The Piano* marks a point on a trajectory from the classical woman's film toward a representation of the woman which includes corporeality in its image of meaningful female agency. On one hand, *The Piano* critiques the violent melodramatic expulsions which cast female subjectivity as the evil that threatens the social order and must be ejected, and it furthermore recognises the enduring power of the woman's body – despite being objectified by the male gaze, sacrificed to articulative production, and mutilated by the agents of social order – to transgress time and space. But, on the other hand, after *The Piano* follows the female body which the patriarchy ejects melodramatically, the otherworldly realm which it then enters cannot yet model clearly for the audience a female subjectivity in which the woman's body is not still under some erasing pressure.

For their help and insightful readings of an earlier version of this chapter, I thank Jolynn Parker, J. Robert Parks, Anjula Razdan, Sarah Reitmeier, James Chandler and, especially, Miriam Hansen.

WORKS CITED

Bilborough, Miro, "The Making of *The Piano*", in *The Piano,* Jane Campion, New York: Hyperion, 1993.

Bordwell, David and Kristin Thompson, *Film Art: An Introduction*, (Fourth edition), New York: McGraw-Hill, Inc., 1993.

Brooks, Peter, *The Melodramatic Imagination: Balzac, Henry James, Melodrama, and the Mode of Excess,* New Haven: Yale University Press, 1976.

Campion, Jane. *The Piano,* New York: Hyperion, 1993.

Cavell, Stanley, "Postscript (1989): To Whom It May Concern", *Critical Inquiry* 16, no. 2 (Winter 1990): pp248-289.

Cavell, Stanley, "Psychoanalysis and Cinema: The Melodrama of the Unknown Woman", in *The Trial(s) of Psychoanalysis* (Ed.). Françoise Meltzer, Chicago: The University of Chicago Press, 1988. First published in a slightly different form in *Images in Our Souls: Cavell, Psychoanalysis, and Cinema*, (Eds.) Joseph H. Smith and William Kerrigan, Baltimore: Johns Hopkins University Press, 1987.

Cavell, Stanley, Ugly Duckling, Funny Butterfly: Bette Davis and Now, Voyager, *Critical Inquiry* 16, no. 2 (Winter 1990): pp213-237.

Cixous, Hélène, "Castration or Decapitation?" (trans.) Annette Kuhn, *Signs: Journal of Women in Culture and Society* 7, no. 1 (Autumn 1981): pp41-55.

Doane, Mary Ann, *The Desire to Desire: The Woman's Film of the 1940s*, Bloomington: Indiana University Press, 1987.

Elsaesser, Thomas. "Tales of Sound and Fury: Observations on the Family Melodrama," in *Home Is Where the Heart Is: Studies in Melodrama and the Woman's Film*, (Ed.) Christine Gledhill, London: BFI Publishing, 1987. First published in *Monogram* 4 (1972): pp2-15.

Heath, Stephen, "The Question Oshima," in *Questions of Cinema,* Bloomington: Indiana University Press, 1981.

Hollinger, Karen, "Embattled Voices: The Narrator and the Woman in Film Noir and the Woman's Film", Ph.D. thesis, University of Illinois at Chicago, 1990.

Johnston, Claire, "Femininity and the Masquerade: Anne of the Indies", In *Jacques Tourneur*, London: British Film Institute, 1975.

Modleski, Tania, "Time and Desire in the Woman's Film," in *Letter from an Unknown Woman*, (Eds.) Virginia Wright Wexman and Karen Hollinger, New Brunswick, NJ: Rutgers University Press, 1986. First published in *Cinema Journal* 23, no. 3 (Spring 1984): pp19-30.

Pipolo, Tony, "The Aptness of Terminology: Point of View, Consciousness and *Letter from an Unknown Woman*", *Film Reader* 4 (1979): pp166-179.

Wexman, Virginia Wright and Karen Hollinger, "The Continuity Script," in *Letter from an Unknown Woman*, (Eds.) Virginia Wright Wexman and Karen Hollinger, New Brunswick, NJ: Rutgers University Press, 1986.

Williams, Alan Larson, *Max Ophuls and the Cinema of Desire,* New York: Arno Press, 1980.

Wood, Robin, "Ewig hin der Liebe Glück," in *Letter from an Unknown Woman*, (Eds.) Virginia Wright Wexman and Karen Hollinger, New Brunswick, NJ: Rutgers University Press, 1986. First published in *Personal Views: Explorations in Film*, London: Gordon Fraser, 1976.

NOTES

1. See Peter Brooks, *The Melodramatic Imagination: Balzac, Henry James, Melodrama, and the Mode of Excess*, New Haven: Yale University Press, 1976. pp11, 14, 56.

2. Ibid. Brooks, '76. p5.

3. Ibid. Brooks, '76. p28.

4. Modified from Jane Campion, *The Piano*, New York: Hyperion, 1993, p31. In quoting from this script, I have removed stage directions and shot descriptions except where important to understanding the dialogue. Where I have modified the dialogue to match that of the film, "mod." follows the citation.

5. Note that shadow play is another indirect form of communication, and so is right at home in melodrama.

6. We have an opposite feeling when we see the chopping of Ada's finger, which this shadow play prefigures. There is no "thrill" in watching that performance on screen – only an unbearable churning in one's stomach.

7. For example, see Karen Hollinger, "Embattled Voices: The Narrator and the Woman in Film Noir and the Woman's Film", Ph.D. thesis, University of Illinois at Chicago, 1990.

8. For example, see Mary Ann Doane, *The Desire to Desire: The Woman's Film of the 1940s*, Bloomington: Indiana University Press, 1987. pp150-152.

9. Stanley Cavell articulates this question as well, "Psychoanalysis and Cinema: The Melodrama of the Unknown Woman", in *The Trial(s) of Psychoanalysis*, (Ed.) Françoise Meltzer, Chicago: The University of Chicago Press, 1988. p254.

10. "The Continuity Script," in *Letter from an Unknown Woman*, (Eds.) Virginia Wright Wexman and Karen Hollinger, New Brunswick, NJ: Rutgers University Press, 1986. p35; hereafter referred to as *Letter*. In quoting from this continuity script, I have removed stage directions and shot descriptions except where important to understanding the dialogue.

11. Ibid. *Letter*, '86. p131.

12. Tony Pipolo, in his essay on *Letter from an Unknown Woman*, emphasises the distinction between optical and narrative points of view. Following J. M. Lotman, Pipolo argues that in film, departures from optical point of view are in fact necessary to achieve narrative point of view, and selects *Letter from an Unknown Woman* to demonstrate his point. Even when the camera strays from Lisa's optical point of view, "Ophuls has made every effort to attune the camera's gaze and mobility to Lisa's temperament, particularly in…crucial moments of her emotional awakening. As a result, he has achieved much more than an approximation between camera view and character consciousness" (Pipolo, "The Aptness of Terminology: Point of View, Consciousness and *Letter from an Unknown Woman*," *Film Reader* 4 [1979]: p172). Moments of directorial intervention, like the commentary of the all-woman band, still do not violate the spirit of Lisa's character (Pipolo p177).

13. Op. cit. Hollinger, '86. pp14, 24.

14. Robin Wood, "Ewig hin der Liebe Glück", in *Letter*, '86. p231.

15. Op. cit. Doane, '87. p5.

16. Op. cit. *Letter,* '86. p60.

17. Op. cit. Campion, '93. p9.

18. I take my understanding of the terms which describe sound's spatial and temporal dimensions – "diegetic" (subcategorised "internal," "external," "onscreen," and "offscreen"; also the "sound bridge"), and "nondiegetic" – from David Bordwell and Kristin Thompson, *Film Art: An Introduction*, (fourth edition), New York: McGraw-Hill, Inc., 1993. pp307-316.

19. Op. cit. Campion, '93. p96. (mod.)

20. See Doane, '87. p56. Although Doane makes this claim during a discussion of the medical discourse subgenre, it applies to the whole woman's film genre as she describes it.

21. Op. cit. Brooks, '76. p66.

22 Op. cit. Doane, '87. pp173-174.

23. See Cavell, "Psychoanalysis and Cinema", '88 and "Postscript (1989): To Whom It May Concern," *Critical Inquiry* 16, no. 2 (Winter 1990): pp248-289; Alan Larson Williams, *Max Ophuls and the Cinema of Desire,* New York: Arno Press, 1980. pp47-69; Stephen Heath, "The Question Oshima," in his *Questions of Cinema,* Bloomington: Indiana University Press, 1981 and Tania Modleski, "Time and Desire in the Woman's Film," in *Letter*, '86.

24. Op. cit. *Letter*, '86. p99.

25. "Woman, though, does not mourn, does not resign herself to loss. She basically *takes up the challenge of loss*…, seizing it, living it, leaping. This goes with not withholding; she does not withhold. She does not withhold, hence the impression of constant return evoked by this lack of withholding. And in the end, she will write this not withholding …, this not writing: she writes of

not writing, not happening", (Hélène Cixous, "Castration or Decapitation?" (trans.) Annette Kuhn, *Signs: Journal of Women in Culture and Society* 7, no. 1 [Autumn 1981]: p49; quoted in Modleski, '86. pp260-261).

26.   'Death-dealing' is Cavell's phrase. See Cavell, "Postscript (1989)", '90. p265.

27.   Doane describes letters in women's films as an "'old-fashioned' means of articulating the effects of such a presence-in-absence," see Doane, '87. p113.

28.   Ibid. Campion, '93. p22.

29.   Ibid. Campion, '93. pp23-26.(mod).

30.   Ibid. Campion, '93. p42. (mod).

31.   Ibid. Campion, '93. p72.

32.   Ibid. Campion, '93. p76. (mod).

33.   Ibid. Campion, '93. p78. (mod).

34.   Ibid. Campion, '93. p94. (mod).

35.   The film lacks scenes in which Baines retrieves the key from the Maoris and has three girls read the key to him:

BAINES: Can you read?
He holds out the piano key. BIG SISTER *takes it with great authority, her friends crowd behind her. She frowns at the writing. She turns it over.*
BIG SISTER: Running writing, we haven't done that yet.
READING GIRL 1: Myrtle can read it, her mother taught her.
The key is snatched from BIG SISTER *and given to* MYRTLE –
MYRTLE (*Frowning*.): D e a r G e o r g e – Y o u – have –
BIG SISTER: That's "my."
MYRTLE: It's not an "M."
BIG SISTER: Yes it is.
MYRTLE AND BIG SISTER: Dear – George – you – have – my –
MYRTLE: – heart? (*She pulls a face as if it doesn't make sense.*) Ada McGrath ...
BAINES: Say it again, just you.
MYRTLE: Dear George you have my heart, Ada McGrath.
BAINES: You say it. (*He points to* BIG SISTER, *who has a deep voice.*)
BIG SISTER: Dear George you have my heart, Ada McGrath. (in Campion, '93. pp107-108)

If these scenes were in the film, the key would, like Lisa's letter, reach its intended recipient despite passing through a mediated postal route. But since the film exists without these scenes, the written meaning of the keys only gets directed, with a different message, at one who can read it: Stewart.

36.   Ibid. Campion, '93. p111. (mod).

37.   Ibid. Campion, '93. pp96-97. (mod).

38.   Ibid. Campion, '93. p104. (mod).

39.   Ibid. Campion, '93. p115.

40.   Ibid. Campion, '93. p115. (mod).

41.   Quoted in Miro Bilborough, "The Making of *The Piano*," in Campion, '93. p147.

42.   Op. cit. Brooks, '76. p18,35-36.

43.   Ibid., '76. p17.

44   Ibid., '76. p32.

45.   A possible counter-reading of the film would argue that the social order is comprised of the characters who leave Stewart behind, and therefore that the twist on melodramatic convention in *The Piano* is that the method by which social order is restored is relocation rather than expulsion. However, I think the film encourages us to read Stewart as the agent through which patriarchy speaks, and that the desire which Ada maintains by leaving Stewart behind is a radical one. Conventional melodrama begins with an established social order which a villain disrupts but which in the end is restored; if we think of Ada, Baines, and Flora as comprising a social order at the end of the film, I believe we must read it as not a *restored* community but instead the foundation of a new one. When I later analyse Ada's near death, it will become even clearer that she does not act to restore a social order but rather survives the efforts of the social order to restore itself in melodramatic fashion.

46.   "In melodrama, violence, the strong action, the dynamic movement, the full articulation and the fleshed-out emotions – so characteristic of the American cinema – become the very signs of the characters' alienation, and thus serve to formulate a devastating critique of the ideology that supports it", (Thomas Elsaesser, "Tales of Sound and Fury: Observations on the Family Melodrama," in *Home Is Where the Heart Is: Studies in Melodrama and the Woman's Film*, (Ed.) Christine Gledhill, London: BFI Publishing, 1987. p62).

47.   Op. cit. Brooks, '76. p168. Since Brooks treats James at length and he is mentioned in Cavell's work on the "melodrama of the unknown woman," an examination of Campion's *The Portrait of a Lady* (1996, UK/US and registered its relationship to melodrama and to James' novelistic flavour of melodrama would be most interesting. I also wonder if the recent spate of James adaptations – *Washington Square* (Agnieszka Holland, 1997, USA), *The Wings of the Dove* (Iain Softley, 1997, USA/UK), and *The Portrait of a Lady* – reflects some felt need for melodrama in the present (or, alternatively, perhaps a desire to take up older melodramas in order to de-melodramatise them or somehow render them tragic – here I am genuinely asking questions without having answers in mind).

48.   Op. cit. Doane, '87. p4.

49.   Ibid. Doane, '87. p179.

50.   Ibid. Doane, '87. p178.

51.   Ibid. Doane, '87. p181.

52.   Doane, '87, pp118–119. See also Claire Johnston, "Femininity and the Masquerade: Anne of the Indies," in *Jacques Tourneur,* London: British Film Institute, 1975. p40.

53.   Cavell, "Ugly Duckling, Funny Butterfly: Bette Davis and *Now, Voyager*," *Critical Inquiry* 16, no. 2 (Winter 1990): pp226-227. Future criticism might re-examine other women's films of the 1940s to see if and how the films articulate subtle but powerful rejections of the social orders re-established in the playing out of melodrama. The question, which exceeds the scope of this essay, is to what degree it would be plausible to add to the singularly short list of elements common to all women's films (viz., address to a female spectator [Doane, '87, p34]), the employment of the melodramatic against the conservatism of its archetype. Does the indictment of the melodramatic characterise the woman's film generally, or do we understand films which make that indictment to be members of a "(sub)genre...which contests that message [the deplorable message conveyed by the woman's film], whose details instead declare that women left alone with their own judgment...are capable of judging the goodness of the 'good' world, and contain untold reserves of desire, which may or may not find worthwhile investment?" in Cavell,'90 "Postscript [1989]". p275.

54.   Op. cit. Cavell, '90, "Ugly Duckling." p233.

55.   Op. cit. Campion, '93. p120. (mod).

56.   This reading was suggested to me by Jolynn Parker, private conversation, 29 March 1995.One could make an interesting case that Ada does drown and that the images of Nelson are the dreams and her floating body above the piano the reality.

57.   Op. cit. Brooks, '76. p35. On a related note, Doane mentions that "the horror film acts as intertext of the woman's film." See Doane '87. p48.

58.   Op. cit. Campion, '93. p115.

59.   Op. cit. Doane, '87. p56.

CHAPTER 3

FEMALE SEXUALITY, CREATIVITY, AND DESIRE IN THE PIANO

RICHARD ALLEN

he Piano is a gothic melodrama whose central complex conceit is the elective muteness of its heroine, Ada McGrath (Holly Hunter). We learn nothing of the origins of Ada's affliction in the film itself, just that she became mute when she was six, but the subsequent behaviour of the character suggests that her mutism has a willed aspect. The etiology of elective mutism undoubtedly has some bearing on Campion's attention to it. Elective mutism is more common in girls than boys and in one widespread variant mutism appears to embody a strategy of active manipulation and control of the environment rather than simply being a symptom of autistic withdrawal.[1] Abstracted from the specific conditions that may have caused it, elective mutism functions in *The Piano* as a conceit through which Campion explores a question that has preoccupied much feminist thought of the last twenty years: the capacity of women to articulate their desire within a culture where they are denied mastery of discourse.

Feminist critics have documented the way in which the gothic melodrama in literature and film depicts the trials of a mute, hysterical, heroine who is driven to despair by a tyrannical patriarch or, in the paranoid version of the female gothic, an apparent tyrant, and is punished if she is faithless or dares to transgress. "Muteness," notes Mary Ann Doane "is in some ways paradigmatic for the genre. For it is ultimately the symptoms of the female body which 'speak' while the woman as subject of discourse is invariably absent."[2] If, in the gothic melodrama, muteness and hysteria offer resistance to male authority they are, nonetheless, forms of madness that must be diagnosed and cured. Submission to male authority in the form of the redeemed patriarch or the rescuing prince is inescapable. *The Piano* adopts the conventions of the gothic melodrama: the mute heroine of the film suffers at the hands of the patriarch Stewart (Sam Neil), she is punished for her transgressive desires; and she is finally 'rescued' by her prince Baines (Harvey Keitel). Yet these conventions are adopted in order to be subverted, for the 'madness' of the heroine is valorised and given a voice.

While Ada is mute she expresses herself through her piano and through the mediation of a private sign language; her wishes are verbalised by her daughter Flora (Anna Paquin). Furthermore, the audience is given access to her thoughts through a voice-over narration that frames the narrative from some time in the future when she has regained the powers of speech. In a context where Ada is at once mute and articulate, her muteness and the forms of self-expression that are associated with it can be interpreted as "a limit case of patriarchal domination, both symptom and countercoup."[3]

The inspiration for Campion's rewriting of the Gothic melodrama is undoubtedly not only the body of feminist writing on the gothic melodrama that seeks to redeem the voice of the mute, hysteric heroine but also feminist re-evaluation of psychoanalytic theory that has explored the way in which classical psychoanalysis forms a kind of parallel cultural discourse to the discourse of melodrama. After all, Freud was also concerned with the problem of female muteness: the institution of psychoanalysis was founded upon the attempt by men to understand the condition of female hysteria. Furthermore, in the Hollywood version of the female gothic the two discourses, psychoanalysis and melodrama, often come together through the figure of the psychiatrist/doctor who rescues the Gothic heroine from her condition.[4] Yet while Freud identified female muteness as a problem, classical psychoanalysis also enshrined a conception of sexual difference in which it seemed that only the male can achieve the instinctual renunciation/phallic focalisation required for mastery over language and cultural achievement while woman is relegated to the dark continent of hysterical, body-centred, inchoate desire. For contemporary feminists the institution of psychiatry (including psychoanalysis) did as much to produce and re-enforce the problem of the silent body-centredness of femininity as to discover it. In an earlier film, *Angel at My Table*, Campion explored the suffering and resilience of writer Janet Frame, after eight years of institutionalisation with wrongly diagnosed schizophrenia. In *The Piano*, by again making her mute heroine so eloquently expressive, she redeems psychiatry's negative characterisation of women's silence by giving that silence a voice. This voice has, nonetheless, a very different relationship to subjectivity and desire from the instrumental form of communication that is culturally identified with the male voice and patriarchal institutions.

Campion succeeds in challenging and transforming the conventions of melodrama and the assumptions about sexual difference that they, together with classical psychoanalytic discourse, enshrine, through the historical and aesthetic self-consciousness she brings to the work. *The Piano* is set in the mid nineteenth century when the gothic melodrama achieved its maturity. However, by staging her story in the newly conquered and colonised New Zealand bush, Campion lays bear the link between the wealth and power of the patriarch in the home and the activity of conquest and colonialism overseas. In the figure of Stewart, the man to whom Ada has been betrothed by her father, the mentality of the patriarch and the coloniser are combined. Stewart seeks to colonise and control the landscape just as he seeks to colonise and control Ada's desire. He lacks the capacity to enter into and empathise with the land he inhabits and the native form of life he finds there. He builds useless fences across inaccessible mountainous land, reduces the forest to charred embers rising out of the mud in order to clear a space around his dwelling. He treats the Maoris as subhuman and finds their direct expressions of sexuality obscene. When he catches Flora pretending with the Maori children to fornicate with trees, he makes her return with soap and water to scrub them clean. The terms of his relationship to Ada are immediately apparent when he refuses to allow Ada, for the time being, to take her precious piano back to his cabin. He has legitimate reasons; it's a rough journey over soggy terrain and, given the number of bearers, it means either leaving the piano behind or leaving behind her clothing and kitchenware. Stewart cannot imagine that Ada would prefer the last option, but we (the audience) already know what the piano means to her. Stewart is unable to hear Ada: he cannot appreciate her music, and he is unable to see her: he opines to Baines that she looks stunted. Although not entirely unsympathetic, for he is a victim of the patriarchal conventions and mores he so thoroughly inhabits, he is condemned by his total lack of imagination that leads him to attempt to dominate and control that which he cannot comprehend.

The film's aesthetic achievement lies in Campion's daring juxtaposition of the impotence of patriarchal authority to an hyperbolisation of the nineteenth century metaphors that link female sexuality to the dark interiors of unconquered continents and the "primitive" peoples that inhabit them. The bush is a muddy, glutinous, fecund landscape, a kind of primal swamp that is filmed in a luminous aquamarine. In Campion's naturalist vision, the bush is a feminine landscape, boldly celebrated as an antidote to the denaturing of the land enacted by a patriarchal colonialism. The indigenous Maori are at home in this environment, not merely in the way they move through and inhabit it, but because they are portrayed as fully dwelling within their own nature, their bodies and their sexuality. In a way that parallels Ada's silence that speaks, the Maori characters display a subversive wit and perspicuity that the representatives of civilisation so conspicuously lack. This is not to claim that *The Piano* revisits the problem of colonialism with the same self-consciousness that attends its exploration of sexual repression. Campion's bold deployment of the metaphor of the dark continent carries its costs. The equation between female sexuality, the dark continent and its native inhabitants creates in Lynda Dyson's words a "fantasy of colonial reconciliation" in which a good colonisation represented by the figure of Baines, a colonial settler who has assimilated native customs and habits, is contrasted with the bad colonisation of Stewart.[5] The costs of the colonial project as a whole are thereby elided and the enterprise vindicated, even as the film, through its literalisation of the metaphor of the dark continent, offers a powerful criticism of patriarchy.

The relationship of Baines (Harvey Keitel) to the land and its indigenous population is in marked contrast to Stewart. His home merges with the marshland rather than being demarcated from it. Even the walls of his home are porous to the environment and natural light. He is linked with the Maori through his facial markings and understanding of their language. He is at home in this world rather than seeking to fashion it in his image. Indeed, he is most at home in their world, eschewing the company of the other colonials. Keitel typically portrays a man whose inarticulateness bespeaks an emotional numbness and pain that issues in violence. But here, his inarticulateness and his wonderfully expressive, gnarled body (echoing the wild knotted trees of the landscape) denote a vulnerability that is both registered by the camera and acknowledged by the character. Here Keitel plays a Lawrentian hero, a man who is willing to submit to his feelings rather than to control and direct them. As I shall explore in more detail, he is impelled by desire to possess Ada but he also wishes to be absorbed and annihilated by her, to be possessed himself. The film's female/feminist point of view thus allows for the articulation of the vulnerability of male desire just as much as it affords the articulation of female desire.

GRAND NARRATIVES OF FEMALE SEXUALITY

But how does Campion portray female desire in *The Piano*? The challenge to a patriarchal conception of sexuality in general and female sexuality in particular enacted in the film is far from straightforward. The problem lies precisely in the film's redemption of female muteness and the self-contained narcissistic universe of experience it entails. How can female muteness function both as a symptom and countercoup to patriarchy? If female muteness is considered a symptom to be diagnosed and cured then the forms of self-expression attendant upon it must be part of the symptom rather than simply a reversal of it. Of course, if we place all our interpretative weight on the fact that Ada "elects" this condition, then her discovery of techniques of self-expression that are an alternative to linguistic communication can be construed as a form of female self-determination and creative self-realisation. It is Ada's self-determination that leads her to choose Baines, the rescuing prince of Gothic melodrama retro-fitted for feminism, rather than the patriarch Stewart as her partner and equal in love.

Yet suppose that we consider Ada's muteness not as a willed condition but as a condition of nature. This connection is made in the opening scene of the film as Ada arises from her seat at the foot of a large tree and walks out underneath its outstreched branches across a leaf-strewn, windswept lawn, and begins in voice-over narration to tells us of her mute condition. Conceived as a natural condition, Ada's mutism is less something elected by her than elected on her behalf by Campion who seeks, so to speak, to throw the myth of the essential femininity back in the face of patriarchal culture, not as a problem but as an antidote. However, in this interpretation of the film none of the features that make Ada's behaviour 'symptomatic' are countered, only their nominalisation. Her mutism and the way it governs her engagement with the world paints a dark picture of female desire in which female sexuality is inextricably wedded to the experience of loss and pain.[6] It is as if, for Campion, the exploration of female sexuality lends us a privileged insight into the peremptory, arbitrary and ultimately self-destructive nature of desire that is disavowed within a rational, goal oriented, and patriarchal social order that seeks to channel and contain its unruly, even deathly, nature.

In this respect, the re-definition of symptom as nature in *The Piano* is not unlike the portrayal of female sexuality in an earlier Campion film, *Sweetie*. The heroine of *Sweetie* is promiscuous and 'hysterical': infantile in her sexuality, body-centred in her identity, lacking a 'proper' sense of interpersonal boundaries, and depressive and suicidal in thought. In one brief scene we see her washing her father in the bath and she 'playfully' drops the sponge between his legs and reaches to pick it up as he passively looks on. Is Sweetie's condition therefore 'symptomatic,' a result of child abuse? It seems to me that this possibility is raised by the film only to be contested, for elsewhere in the film Sweetie is strongly connected to nature, instinct, and fertility in contrast to her frigid, repressed, boundary obsessed, though ostensibly normal sister, who chops down the tree that grows in the back garden and leaves it to die under her bed. Sweetie is a creature of nature not culture and in this respect her tolerant, if indulgent, father compares favourably in his treatment of her with her hostile, even murderous, sister.

If I am right, there are, then, two rather different narratives at work in *The Piano* working both with and against the idea of female mutism as a malady and symptom. Both have their origins in feminist appropriation and reconsideration of post-Freudian developments in psychoanalysis.[7] The first narrative is predicated upon object relations psychology redefined by a cultural feminism. A key thinker for cultural feminism and, I believe, for Jane Campion, is the British pediatrician and psychoanalyst, D.W. Winnicott. For Winnicott, the role of the mother is a traditional one: she provides a facilitating environment for the child's growth and development, in particular the realisation of her or his creative imagination. Winnicott describes the mirroring relationship between mother and child from which a sense of self emerges and he analyses the role of the so-called transitional objects, such as blankets and toys in fostering the child's creative interaction with the world and nurturing her sense of self-identity apart from the mother. As we shall see, the idea of mirroring and creative play are strongly evoked in Campion's portrayal of the relationship between Ada and her daughter Flora and its link to their shared experience of Ada's music making.

The feminist spin that is given to object-relations psychology within cultural feminism is that the processes described by Winnicott play an especially crucial role in the formation of female subjectivity. Winnicott himself implicitly acknowledged this when he contrasted a 'feminine' form of relatedness to the world he called 'being' with a 'masculine' form of instinct governed behaviour that is predicated upon separation from the world and hence the need to control, associated with 'doing.'[8] Nancy Chodorow explores the way that in a culture where mothers perform the nurturing function, boys are required to define themselves against the mother in a way that girls are not. As a result "feminine personality comes to be based less on repression of inner objects, and fixed and firm splits in the ego, and more on retention and continuity of external relationships" and "more flexible and fluid ego boundaries."[9] Jessica Benjamin draws explicitly on Winnicott in order to articulate the extent to which self-identity and the capacity for creative self expression are forged in the interaction between mother and child rather than in the instinctual renunciation that defines the Oedipus complex, and the acquisition of linguistic command that coincides with it.[10] In this context, Ada's mutism/self-expression, together with the relationship she establishes with her daughter, evokes a sphere of feminine experience that has flourished in the absence of, and even in resistance to, patriarchal presence or intervention. Benjamin stresses, above all, the need for the mother to possess an autonomous identity in the eyes of the female child. The autonomous identity of the mother affords in turn the female child an identity that she can recognise as one that belongs to herself as a woman. In this way femininity could no longer be defined simply as lack in relationship to the culturally bestowed plenitude of the male phallus, for a strong identity would already be bequeathed to the female child which paves the way for an adult object choice that is relational rather than hierarchical, one based on shared feeling rather than domination and submission. Such a narrative is enacted in *The Piano* through Ada's choice of Baines and rejection of Stewart.

The second narrative is that of a psychoanalytic feminism whose origins lie in Lacanian psychoanalysis. Lacan's conception of subjectivity is in radical contrast to Winnicott and returns to Freud with a vengeance. By concentrating on the role of object-relations and the formation of self, Winnicott sought to play down the role of instinct theory within psychoanalysis, indeed he wrote that there is "no sense in making use of the word *id* for phenomena that are not covered and catalogued and experienced and eventually interpreted by ego functioning."[11] For Lacan, in contrast, the ego takes the place of an id that remains completely alien to it and consistently threatens to subvert it. Lacanian mirroring, like Winnicott's, engenders a sense of self, and in a certain sense for both thinkers, the self that is engendered is a fiction, but for Lacan, the ego is not simply a fiction but a fantasy that is predicated upon deception and narcissistic illusion. The significance of Lacanian psychoanalysis for feminist thought in this respect is that it seems to offer a way of exposing the fiction of subjectivity upon which a patriarchal social order is founded. A patriarchal culture that deems women mad, mute, body-centred hysterics, beyond the pale of culture is predicated upon a fantasy of linguistic mastery and autonomy. It is women's 'madness' that gives lie to this fantasy by speaking the truth of subjectivity and revealing the proximity of life to a mortality that the patriarchal social order consistently seeks to deny.

French feminist and Lacanian psychoanalyst Julia Kristeva explicitly connects female muteness to creativity. She posits a form of vocal and gestural significa- tion that exist prior to language or what she calls, after Lacan, the symbolic. Kristeva terms this form of signification the "semiotic" and associates it with the infant's experience of the mother's body as container or receptacle for bodily processes she calls the *chora*. This realm of experience, immeasurably pleasur- able, is nonetheless, one of pure unbounded negativity. "The mother's body," she writes, "is the ordering principle of the semiotic *chora*, which is on the path

of destruction, aggressivity and death."[12] Art, for Kristeva, represents a "semioti-
sation of the symbolic" and the "flow of jouissance into language," thus, for
Kristeva, music is presumably the art that bears the most direct relationship to
the experience of the drive and the mother's body.[13] She writes that "intonation
and rhythm" which define music "lead us directly to the otherwise silent place
of the subject."[14] Ada's mutism signals her attachment to what might be termed
a body-centred subjectivity that is defined by instinct which blurs the boundary
between self and other, self and world: it finds expression in her piano playing,
and it is resistant, not to say antithetical, to the boundary maintenance and agent
centred subjectivity required of an adult, patriarchal world. In this context, the
piano functions not as a transitional object but more like Lacan's object (a);
something that represents, in the sense of standing in for, an imaginary wholeness or plenitude that is represented by Kristeva's idea of the *chora*. By standing
in for an imaginary wholeness the object (a) precipitates a yearning for it, and
by sustaining that yearning, guarantees that desire cannot be satisfied.[15]

This way of conceiving the significance of Ada's creativity is fundamentally at
odds with the cultural feminist narrative, for her piano playing is not part of her
"development" but embodies her resistance to it. Rather than leading to a more
relational form of "object choice," Ada's subjectivity, according to this narrative,
is one that resists all "object choices." Any kind of "relation" is a form of
self-annihilation, entailing the loss of the imaginary wholeness that defines the
subject's pre-symbolic or real identity. In this psychoanalytic narrative, the
subject's entry into language and the realm of adult object choice is inevitably a
fall from the narcissistic illusion of self-object or self-other identity to the
realisation of the unbreachable chasm between self and other. The pleasure
principle that underpins narcissism is modified by the reality principle which, for
Lacan and Kristeva, is the beyond of the pleasure principle, the impossibility of
desire's satisfaction and hence the recognition of the death that inhabits life. If
we transpose this pessimistic narrative onto *The Piano*, Baines appears no better
as an object choice than Stewart for he too destroys Ada's narcissistic sense of
self sufficiency. So much so, that when Ada is faced with the loss of illusion that
the good life with Baines entails she seriously entertains the possibility of
self-annihilation.

PIANO PLAYING IN A PRE-OEDIPAL WORLD

The enigma of female sexuality in *The Piano* and, no doubt, the widely differing
critical responses to the film arises, I believe, from the coexistence of two
apparently incompatible narratives of the relationship between femininity, crea-

tivity and desire. The ambiguity centers on the role of the piano. The piano is something that Ada brings to the present, and to the Bush, from her childhood and it is established as an object that Ada needs in order to negotiate the journey away from home. We first witness Ada playing in a darkened room, where the piano is surrounded by packing cases suggesting imminent departure. Ada begins to play with great concentration and intensity until she is abruptly interrupted by a woman who is clearly not her mother. Moments of screen time later, when Ada and Flora land on the beach, Ada stands pensively by the piano to reassure herself after the ordeal of the journey. In this way, the piano helps establish Ada's psychological separation from home and supports her sense of self-identity. Her attachment to the piano gains in intensity once she is threatened with its loss, and this is strikingly dramatised through Campion's cinematography and the swelling soundtrack once Stewart refuses to bring the piano home and she is forced to abandon it on the beach. Beginning with a high angle, long shot over the shoulder of Ada looking down to the piano isolated on the vast expanse of the beach, the camera slowly zooms in to a closer view and Nyman's music swells as Ada emotionally cleaves to the object. The flaps of Ada's hood still remain visible in the immediate foreground evoking a psychological, rather than simply a physical, presence. A reverse-field of Ada looking at the piano on the beach is shot as a slow lateral circular dolly movement through a telephoto lens that blurs the background. The shot serves to completely detach character from environment and complete the sense for the viewer that she inhabits a self-enclosed psychological space together with the piano. When Ada arrives at Stewart's house and marries, she rushes back into the house in her sodden wedding dress and looks out through a rainswept window to imagine the piano on the beach (the audience actually sees the piano on the beach). Finally, denying herself to him, even after they are married, she compulsively recreates a facsimile of the piano out of his kitchen table when he continues to refuse her request to bring it to the house.

How are we to understand the role of the piano in the film? On the one hand, by affording Ada a creative interaction with the world in a context where she is undergoing separation and transition, the piano evokes Winnicott's transitional object. The transitional object is a toy played with by a child that, according to Winnicott, provides the child with its first contact with a reality that is beyond the orbit of merely subjective perception; it is experienced by the child at once as 'me' and as 'not-me.' The sense of otherness that it affords reciprocally engenders in the child a sense of self. For Winnicott, it is in the child's transaction with the transitional object that the origins of volition, creativity and hence of self-identity lie. Of course, when we encounter Ada in *The Piano* she is not a child playing with her toys but, already, an adult pianist. However, the link between the two kinds of playing and between adulthood and childhood is secured by the symbolic identity that Campion creates between Ada and her little girl Flora. Ada and Flora are doubled in many ways. They consistently echo each other in their position in the frame, and in their costume, gesture and mannerisms. Flora is roughly the same age as Ada when she went deaf and she is also Ada's voice to the outside world. Through this doubling, it is as if Ada's relationship to her own (absent) mother is reproduced in the relationship she bears to Flora. Just as Flora speaks for Ada, Ada 'speaks' through her piano of her relationship with her own mother and therefore she also speaks for Flora's relationship with herself. Ada is thus at once child and mother.

The scenes on the beach imaginatively establish the creative, playful, and self-affirming relationship between the mother and daughter, and the role of Ada's piano playing in expressing this. Winnicott uses the term "transitional space" to refer to the area of experience in which the transitional object is creatively manipulated. It is neither wholly inner (the condition of existence for the child who has not yet felt the mother's absence), nor wholly outer and external to the child (the experience of reality of the child who has been weaned), but partaking of both. This idea of transitional space is brilliantly figured in the film's most memorable images: those that feature Ada and Flora playing with and alongside the piano on the beach, situated between the undifferentiated expanse of sea (the link with an absent mother) and the dark, seemingly impenetrable barrier of the bush (the world of adult desire). As Baines looks on, Ada plays the piano with passion as Flora constructs a beautiful sea horse out of shells found on the beach, creatively playing beside her mother who creatively plays alongside Baines. Then mother and daughter play a duet together, and finally from a high angle shot we see their footprints on the sand cross and unite around the sea horse, with Baines looking on behind them. Campion depicts the mother daughter relationship as the well-spring for a reciprocated, non-exploitative form of love that is itself a model of creativity. Winnicott, as Benjamin relates, often quoted a line from Rabindrinath Tagore to express the idea of transitional space, of a boundary that opens onto unbounded possibility, that resonates with these scenes: "on the seashore of endless worlds children play."[16]

Winnicott is careful to distinguish a child's imaginative play with the transitional object from the psychoanlytic concept of the fetish. In general terms, terms which Lacan attempts to capture in the idea of the object (a), a fetish object in psychoanalytic theory is a substitute for something lost, though never attained, that serves to support and sustain wish-fulfilling fantasy where desires that cannot otherwise find fulfillment, and hence are a source of anxiety, appear satisfied by imagination alone. For Winnicott, the instinct driven fantasy that supports such a fetishistic substitution is the antithesis of creative imagination because it short circuits the role of the ego in its creative exchange with the physical world. The transitional object contributes to the cultivation of the imagination and the development of the individual, it is forward looking; the fetish binds and inhibits the imagination in fantasy, it is regressive.[17] And yet, Ada's attachment to her instrument does have a fetishistic aspect, an aspect in which it appears to serve as prop for a narcissistic fantasy of self-sufficiency. Ada is not a child, learning to negotiate separation, but an adult who has supposedly separated! Her attachment to the piano in the context of her adult responsibilities thus begins to seem less a means of effecting a transition to adulthood, than a means of arresting or refusing the transition, of sustaining narcissitic defenses against the threat of difference and otherness. In this regard, while *The Piano's* music evokes the inner life of the protagonist, it suggests less an inner life that is governed by the free play of imagination than one that is organised around the highly repetitive, obsessive theme of fantasy, of imagination governed by desire.

As I have already mentioned, an influential tradition of psychoanalytic theory links the appreciation of music to the infant's experience of the mother's voice in the context of the tactile environment of the mother's body, not as yet differentiated from the self. Music seems to short-circuit language and somehow evoke raw, unmediated feeling.[18] The relation of music to the mother's body and a pre-rational body centred subjectivity is evoked both by the character of Ada's relationship to the piano, her music making, and the connotations that are attached to it. Michael Nyman's choice of non-period music is crucial to the emotional impact of the score. Had Nyman used period music, even music supposedly written by Ada herself, the film would have conveyed the sense that Ada had mastered a musical corpus. The choice to use non-period music not simply emphasises the connection between music and Ada's inner life, but it highlights that life as a solipsistic internal world rather than the life of a mind that transacts with a larger culture of which Ada is, nonetheless, clearly aware, as is made evident in the moment when she hammers out Chopin's *Prelude in E major* (a standard in the piano repetoire), in defiance of Baines. Ada's own musical composition is marked by a high degree of repetition: we do not simply hear a repeated melody, with little development of theme, the music also uses a very repetitive, rolling, left hand accompaniment figure to accompany the signature melody.[19] This repetition suggests the obsessiveness of unfulfilled desire that is explicitly underscored as Ada gazes down longingly at the piano on the beach in the scene I have already described, one that evokes a sense of unfathomable loss. Music making in *The Piano* seems less a rational, purposive activity than a welling up of instinct minimally constrained by reason and form. The music also betrays a series of sometimes vague associations with the sea that is perhaps evoked in the film as a metaphor for the maternal-feminine. Sea shanties were purportedly an inspiration for the work and the sea is arguably evoked in the rolling left hand accompaniment. Furthermore, the piano is connected metonymically with the sea as it rests on the beach, and the sea also becomes its *final* resting place.

The figuration of the piano in the film contributes to the transitivity of mother-daughter relationships in which Ada is both mother and daughter. It does not simply stand in for Ada's lost or absent mother, it also seems to stands in for Ada herself, in the sense that it is both metaphorically and metonymically linked to her own body. Since narcissism involves a denial of the difference between self and other it is consistant with narcissism that the fetish used to support it is *understood* as a physical extension of the self, even though it is not. Ada's attachment to the piano is a strongly physical one, she needs to be near it, not simply to play, but just to be near it. Ada's declaration of love for Baines is made through dismembering a piano key, and Stewart responds by cutting off Ada's fingers, acting out, even if he does not realise it, the symbolic equation between piano keys and fingers, the piano and Ada's body. Baines is more self-conscious. For him, the piano is a way of obtaining Ada, and their erotic contract devised by Baines consists in an exchange of piano keys for access to Ada's body parts. In one scene the piano as a whole acts as a fetish substitute for the body of Ada as we spy Baines from behind, emerging naked from his bedroom to clean and then to caress the piano while we hear music making from Ada's previous recital in his house.

Any interpretation we give of *The Piano*'s complex motif of touching depends on whether we point to the role that touch plays in cementing the differentiation of and relationship between self and other – the child's interaction with the transitional object that is centred upon touch (and smell) rather than vision – or emphasise the extent to which touch suggests a pre-linguistic realm of essentially female body-centred immanence. Touch is central in the film to establishing the reciprocity between child and mother: it is emphasised as the immediate source of creativity in Ada's piano playing, and the manual dexterity required for Ada and Flora's private sign language and Ada's piano playing alike, and links Ada's creativity to the mother-child relationship. We first see Ada as she looks through her fingers at a visual field of white light that gives way to the sight of her little daughter trying to ride a resistant pony. The shot suggests a proximity between the senses of vision and the senses of touch, and evokes in this way, too, Ada's own connection with the world of childhood and Flora whom she at once sees and identifies with. The connection between Ada and Flora and creative self expression is evoked in a gesture on the beach where Ada cradles Flora and strokes her forehead and then, continuing the gestures, plays a few tender notes on the piano alongside them through a small gap in the packing crate.

At the same time, touch in *The Piano* also intimates a more primordial link between the self and other that evokes the body of the mother as the site of a pre-linguistic, pre-oedipal, utopian fusion. In a manner that is directly apposite to the mother-child role reversal that characterises *The Piano*, Kristeva writes that "by giving birth, the woman enters into contact with the body of *her* mother; she becomes, she is her own mother; they are the same continuity differentiating itself. She thus actualises the homosexual fact of motherhood, through which a woman is simultaneously close to her instinctual memory, more open to her own psychosis, and consequently, more negatory of the social, symbolic bond."[20] Campion links Ada's and Flora's private sign language with the body of the mother when, in the liminal space of the beach between the sea (mother) and the Bush (adult desire), we spy Ada engaged in an animated act of story-telling. She communicates with Flora in her private sign language in a womb like tent constructed out of one of Ada's hooped petticoats that is surrounded by a little mound of sand decorated with white shells no doubt sculpted by both mother and child. This scene serves as a visual figuration not only of Kristeva's idea of the *chora*: the container that encases and defines a body-centred "feminine" subjectivity where the child is a part of the mother's body, but of the "semiotic," non-linguistic, tactile, form of "communication" which defines it.[21]

PIANO PLAYING IN AN OEDIPAL WORLD

Cast up on land, Ada enters the world of adult desire and the claims made on her by Stewart and Baines. The interpretative conundrum posed by Ada's relationship to Stewart and Baines is this: does Baines simply represent a contrast to Stewart, a feminised man whom she can love as an equal? Or is Baines a wolf in sheep's clothing and really, like Stewart, someone who seeks to corral and own a femininity which defies and resists his understanding? To the extent that we view the masculinity of Baines in contrast to Stewart, Baines represents the possibility of a new kind of male heterosexual partnership. In this regard, *The Piano* offers a decidedly different conception of heterosexual romance than is typically portrayed on the silver screen. However, to the extent that Baines is, in the end, just another representative of patriarchy, marriage to him signals another form of imprisonment that is all the more oppressive in the sense that Ada is seduced into giving up her freedom and acquiescing to the theft of her heart.

As we have already seen, the contrast between Stewart and Baines is one that is sharply drawn. Stewart embodies the classical, though not caricatured, male response to the threat of difference and otherness of femininity. He preserves his self esteem by the effacement or diminution of the other. On the way to meet Ada on the beach, Stewart halts the party of bearers in order to gaze upon, furtively, a small framed photographic portrait of the woman to whom he is betrothed but has never seen. Looking at the picture lost in reverie, he meticulously pastes his hair across his forehead with a comb and we see that the glass cover of the portrait has become a mirror that effaces the image of Ada, thereby articulating Ada's function as a reflective surface for Stewart's narcissism. In contrast to Baines who seeks contact with and proximity to the object of desire, Stewart is a voyeur who craves proximity but can only tolerate proximity at a distance. This is made evident when he crawls his way under Baines house to get a really close look at their love-making. Stewart refers to Ada as a stunted human being, projecting onto her his own sense of himself. Unable to keep Ada caged up in his house like a trapped bird or to submit her will to his, he cuts off her finger, stunting her creativity in a desperate effort to preserve his own wounded narcissism. Then, when she is lying unconscious, he first sings her a lullaby, before attempting to penetrate her prostrate, lifeless body. At this point Stewart becomes metaphorically speaking a monster, one of the living dead; the charred, burnt out tree-trunks that surround his cabin provide an expressionist comment upon the relationship to death that negatively informs Stewart's life. By constantly refusing to recognise the loss and lack of wholeness that is a part of life, his life becomes governed by lack and death.

However, it is important that Stewart is not a caricature, but a character with whom we have some sympathy. It is reasonable in the circumstances for Stewart to expect that his new wife will comply to his will and lie with him. His expectations are framed by the conventions of an arranged marriage and he reasonably assumes that Ada is in agreement with these conventions since she complies with her father and makes the trip all the way to New Zealand from Scotland. The film makes clear that Stewart's monstrosity is really the monstrosity of the social order that he represents more than just the character. Blind to the way the social order constrains and confines his behaviour Stewart seeks to identify himself so completely with that social order that he reproduces it like an automaton. It is for this reason that he is, imaginatively speaking, dead. He lacks irony, creativity, a sense of humour, spontaneity and appreciation of music. He lacks, in fact, all that is represented in the creative piano playing and, we might surmise, the "core self" that is nurtured in the mother-child relationship. In Winnicott's vocabulary, Stewart lives a "false self" whose life is governed by defensive adaptation to environment rather than a creative interaction with it.

Baines, dumped by his wife, is a man who has retreated to the bush to wallow in instinct and the flesh. His orientation is completely towards realisation of the pleasures of the flesh to the point of erasing his own subjectivity. Musically illiterate, Baines nonetheless responds to Ada's piano playing as a direct expression of her self. As Stella Bruzzi has emphasised, Baines's desire is to enter into her world, to achieve proximity through touch, in contrast to the voyeuristic Stewart for whom boundaries and the differences they define are such a source of anxiety.[22] In this respect, it could be argued that Baines is a man who practices a way of being with the other that is culturally identified as feminine rather than masculine, and affords Ada a partner in love rather than someone who dominates or subordinates her to his desire. Although the circumstances of his courtship to Ada are contrived by Baines, he is captive as much as conqueror, for it is Ada through her piano playing who orchestrates the romance. It is also true that the film establishes a way of looking at Baines that at once places him in the traditional feminine role as object of the camera's gaze, and yet at the same time strips that gaze of the detached, voyeuristic objectifying quality that tends to accompany looking at the female body in commercial cinema. When we see Baines naked in the half light as he caresses the piano in Ada's absence, we are forced to acknowledge and respond to the character's vulnerability, even as we are invited to contemplate his compact, muscular body.

Yet the relationship between Ada and Baines is more complicated and ambivalent than the straightforward contrast between Stewart and Baines might lead us to believe. For this interpretation requires us to believe in the possibility of love, of a relationship with another that is not simply driven or subtended by narcissistic desire. This possibility is consistent with, and follows from, the narrative of cultural feminism which also renders "object relations," the relationship of self and other, conceptually independent from the psychic role of instinct. As we have seen, the point of Winnicott's narrative of child development is to challenge the psychoanalytic narrative of object relations that reduces the relationship to another, including the adult love relationship, to a function of the drives. However, just as the counter narrative of psychoanalytic feminism seems to inform the film's depiction of the mother-daughter interaction and its relationship to creativity, it also seems to inform the film's portrayal of the love relationship between Ada and Baines, and invest that relationship with a profound ambivalence. If Ada's muteness signifies an essential femininity that Ada and Flora share and Ada's piano playing serves to express, it is a narcissistic body-centred subjectivity which resists the differentiation of self and other. Thus Ada cannot but be resistant to the call of desire that is predicated upon the differentiation of self and other rather than upon refusal of that differentiation, since it requires her to relinquish her narcissism. However much Baines seeks to establish proximity to Ada through touch, one could argue, he cannot hope to get near her – he is always acting like Stewart, at a distance, and he cannot hope to respond to her subjectivity other than in a form that controls, possesses, and hence denatures it.

The relationship between Baines and Ada is overshadowed by the fact that Baines effectively steals the piano from Ada, when he arranges to purchase it from Stewart, and then extorts sexual favours from her in exchange for returning it. These are the circumstances in which Baines contrives to get close to Ada and in which Ada's own desire is aroused. While Baines' body-centred subjectivity contrasts him with Stewart and aligns him with Ada, his desire to touch her is just that, desire: desire that is inflamed and sustained by the apparent unattainability of the object. When Baines rather humourously grovels around at Ada's feet, desperate to find a spot of her body not covered by clothes, he seems very like Stewart debasing himself in the act of trying to get a good look at Ada and Baines making love. There is a difference between these two scenes: the exchange between Ada and Baines involves a certain reciprocity. However, it is a reciprocity conditioned by the terms of a contract. Ada does indeed begin to take pleasure in Baines' attention as her piano playing seems increasingly to become a solicitation, but it is a pleasure that does seem to be conditioned by her willingness to be objectified within a perverse scenario of control and submission. Of course, whether or not the relationship between Ada and Baines is accurately described as perverse is just what is at stake in interpreting these scenes. As Jessica Benjamin has written,

> "Eros is certainly not free of all that we associate with aggression, assertion, mastery and domination. But what makes sexuality erotic is the survival of the other with and despite destruction. What distinguishes Eros from perversion is not freedom from fantasies of power and surrender, for Eros does not purge sexual fantasy – it plays with it."[23]

It is certainly possible to view the "perversity" staged in the film as an hyperbolisation of romance, as a way of portraying the frisson, the electricity of erotic fantasy.

Baines confesses that the terms of the contract with Ada are making him wretched, nonetheless, he is a character who is quite at home, but perhaps too much at home, in the world of the flesh. Ada's response seems more complicated, more ambivalent, as if to expose Baines' uncomplicated pursuit of pleasure as a form of self-deception. After they have consummated the relationship it is easy for Baines to declare his love, but Ada's response is to look at her own image in the mirror, hesitant, before she turns back to him and passionately kisses him. For Ada, in contrast to Baines, desire involves a sense of risk, a sense that something, her self, is being lost. Insofar as Ada's subjectivity in the film is defined by a bodily narcissism, her awakening to the world of sexual desire comes at a great cost, for she is also awakened to the fact of her own lack of self-sufficiency. She now depends upon another to fulfil her desire, and the piano can no longer satisfactorily stand as a prop to her subjectivity. Her dependency is dramatised in the scenes where she is incarcerated in Stewart's house and her desire for Baines is frustrated. Approaching her piano, that has now been returned to her, she strokes the keys with the back of her hand, miming the caress of the piano that had earlier been made by Baines and she begins to play romantically. But the desire that impels her to play overwhelms the activity and she stops in frustration. Then, pressing her face against her own mirrored image, she kisses herself. Later, sleeping with her daughter, Flora, she presses her body close and begins to caress her until she awakens from her dream. Finally, while she denies her body to Stewart, she approaches him with the same caress. The overriding motivation, here, as in the other cases, is to use the object as a fetishistic substitute for the absent Baines. Now one might well want to emphasise the way in which these scenes portray an active fetishistic female sexuality that is at odds with traditional representations of female desire, and that complements the portrayal of male sexuality in the figure of Baines. However, while Baines readily returns to his Maori mistress when he is denied contact with Ada, for Ada, the separation from Baines is accompanied by an acute sense of loss, frustration and anxiety which dramatise the intensity and cost of her new attachment to Baines.

The costs of Ada's awakening to desire are also registered in the fate of her relationship to Flora which continues to parallel her relationship with the piano in the film. The status of the piano in this string of metonymic substitutions for the body of Baines is instructive. Once Ada acknowledges that her piano playing is functioning as a conduit to Baines' affection, by itself, it no longer provides a satisfactory support to her subjectivity. As if in recognition of this, Ada disengages a key from the piano and inscribes it with a testimony of her love for Baines. The fact that Flora's proximity to Ada inflames her desire dramatises the threat that the encroachment of adult sexuality poses to the mother-daughter relationship. Ada no longer needs Flora in the same way as she no longer needs the piano, and just as she uses the piano key as a way to Baines' heart she unconscionably uses Flora as her delivery girl, like a lover who uses an unseated rival to deliver a message of love to his beloved. Flora, on her part, sees Ada's passion for Baines as a threat to her own place in Ada's heart. She has manifest ambivalence to the relationship from the start, teasing and petting Baines' dog by turns as she is forced to wait interminably outside Baines' house while Ada plays within. Her hostility increases dramatically after she spies on them lying together. Once she is forced to act as go between she responds to her narcissistic wound by impulsively running to Stewart with the piano key that Ada has entrusted to her. This action is utterly comprehensible if it is understood as a response to jealous impulse rather than a considered response to consequences. Failing to comprehend her own narcissistic wound Flora cannot comprehend the wound inflicted upon Stewart and anticipate the calamitous rage that results from it.

I have argued that the *The Piano* can be interpreted as a story about the realisation of female desire and female self empowerment, and yet the film also supports a different, metaphysical understanding of female sexuality in which the female experience is privileged in exposing the impossibility of desire's satisfaction and, ultimately, the link between desire and death. I would argue that it is not a question of choosing between these interpretations on the grounds, say, of intellectual disagreement with a psychoanalytic understanding of human behaviour, because it seems to me that a metaphysical interpretation of psycho-analytic psychology is inscribed in the metaphors and symbols that govern the depiction of human action and interaction in the film. Although, as I have tried to show, the film is not reducible to this kind of psychoanalytic interpretation, I believe that a metaphysical picture of human motivation inhabits Campion's conception of the work. This is nowhere more apparent than in the closing scenes of the film.

As Baines and Ada leave the shores of New Zealand with the piano, Ada calls for it to be thrown overboard, ostensibly because of the danger that it might sink the boat with its weight. However, caressing the ocean with the back of her hand, she hints at a desire to abandon her life with that of the piano. As the piano slides overboard, she sees the coiled rope attached to it rapidly unfurl and impulsively places her foot within the coil. Moments later she is being dragged down to the bottom of the sea. After a protracted delay in which she entertains death, she lets loose the rope that attaches her to the piano and swims up to the glittering surface of the water. Then the film cuts abruptly to her new life with Baines in Nelson where she is a piano teacher and, with difficulty, is learning to speak. In order to grow up Ada has to give up her relationship to the piano insofar as it has functioned as a narcissistic prop to her subjectivity. To be sure, she could die with it, but the point Campion wants to make is more subtle. In the adult world of desire, the piano can no longer serve as a prop or guarantee for her wholeness in the way it did in her pre-Oedipal universe. On the contrary, what was once indispensable to the expression of her subjectivity has become a ball and chain, too palpable a reminder of her lack of wholeness. At the same time, when Ada goes with Baines at the end it is a choice she makes that is governed by an awareness of the death that awaits those who live with the social order, an understanding of the contingency of life. Perhaps having given up her narcissistic prop she is in a position to understand its symbolic significance in her life. Her fall into the water is what Lacan would call the encounter with the Real, an experience of non-being that demarcates the arbitrariness of being. The relatively normal and banal life we surmise that she then goes on to lead is a life that understands the place of death within it. When she plays the piano at the end she plays it with a silver finger that clicks every time it hits the key, as a reminder of imperfection and loss – a kind of baffle or stain in the field of sound. When we see her with Baines, practising her phonemes, finally learning to speak, the cloth draped over her head is a dark veil, as if she were in mourning, and the final image is one in which she imagines herself still suspended over the piano in its ocean grave as she speaks the lines of Thomas Hood:

> There is a silence where hath been no sound
> There is a silence where no sound may be
> In the cold grave, under the deep deep sea.

This paper originated in a presentation at Washington Square Institute, New York entitled "The transitional Object, Fetishism, and *The Piano*" that was subsequently published in their in-house journal *Issues in Psychoanalytic Psychology* 17:2 (1995). I thank my respondent on that occasion Dr. Judith Eckman-Jadow. Thanks also to Ira Bhaskar, Dr Martha Liebmann, Denise McKenna, Toby Miller and Jeff Smith

NOTES

1.   See Larry B Silver, "Elective Mutism," in Harold I. Kaplan and Benjamin Sadcock (Ed.) *Comprehensive Textbook of Psychiatry V*, Volume 2, 5th edition, ch. 42. p1. A reference to this work is made in Harvey Greenberg's review of the film in *Film Quarterly* 47:3 (1994). p46.

2.   Mary Ann Doane, "The 'Woman's Film' Possession and Address," in Christine Gledhill, (Ed.) *Home is Where the Heart Is: Studies in Melodrama and the Woman's Film*, London: BFI, 1987. p. 292. For further analysis of female muteness in the woman's film see Amy Lawrence, *Echo and Narcissus: Women's Voices in Classical Hollywood Cinema*, New York: University Of California Press, 1991.

3.   Harvey Greenberg, "The Piano," *Film Quarterly* 47:3, p48.

4.   See Mary Ann Doane, *The Desire to Desire: The Woman's Film of the 1940s,* Bloomington: Indiana University Press, 1987. pp39-69.

5. See Linda Dyson, "The return of the repressed? Whiteness, femininity and colonialism in *The Piano*," Chapter 7. p113.

6. This interpretation of the film has also been suggested by Suzy Gordon in ""I clipped your wing, that's all": auto-eroticism and the female specatator in The Piano debate" *Screen* 37:2 (Summer 1996). pp193-205, but not in terms that I find comprehensible.

7. Nancy Chodorow identifies and compares these two narratives of psychoanalytic feminism in *Feminism and Psychoanalytic Theory*, New Haven and London: Yale University Press, 1989. pp178-198.

8. See D.W. Winnicott, *Playing and Reality*, London: Routledge, 1971. p81.

9. Nancy Chodorow, *The Reproduction of Mothering: Psychoanalysis and the Sociology of Gender*, Berkeley: University of California Press, 1978. p169.

10. Jessica Benjamin, *The Bonds of Love: Psychoanalysis, Feminism and the Problem of Domination*, New York: Pantheon Books, 1988.

11. Op. cit. Winnicott, '71. *Playing and Reality*, p85

12. Julia Kristeva, *Revolution in Poetic Language* (trans.) Margaret Waller, New York: Columbia University Press, 1984. pp27-28.

13. Ibid. Kristeva, '84, *Revolution in Poetic Language*, p79.

14. Julia Kristeva, *Desire in Language: A Semiotic Approach to Literature and Art*, (Ed.) Leon S. Roudiez, (trans.) Thomas Gora, Alice Jardine and Leon S. Roudiez, New York: Columbia University Press, 1980. p167

15. On the role of the object (a) in Lacan's thought see *Seminar XI: The Four Fundamental Concepts of Psychoanalysis*, (trans.) Alan Sheridan, New York: Norton, 1978.

16. Op. cit. Winnicott, *Playing and Reality*, p95.

17. On Winnicott's relationship to Freud see Jay R. Greenberg and Stephen A. Mitchell, *Object Relations in Psychoanalytic Theory*, Cambridge Ma: Harvard University Press, 1983. pp188-209.

18. In addition to Kristeva, Guy Rosolato, Luce Irigary and Helene Cixous stress the link between emotional response to music and nostalgia for the mother. This tradition of thought is discussed by Carol Flynn in *Gender, Nostalgia and Hollywood Film Music*. Princeton: Princeton N.J., 1992. pp51-69.

19. Thanks to Jeff Smith for pointing this out to me and for his many other cogent observations on the film.

20. Op. cit. Julia Kristeva, *Desire in Language*, p239.

21. I owe this insight to Kyungwon Song who wrote a paper on "Female Jouissance and *The Piano*" for my class Psychoanalysis and Cinema.

22. See Stella Bruzzi, "Tempestuous Petticoats: costume and desire in The Piano," in Chapter 6. p104.

23. Jessica Benjamin, *The Bonds of Love*, New York: Pantheon Books, 1988. pp73–74.

CHAPTER 4

THE SICKNESS UNTO DEATH: DISLOCATED GOTHIC IN A MINOR KEY

KIRSTEN MOANA THOMPSON

I am terrified by this dark thing that sleeps in me.
All day I feel its soft, feathery turnings, its malignity

Elm, Sylvia Plath[1]

What lies at the heart of *The Piano* is a dark and monstrous secret, wrapped far beneath the tight Victorian clothing that haunts the mise-en-scène and the mute body of Ada McGrath. Investigating the thematic importance of the *secret* of Ada's muteness in *The Piano* is a way of tunneling beneath the locked houses, and enclosing spaces of bush and sea that permeate the private spaces of Ada's 'dark talent'. Jane Campion's 1992 film is a musical and visual inflection of Romantic gothic, a European cultural form that becomes allegorically displaced and refigured in the cultural location of nineteenth century colonial New Zealand.

Campion's gothic inflection traces the way in which music, sound and silence function as aural emblems, riddled with allegorical resonances that evoke the physical and psychological confinements in which Ada McGrath is placed and to which she responds. Three melodies in Michael Nyman's score form a narrative fulcrum upon which the songs *Big My Secret, The Heart Asks Pleasure First* ,and *Bed of Ferns* balance, winding their way through the film in shifting repetitions of diegetic and non-diegetic leitmotifs.[2] The narrative movement between these three central compositions emblematises Ada's conflicts and struggles; the melancholia of the secret sadness she bears, the ambivalence between her dark will that would take flight in self-destruction and her continuing struggle for passion and life.

THE GOTHIC

> *"And what would we see then Kleist, if we looked through the rents into*
> *the abyss behind the beauty, that would turn them mute."*
> Caroline von Günderrode[3]

The Piano shares elements of the mise-en-scène of both the cinematic and literary Gothic genres[4]. Later developments of the Gothic genre shifted from a medieval mise-en-scène (with its displacement of emotions of fear and horror within dark architectural spaces, labyrinthian passages and mountainous land-scapes) into a more tortuous and internal psychological realm of irrational passions and dark fantasies.[5] The predominant atmosphere of the Gothic was one of supernatural terror, mystery and uncanny horror. This literary and intel-lectual movement was in part a reaction to the eighteenth century's rationalism and neoclassicism. *The Piano* invokes the psychological grotesquerie of the Gothic together with the classical elements of Romanticism, where the power of emotions and the imagination are privileged with a sense of the sublime.

The Piano consciously inflects Romantic codes of musical expressivity with the dark tones of Gothic horror through its investigation of the violent consequences of the triangular relationship which connect the central characters Ada McGrath (Holly Hunter), George Baines (Harvey Keitel) and Alisdair Stewart (Sam Neill). The Gothic literary genre was centred on the family home as a site of psycho-logical terror, frequently thematised through the unspoken secret of incest by the father. This threat within the family is one signaled by the entrapment of the mise-en-scène, a theme which is traced within the claustrophobic spaces of *The Piano*. The allegorical displacement of the Romantic onto this colonial period piece, with the raw and unruly landscape of New Zealand's bush and sea, is a fitting site for the tumultuous emotions of passion, jealousy and love that unfurl, mimicking Ada's stormy and passionate will. Campion's Gothic inflection of Romanticism is structured through the allegorical hints of the film's score. What is the terrible secret that turned Ada mute and in what way does musical form and genre code her piano playing as central to the Gothic condition with its privileging of interiority?

MUTE SECRETS

> "I have not spoken since I was six years old. No one knows why, not even me. My father says it is a dark talent and the day I take it into my head to stop breathing will be my last." [6]

The film's opening is a privileged moment of narration; Ada McGrath's voice-over paradoxically tells us "the voice you hear is not my speaking voice, but my mind's voice".[7] Not uncoincidentally, it was as a child of "five or six"[8] that Ada first began to play the piano. *The Piano* brackets the narrative's beginning and end with Ada's voice-over, a formal structuring of Ada's subjectivity through optical and aural point of view. The first image we see is from her point of view: a mysteriously blurred image framed through her fingers. An eyeline match reveals an old man tugging at an obstreperous pony upon which Flora (Anna Paquin), Ada's only child, sits. This shot is murky in its legibility; the lighting and color are sombre autumnal tones, a fitting match for the harsh Presbyterian world of its Glasgow setting of the 1850's. Emblematically, these opening shots point to the willfulness of Ada's child who refuses to take off her roller skates and whose pony seems to resist her grandfather's control. The bond of their shared qualities of stubbornness, imagination and creativity are underscored by their parallel costumes and the echoing of physical mannerisms, a visual duet that winds its way throughout *The Piano* like a leitmotif. Both share a close non-verbal bond, a secret world of fairy stories and tale telling, and both have a will that brings frightening and unexpected results.

Although the film's opening sequence remains cryptic, it seems likely that the old man is Ada's father, a figure who lies symbolically and visually at the peripheral edges of the narrative. Seen only briefly in this shot, the father's presence is, I would argue, allegorically inscribed through the diegetic and non-diegetic recurrence of the melody *Big my secret*, and hints at the source of Ada's muteness. Its importance is marked by its position as the film's first diegetic melody, as we see Ada play this piece before she leaves Scotland. The cause of Ada's turn into muteness is an unanswered question in the narrative; a suggestion of childhood trauma and an idiosyncratic will that characteristically refuses conventionality throughout her life. The historical onset of Ada's muteness and the inception of her passionate relationship with music is suggestively linked in terms of its explanatory power; her withdrawal into music is an alternate mode of non-verbal expressivity. Ada's piano therefore functions as a metonymic substitute; as she herself acknowledges, the piano is an extension of her identity: *"The strange thing is I don't think myself silent, that is, because of my piano. I shall miss it on the journey."*[9] Even Ada's name is a musical palindrome, a triplet play on the keys of A and D.[10] For Ada, playing the piano is a 'weird lullaby' that she sings to herself, a metonymic indice of much that remains secret and elliptical in her past. It foregrounds the Romantic genre's play with the boundaries between the interior emotional life and its externalisation in nature. Yet this discursive system is not an inaccessible private language, for as musicologists have recognised, the expressive qualities of music itself contain semiotic codes that structure and inform narratives.[11]

As she begins to play *Big My Secret,* a slow and passionate mood piece with the shifting rhythms and tempo typical of Michael Nyman's idiosyncratic style, we sense the melancholic sadness that besets her and alludes to the mute secrets that she bears from her past. Ada's playing abruptly ceases as we cut from a close up of her face to a point-of view shot of an older woman who has entered the room. From the screenplay, this woman is identified as a maid, and her entrance into the room interrupts what is narratively positioned as the privacy and intimacy of Ada's performance.[12] The predominant impression of these prefatory scenes in Scotland is of an environmental austerity that Ada leaves behind; already her musical expressivity is situated as unwelcome and transgressive.

> *"Not only the circumstances of my life, but also my own nature, have imposed stricter limitations on my actions than yours have done on you, Kleist."*
> Karoline von Günderrode[13]

A gifted woman of immense musical and imaginative creativity, Ada is a woman out of her time, displaced and alterior. She is indicative of Campion's idiosyncratic investigation of fictional nineteenth-century characters with a historically specific relationship to sexual passion that is very different from twentieth century sensibilities.[14] Ada is sexually unconventional and as displaced as the film's central disjunctive image: a grand piano on a rugged isolated shore. Ada is a woman who has transgressed Presbyterian bourgeois mores, having born a child out of wedlock to a man who has left her. The only trace of her former lover that remains narratively explicit (notwithstanding Flora's many fantasies[15]), is the inscription upon one of the keys of Ada's piano; "A ♥ D" (which is later echoed by the gift of her key to George Baines). The piano is the locus for Ada's passions and acts as a messenger of her desire.[16] Yet if the piano also carries with it the repressed secrets of incest or of lost love, then her relationship with it is fraught with ambivalence.

Through an arranged marriage, Ada passes from the entrapment of her father and her past into a classically Gothic form of confinement; *"Today he married me to a man I've not yet met ..."*[17] This marriage to a stranger in a foreign land proves to have violent consequences. Her father's motive for this arrangement is never stated, yet it seems that Ada's marriage is one way for her father to dispose of her and her illegitimate child, or it could be a form of flight for Ada herself. The violent images of Ada's arrival by boat in New Zealand on an isolated coastline with the crashing sound of the sea's waves, the roaring wind, and the keen of seagulls exemplify the harshness of this new land for this Pakeha[18] outsider. This water sequence foreshadows and contrasts the calm and peacefulness of the underwater shots that bracket the film with Ada's near death.

On the first night that she stays on the beach, the second piece that Ada plays is a few notes of *The Heart Asks Pleasure First*, but the inrushing tide forces her to withdraw onto dry shore. Both *Big My Secret* and *The Heart Asks Pleasure First* are diegetic pieces that are narratively interrupted; her longing for her piano, like her desires, are at first frustrated. The next morning, the latter piece then recurs non-diegetically as part of the orchestral score, articulating a striking image of loss; Stewart insists that she must leave her piano behind on the beach. An over the shoulder shot of Ada zooms in to her point of view shot of the tiny piano left behind on the beach. The wide depth of field of this shot includes Ada's ribbon flapping out of focus in the lower right of the frame, thus linking the two visually and emotionally. In this farewell sequence the camera then begins a slow 180-degree pan close-up of Ada staring fixedly at the beach. Campion uses this characteristic rotating camera movement repeatedly throughout the film, acting as a visual parallel to the swirling strings in the melody. In this long take her close-up privileges the darkness of her eyes and the unblinking intensity of her gaze.[19] The ensuing high angle long shot is a strikingly beautiful image of Ada and Flora still looking out to the beach, amidst the brilliant green and blue colours of bush and sea, intensifying the sorrow and loss that she feels upon leaving her piano.

The longing invoked by this sequence's combination of lyrical camera movement and the insistent repetitions of *The Heart Asks Pleasure First* is finally answered in the joyfulness when Ada succeeds in returning to her piano on the beach. Here Ada's pleasure abounds, a flight of musical delight inspiring Flora to dance a ballet with seaweed, ultimately joining with her mother in a duet on the piano. In this sequence the above melody returns as a diegetic piece, a piece that Ada is finally able to play completely, and indeed as the editing structure suggests, plays repeatedly through the entirety of the day. Close-ups of Ada's face show a new openness and passion to which Baines responds in reaction shots with puzzled fascination. Ada's delight and passion are signaled through a repetition of dynamic camera movements around her that echo the energy of her performance. The melody in A minor shifts in characteristic Nyman style from 12/8 to 9/8 to 6/8 time and is written *marcato cantabile* (accented with a singing style). Its simple yet insistent central melody is marked by a regular and highly accentuated line in the treble, together with accented chords in the bass. As the song increases in complexity, so too does the tempo shift, and Ada's performance increases in intensity and passion as the *marcato* leitmotif is recapitulated. The swirling camera movements in 180 degree semi-circles mirror the restless dynamism of the melody.

As Ada plays, Campion edits the sequence with alternating close ups of Ada, medium shots of an intrigued Baines, and full shots of her daughter. The dominant impression is one of movement, accentuated by Campion's constant use of camera movement within shots, mimicked through the visual arc Baines paces around Ada, and echoed in the lyrical movements of her daughter's ballet. As the melody ends the non-diegetic score begins a new melody that underscores the harmony created by all three characters finally framed together in one shot. The final shot of this central sequence is a crane shot showing the three in long shot, mother and daughter walking off together, with Baines slowly joining the two ahead. Their footprints in the sand form a triangle, counterpointed by the spiral swirls of Flora's seahorse sculpture. This graphic patterning allegorically foreshadows the future narrative formation of this particular family.

ENTRAPMENT IN THE UNDERWORLD

Ada's sense of entrapment within the domestic space is codified by Campion's transformation of the New Zealand bush into a murky underwater world. Inspired by a nineteenth-century color stills process called autochrome,[20] cinematography and production design create a barren and cold setting around Stewart's house, with burnt-out tree stumps underlining its sterile harshness. The disjunctive and artificial quality of the arranged marriage is exemplified in the marriage portrait scene. Amidst pouring rain and deep sucking mud, Ada and Stewart pose for a daguerreotype in full formal dress before a fake backdrop. Ada's wedding dress is itself a simulacrum pulled on over her own clothes. The disjunctive irony of this *façade* of cultural ritual is underlined by Morag's oblivious comment: *"If you cannot have a ceremony together, you have at least a photograph."*[21] Ada's contempt for this empty cultural practice is made evident as she angrily tears off the confining wraps of her wedding dress afterwards. Both literally and figuratively, the house and the landscape act as psychic spaces of confinement,

as Stewart boards up the house to prevent Ada seeing Baines. The real threat
for Ada comes, not as Stewart's Aunt Morag (Kerry Walker) fears from a Maori
'threat', but from *within* the marriage, for Ada is married to a man who, like
Bluebeard, wields an axe.[22]

> "Morag: Have the natives aggressed you? I have to say you have done
> the wrong thing here, you see you have put the latch on the outside.
> When you close the door, it will be the Maoris that lock you in, see? With
> the latch on that side, you are quite trapped...
> Nessie: (nodding her head) : ... quite trapped"[23]

Indeed *The Piano's* allusion to the confining consequences of Victorian marriage
is invoked by an interesting sequence which was cut from the film. This sequence
concerns a conversation between Baines and a blind piano tuner. Like Ada, this
man's wife was immensely gifted:

> "My wife sang with a bell-clear tone. After we married she stopped. She
> said she didn't feel like singing, that life made her sad. And that's how
> she lived, lips clamped closed over a perfect voice, a beautiful voice."[24]

Through the enclosing spaces of self-imposed muteness, the snare of Victorian
marriage for women bears the death of creativity.

THE INSTRUMENT OF MY DESIRE

If the gothic dimensions of Ada's entrapment within a series of patriarchal
domestic spaces constitutes a kind of psychic death underpinned by the entrapment of the house and marriage, then Ada's choice of music as an alternate mode
of discourse foregrounds the expressivity of her subjectivity, upon which the
emotional significance of her music bears its traces. Allegorically the piano
functions to communicate secrets in a different realm of musical codes (the
minor key, the romantic musical genre), as a symbolic replacement for her voice,
and as an aural signification which almost allows us to hear what is in her mind.
Ada's piano functions as an expression of her character, suppressed passions
and emotional desires; in the film's opening shots we already see her caressing
it. It is the first and only thing she cares about in the motley collection of
possessions left adrift on the beach. Sensually the piano is also figured as an
erotic object for Ada, blurring the boundaries between her own body and her
music as discursive form. The intimate close-ups of Ada's hands stroking the
piano's keys are the central expressive indice to the emotions that rage within
her mute body. Like Ada, the piano is surrounded by a protective casing, one
that must eventually be unpacked through her reawakening sexual desire.

LESSONS OF SEDUCTION

The story of Baines' and Ada's erotic relationship is charted through the narrative structuring of six piano lessons, the final one of which ends with the two making love. The subtle transformations are marked in this relationship by the shift in music played by Ada, beginning with scales (first visit), *Silver fling* (the first lesson), *Big My Secret* (the second lesson), and *The Attraction of the Pedaling Ankle* (the third lesson). The piano lessons form part of a continuing series of exchanges in which Ada functions as a sexual and material commodity between two men; it is the first of multiple exchanges that will figure between George Baines and Alisdair Stewart. In this exchange economy, Ada's piano operates as currency. Stewart trades Ada's piano for land, and as part of this bargain, Baines is to receive piano lessons from Ada. Yet Baines initially obtains Ada's piano as a sexual bargaining chip. His actual bargain with Ada relies upon sexual blackmail; for each black key, "there are things I want to do".[25]

Baines' increasingly passionate obsession with Ada is signaled through a subjective use of a sound dissolve from the second lesson. The sound bridge of *The Heart Asks Pleasure First* aurally links the preceding scene to Baines' point of view shot of the piano without Ada. Baines then disrobes to caress and clean the piano with his shirt, and with this sensual gesture again foregrounds the piano as a metonymic stand-in for Ada. By the fourth lesson (in exchange for two keys), Baines forces Ada to remove her dress sleeves. She reveals her displeasure at the bargain by abruptly shifting from a slow moody nocturne to a brisk march. This shift in melodic genre is a discursive defense which abruptly terminates Baines' advances. By the fifth lesson, Ada's anger has grown, as she shows her revulsion at Baines smelling her dress. In an earlier lesson, Ada had shown her displeasure for Baines' ownership of the piano by opening its lid onto his fingers. Now in this lesson Baines jealously perceives the piano as his rival for Ada's affections. Upon her caressing the keyboard instead of him, he snaps the lid shut on her fingers.

The piano is both the narrative premise for Ada and Baines' initial relationship and the site of erotic tension and struggle between them. At first Ada sees Baines as an illiterate oaf with dirty hands who, by culture and class, has no right to her piano, and by broader ideological implication, has no right to this social indice of culture and wealth.[26] What began as an act of sexual blackmail becomes an act of sexual frustration as Baines returns the piano to Ada. The thematic implications of this exchange economy are ideologically connected to a critique of patriarchal colonialism, where pianos, buttons and guns are traded for land, and where women function as sexual commodities for exchange (Stewart gives

Ada to Baines to take away by film's end). The implications of this economy are laid bare in Baines' outburst of patriarchal *ressentiment*: *"The arrangement is making you a whore and me wretched."*[27]

Baines' initial fascination with Ada's passionate love for music is in stark contrast to the other characters' reactions. Alisdair Stewart, his aunt Morag and his cousin Nessie are deeply uncomfortable with the differences that Ada's playing represents for them, so removed is it from their own musical codes. In this regard, Ada's playing mirrors her own passionate individuality; in keeping with the Romantic genre, Ada's playing intimates a sense of transcendence over the very cultural limitations to which she is bound. The silent disapproval of the maid that we see in the film's opening scene that abruptly silences Ada's playing foreshadows Stewart's Aunt Morag, who finds Ada's playing strange and inappropriate:

> Aunt Morag: *"You know, I am thinking of the piano. She does not play the piano, as we do, Nessie ... No, she is a strange creature and her playing is strange, like a mood that passes into you ..."*[28]

Morag's attitude to music is paradigmatically opposed to Ada's. For Aunt Morag, playing the piano is one of the cultural accomplishments appropriate for young Victorian women, an accomplishment that is intrinsic to the superficial competence of drawing-room manners in keeping with Coventry Patmore's notion of the angel in the house.[29] This construction of Victorian femininity positioned women as cultural trophies whose education was carefully delimited within a framework in which women functioned as cultural accessories within a bourgeois patriarchal economy. Upper-class and bourgeois education for women was restricted to singing, painting, needle-work, novels and (often) learning the piano. Ada's playing is the obverse of the angel in the house, in so far as it foregrounds her personal expressivity and the potential enactment of dangerous social desires:

> Morag (to Nessie): *" ... Your playing is plain and true and that is what I like. To have a sound creep inside you is not at all pleasant."*[30]

It is interesting that Morag unconsciously describes the threat of Ada's music as corporeally invasive, for Ada's music is symptomatic of the secrets she carries. Indeed the melody that Morag hears at the Stewart house is *The Mood that Passes Through You*. In 4/4 minor key, its style is *pesante* (heavy, ponderous) and strangely atonal in quality. The piece bears very similar formal and atmospheric qualities to that of *Deep Sleep Playing*, the somnambulist melody Ada plays unconsciously, and like the former piece, shares the ethereal and unsettling qualities of a ghost story. *Deep Sleep Playing*'s heavy modulating chords in the treble wander in a kind of psychological fugue-like state, as the bass insistently repeats an ascending chord structure; the atmosphere is one that seems to figure the hauntings of the unconscious. Suddenly, in the sixth measure, an *accelerando molto* (much faster) of agitated triplet chords erupts. Disrupting the soporific and hushed qualities of its opening musings, this unruly shift in tempo seems to speak to the anguish and turmoil that comes surging out of Ada's repressed memories (her childhood, her latent sexual desires), that can only be communicated through her playing. The expressivity and anguish rendered through the formal devices of this atonal structure and abrupt transition code the music we hear through a romantic musical genre verging on modernity insofar as it evokes the power of her emotions and passions. Yet its atonal qualities seem to inflect romanticism with the unsettling elements of a twentieth century sensibility, perhaps signifying the uneasy unconscious of the narrative's gothic displacement.

The most symptomatic example of Campion's ironic commentary on the repressive anxieties of this displaced Pakeha settler culture, whose limit points Ada makes evident, is in a scene which occurs early in the film. Here, Stewart, astonished to find Ada silently playing an engraved keyboard on the kitchen table, reports his discovery to Morag in a scene redolent with Austenian wit. Aunt Morag's character is adroitly captured through her controlling and terse commands to her daughter Nessie: "Tea! Biscuits!". The skillful alternation of the editing structure with the dialogue's ascerbic pacing enables an ironic commentary on Morag's inability (with Stewart) to comprehend Ada's actions. Stewart, in a classic Gothic trope, can only explain Ada's differences in terms of madness, a generic consequence of the entrapment within the patriarchal space of marriage:

> Stewart: "I knew she was mute, but now I'm thinking it's more than that. I'm wondering if she's not brain-affected."[31]

In this scene, intimate close-ups, the visual hallmarks of Campion's surreal style, alternate with shot/reverse shots of Morag and Stewart. An extreme close-up shows us Stewart's point-of view. He stirs his teacup and clinks his tea spoon, marking his extreme discomfort with Ada's behaviour. Stewart's off-screen observation, "There is something to be said for silence..."[32] is comically accented by a close up of the agitated fluttering of Morag's fan. Morag replies with a non-sequitur worthy of her social discomfort:

> Morag: "Certainly, there is nothing so easy to like as a pet, and they are quite silent." (my emphasis).[32]

The thematic importance of silence and the very emptiness of this social exchange are further reiterated through a dolly back that reveals George Baines, semi-obscured in the door frame, silently listening. His own social marginality in this Pakeha culture is made quite apparent through the staging of this scene.

Morag's and Stewart's puzzled responses to Ada's impassioned eccentricities are counterpointed, as the film subsequently demonstrates, by Baines' increasingly erotic fascination with Ada, her piano and her music. To further reinforce Morag's positioning within the repressive and imperialist dimensions of this colonial culture, Campion adroitly shows Morag abruptly hush Mary and Heni's Maori rendition of "God Save the Queen". Through ironic editing, Morag's desire for silence is situated as quite different from that of Ada's and acts as a mordant critique of Morag's colonialism by invoking the historically overdetermined national anthem of England. For Ada, the empty social exchanges symptomatic of the above scene are, as Flora reports, where "most people speak rubbish and it's not worth the listen."[33] Campion positions Stewart and Morag as firmly part of a repressive culture inconsistent with Romantic ideology and structures Ada's music as part of a paradigm which invokes the *possibility* of sublime transcendence at the very moment when such transcendence is shown to be naively ideal in the light of a colonialist and patriarchal culture. Through subtlety of performance, dialogue and editing, this scene outlines the discursive and ideological boundaries that separate and confine the characters in this narrative.

The continuous comical duet of Morag's inane remarks, so adroitly echoed by Nessie,[34] mark their language as a repressive paradigm of conventionality. Ada's choice of muteness as well as sign and body language operate as a *willfully* different discursive system. Indeed, in the whole film, we hear Ada's voice only twice, in brief voice-overs that bracket the narrative. Otherwise the spectators, like the characters, are restricted to subtitles, body language and Flora's translation of sign language. In Ada's discursive paradigm language is an intuitive and non-verbal psycho-phenomenological process; the mute speaking body is an oxymoron which has uncanny communicative powers.[35] She tells Flora how she communicated with her father, the cryptic figure 'D', who was a music teacher:

> Ada [subtitled sign language]:"I didn't need to speak, I could lay thoughts out in his mind like they were a sheet....[but] after awhile he became frightened and stopped listening."[36]

The complexity of Campion's characterisation is pointed to in the fact that it is *Stewart*, not Baines, who can hear Ada's mind-voice:

> Stewart: "I heard her speak, in here (pointing to his head)
> She said: "I have to go, let me go, let Baines take me away, let him try and save me. I am frightened of my will, of what it might do, it is so strange and strong."[37]

The key turning point in the narrative, as Ada makes her choice for Baines, is marked by the entrance of the non-diegetic melody *A Bed of Ferns*, signaling Ada's troubled mind and emotional yearnings. This sequence begins in a full-shot with Ada facing away from the camera. As the camera dollies in and tilts up to an extreme close up on her tightly coiled hair, the image lap-dissolves to a high angle shot of the bush stirring with the beginning of a strong breeze (and her nascent sexual desire). A subsequent dissolve takes us inside the house and as *A Bed of Ferns* fades out we see that Baines has returned the piano to Ada. She caresses the keys pensively and plays a few notes of a melody *(Little Impulse)*, then stops and looks around as if she expects Baines to be behind her. Her inability to complete the melody reflects her emotional preoccupation with Baines. *A Bed of Ferns* features an oboe solo in minor key, plaintive and yearning. This melody occurs earlier in the soundtrack in a slow sweeping crane on Flora and Ada, sitting pensive and physically separate in the bush. At this point Ada is mourning the loss of her piano, which remains abandoned on the beach, thus linking this melody with a sense of loss and sadness. It is this melancholia which forms the third and final part in the triad of melodies which structure her character.

I CLIPPED YOUR WING

The Gothic melancholia which inflects the romanticism of Ada's characterisation underscores the ambiguous relationship she shares with her piano as the container of the secrets of her past. Her gift of a piano key to George Baines is betrayed by her daughter and results in the narrative's most violent, yet aes-thetisised scene. Enraged by his cuckoldry and sense of castration, Stewart returns to the house with an axe, first chopping Ada's book and then the piano he hates. Heightened sound intensifies the violence of this scene as he drags her outside, to the accelerated non-diegetic score of *The Sacrifice*. The scene is infused with the dread of death and terrible retribution and abruptly terminates with the chopping sound of the axe. As with the earlier scene when Stewart attempts to rape Ada, film speed markedly decreases as the score begins a *ritardando*. Ada's mute shock, disbelief and slow turn of her head as she feels the rain on her face is a silent horror in slow motion. Her staggering and final collapse in a pool of mud is like that of a dying swan as her dress billows out around her.

THE SICKNESS UNTO DEATH

"... *Worse even than your maddening*
Song, your Silence. At the source

Of your ice-hearted calling –

Drunkenness of the great depths.
O river, I see drifting

Deep in your flux of silver
Those great goddesses of peace.
Stone, stone, ferry me down there."[38]
Lorelei, *Sylvia Plath*

Like Plath's poem which eerily foreshadows her own powerful attraction to death and ultimate suicide, the silence of the sea represents the ultimate mise-en-scène of a hushed stillness for Ada. The film's final scenes deal with the choice she must make; in throwing the piano overboard, she must decide whether she too will be buried with it. The placement of the piano as a coffin that must be buried is recognised by an unnamed Maori oarsman: *"Ae! Peia. Turakina! 'Bushit'! Peia te kawheha kite moana!"*[39] and by Ada's description of it as 'spoiled'. Ada's final and curious double choice is in keeping with her character's unconventionality. Her 'leap of faith' in choosing to surface is not that of Kierkegaard's existential belief in a God, but in a double life and death. Experiencing the stillness of the ocean and near-death as she is pulled down with her coffin piano, she chooses to let go and come to the surface in a form of resurrection. Long outside the European domain of sexual respectability, Ada chooses passion and life with Baines, yet the film's double ending remains ambivalent because her relationship with Baines is nonetheless informed by the codes of patriarchy and imperialist colonialism.

> *"But for this reason I fancy that I see myself lying in the coffin, and my two selves stare at each other in astonishment."*
> Karoline von Günderrode[40]

Ada's final choice is a curiously split one; one self chooses to return to the Pakeha provincial town of Nelson to become a piano teacher, and the other preserves part of herself in an imaginary death: *"At night I think of my piano in its ocean grave, and sometimes of myself floating above it"*.[41] Her new bourgeois life in a culturally transgressive union with Baines is an ambivalent resolution, and so Ada continues to hold on to the strange image of her own death, a death which is curiously described through an aural metaphor: *"It is a weird lullaby and so it is; it is mine"*. This sense of uncanny alterity is preserved in the metallic clicks she makes in playing with her new metal fingertip: *"I teach piano now in Nelson … I'm quite the town freak, which satisfies."*[42] Ironically, Ada has chosen a new life of respectability, a life which Baines too has chosen by re-entering the boundaries of Pakeha settler culture. It seems appropriate then that in singing a Waiata of farewell to Baines, Hira alludes to the psychic loss involved in this choice as Ada and Baines leave in their journey across the sea and ultimate lifelong journey together to death:

"He rimu teretere koe ete. Peini eeeii,
Tere Ki Tawhiti Ki Pamamao eeeii
He waka Teretere He waka teretere.
Ko koe ka tere ki tua whakarere eeeii."

[you are like seaweed drifting in the sea Baines.
Drift far away, drift far beyond the horizon,
A canoe glides hither, a canoe glides thither,
But you though will journey on and eventually be beyond the veil.][43]

The psychic consequences of all the baggage that Ada brought with her to this new land has meant that much of her inward journey was coloured by the despair of Kierkegaard's *Sickness unto Death,*[44] yet *The Piano's* curious double ending of death and life recognises the central paradox of Romanticism. If the most sublime experience is that of death, it cannot be simultaneously represented and experienced. Through the focal lens of the Gothic, collapsing the boundaries between image and music and between life and death into a strange synaesthesia, Ada's journey has been towards that lullaby of herself floating above the piano.

There is a Silence where hath been no sound
There is a Silence where no sound may be
in the Cold grave, under the deep deep sea
Thomas Hood[45]

NOTES

1.   Sylvia Plath; *Collected Poems,* (Ed.) Ted Hughes, London:Faber & Faber, 1981.p192.

2.   Original Music arranged, composed and produced by Michael Nyman, 1993 Virgin Records. Sound Designer Lee Smith. In general chronological order the musical sequences are: To the Edge of the Earth (credit sequence); *Big My Secret; A Wild and Distant Shore; The Heart Asks Pleasure First; Here to There; The Promise; A Bed of Ferns; The Fling; The Scent of Love; Deep into the Forest; The Mood That Passes Through You; Lost and Found; The Embrace; Little Impulse; The Sacrifice; I Clipped Your Wing; The Wounded; All Imperfect Things; Dreams of a Journey* (departure to Nelson).

3.   Karoline von Günderrode (1780-1806), a Romantic poet and various lover of Clemens Brentano, Friedrich Karl von Savigny and Friedrich Creuzer, stabbed herself to death at 26. This fictitious quotation is taken from Christa Wolf's *No Place on Earth,* translated from the German by Jan Van Heurck, New York: Farrar, Strauss & Giroux, 1979, (1982).p96. Wolf's novel is an imaginary account of a meeting between Günderrode and Heinrich von Kleist (1777-1811), who also killed himself. In actuality the two never met.

4.   I use mise-en-scène in a metaphoric sense to point to the thematic importance of the *staging* of

space. The centrality of architectural spaces in the Gothic genre are densely suggestive in terms of psychological states of entrapment in Victorian marriage.

5. The Gothic novel cycle was initiated with Horace Walpole's *Castle Of Otranto (1764*), followed by Ann Radcliffe's *The Mysteries of Udolpho (1794,)* and Matthew Lewis' *The Monk* (1797). Later works like Mary Shelley's *Frankenstein* and the short stories of Edgar Allen Poe marked a shift in the genre to brooding atmospheres of uncanny, macabre or melodramatically violent events through the foregrounding of aberrant psychological states. Fear of the unknown coincide with Romantic obsession and are emblematised in the Gothic heroes of Charlotte Brontë's Mr. Rochester and Emily Brontë's Heathcliff, and are carried over to the melodramatic cinematic adaptations of *Wuthering Heights* and *Jane Eyre.*

6. All quotations are taken from Campion's screen play *The Piano,* London: Bloomsbury; 1993. p 9, unless otherwise noted. All subsequent notations from the screenplay will be referred to as *TP*

7. Op. cit. *TP*; p 9.

8. Op. cit. *TP*; see p 41 Stewart(to Baines): "I have it in a letter she plays well, she's been playing since she was five or six."

9. Op. cit. *TP*; p 9.

10. Discussed in Showtime Network's transcript of interviews with Jane Campion, Mary-Joe Kaplan (Producer), Michael Nyman and the members of the cast. (Unpublished author's copy)

11. See for example Susan McClary's *Feminine Endings; Music, Gender and Sexuality*, Minnesota:University Of Minnesota Press, 1991, Jean-Jacques Nattiez's *Music and Discourse; Towards a Semiology of Discourse*, (trans.) Carolyn Abate, New Jersey: Princeton University Press, 1990, and Leonard B. Meyer's *Emotion and Meaning in Music*, Chicago & London: University of Chicago Press, 1956.

12. Ada's mother never appears in these early scenes and is probably dead.

13. Op.cit. Wolf ; p103.

14. Jane Campion: "I have enjoyed writing characters who don't have a twentieth century sensibility about sex. They have nothing to prepare them for its strength and power." See "The Making of The Piano" afterword in *TP*, p135.

15. Flora at first claims that her father was a famous German composer and her mother a famous opera singer, who met in Luxembourg. They married with 'fairies for bridesmaids'. Aunt Morag's disbelief at this story produces a new Romantic invention of Flora's; her father and mother were singing in the Pyrenees when lightning struck at the peak of their duet. Her father was struck dead and her mother struck dumb: "she never spoke another word". Flora has herself heard from her mother that her father was a music teacher.

16. According to Sam Neill one of the original titles for the film was *Pleasure*. See Showtime transcript, p.14

17. Op. cit. *TP*; p9.

18. Pakeha, translated as "person of fair skin" is the Maori word for the European settlers that first came to New Zealand.

19. Indeed, as Campion has acknowledged, that at first "Ada was going to be a tall woman with a strong, dark, eerie, Frieda Kahlo sort of beauty", she selected Holly Hunter in part for the rich possibilities in the expressive directness and haunting qualities in her steadfast gaze. See *TP*; p149.

20. Stuart Dryburgh, the film's cinematographer, noted:

"...We've tended to use strong color accents in different parts of the film, drawing out the blue-greens of the bush and the amber-rich mud. Part of the director's brief was that we would echo the film's element of underwater in the bush. 'Bottom of the fish-tank' was the description we used for ourselves." See "The Making of The Piano", *TP;* p141.

21.   Morag's comment does not appear in the published screenplay.

22.   Charles Perrault's fairytale *Bluebeard* is a classic Gothic tale of the dangers of marriage and the murderous potential of the husband. The house in this fairytale contains a room to which Bluebeard's wife Fatima is expressly forbidden from entering. Her violation of this taboo and her discovery of the room's horrors – the murdered former wives of Bluebeard – is directly invoked in *The Piano* in the community play of the tale. Fatima, played by Nessie (Geneviève Lemon) opens the secret room with a key, behind a curtain to see the room's secret horrors. This sequence of the play occurs behind a curtain in silhouette, where she is confronted by Bluebeard who cuts off her hand. This sequence causes uproar amongst some of the Maori spectators who fail to discern the distinction between the play's simulation of this violence and its reality. The amputation of Fatima's hand ironically foreshadows Stewart's brutal chopping of Ada's finger; a violent retaliation for his own sense of castration.

23.   Op. cit. *TP;* p 90.

24.   Op. cit. *TP;* p49.

25.   Quotation from dialogue used in the film.

26.   See *TP* p 42 ff. & p46. A scene in the screenplay which did not appear in the film shows Flora, on behalf of her mother, insisting that Baines scrub his hands before beginning the lessons.

27.   Op. cit. *TP;* p76.

28.   Op. cit. *TP;* pp91-92.

29.   See Sandra Gilbert & Susan Gubar's discussion of Coventry Patmore's *The Angel in The House* (1854) in *The Madwoman in the Attic; The Woman Writer and the Nineteenth Century Literary Imagination,* New Haven: Yale University Press,1979. Revised edition 1984. pp22-29.

30.   Op. cit. *TP,* p92.

31.   Op. cit. *TP;* p39.

32.   Op. cit. *TP;* p40.

33.   Flora translates her mother's observation to a shocked Nessie and Morag. See *TP;* pp56–57.

34.   Echoes in dialogue recur like duets between Morag and Nessie. See "very dramatic" (film dialogue); "Used her teeth and wiped her feet on it" *TP* 40; "quite trapped" *TP* 90. Flora invents a romantic story about her father and mother, claiming that her father was struck dead by lightning and at that very moment her mother was struck dumb. From that moment on, she never spoke another word. Morag echoes: "never spoke another word". Physical mimicking also occurs, most noticeably with Ada and Flora dressed alike in dress and bonnet, tilting their heads sideways. An unnamed Maori also mimics Stewart's testy behaviour, when he first meets Ada on the beach.

35.   A further irony is the fluency of Ada's "mind's voice" which only the spectator can hear. The narrative's final scene shows Ada veiled as she practices to speak 'externally'; "I am learning to speak. My sound is still so bad I feel ashamed. I practise only when I am alone and it is dark." *TP;* p122.

36.   Op. cit. *TP;* p 51.

37.   Op. cit. *TP;* p115.

38.   Op .cit. Plath, *Lorelei;* pp94-95.

39.   The screenplay renders this dialogue as "Yeah, she's right, push it over, push the coffin in the water", but the final shooting script's dialogue differs slightly: "The woman is right. It's a coffin. Let the sea bury it."

40.   Karoline Von Günderrode epigraph in *No Place on Earth* by Christa Wolf, New York: Farrar, Strauss & Giroux, 1979,1982. p xii.

41.   Op. cit. *TP;* p 122.

42.   Op. cit. *TP;* p 122.

43.   Op. cit. *TP;* p 117. Verse courtesy Selwyn Muru.

44.   See *Fear and Trembling and The Sickness Unto Death* by Søren Kierkegaard for his exposition of despair, New York: Doubleday Anchor; 1985.

45.   Op .cit. *TP; p*123. Sonnet ' Silence', by Thomas Hood (1799–1845).

Fig. 1. (above). The film continually privileges whiteness through the play of light against dark, emphasizing the binary oppositions at work in the text.

Fig. 2. (below). Baines and Ada.

Fig. 3. (above). The caged hoops of Ada's skirts are echoed in the black supple jack vines.

Fig. 4. (left). Stewart, who seeks to colonize and control the landscape.

Fig. 5. (above). Baines has an understanding of the indigenous culture.

Fig. 6. (right). Ada and Flora spend a night on the beach sheltered by a hooped petticoat held down with shells.

Fig. 7. (above). Like flotsam and jetsam heaved out of the sea, Ada stands amongst the debris of her old world.

Fig. 8. (below). Baines' desires become enmeshed in her playing.

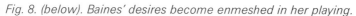

Fig. 9. (above). The ominous looming cliffs add a romantic vision of nature.

Fig. 10. (right). 'Whiteness' is represented through a matrix of race, gender and class differences.

Fig. 11. (above). Baines, whose desire for Ada has been ignited by her playing, follows Ada and Flora from the beach.

Fig. 12. (left). Like a beachcomber collecting driftwood, Stewart forages amongst the offerings purged from the sea.

Fig. 13. (above). As Stewart meets Ada on the beach, a character stands behind him with a straw hat mimicking his actions.

Fig. 14. (right). Ada and Flora with the piano, around which the story unfolds.

Fig. 15. (above). Baines awakens Ada's sexual desires.

Fig. 16. (below). In the 'wedding photo' scene, curtained backdrops shield what
was often described in colonial journals as barbaric, irrational and inferior
civilizations.

2

CULTURAL STUDIES

CHAPTER 5

IN THE BODY OF THE PIANO

FELICITY COOMBS

A group of Maori men, struggling with its bulk, haul a piano from the beach up a steep mountainside. It slips from their hands in the dampness and, crashing against a tree, thunders out a low jarring bellow. While the men scatter one remains and, in Maori, calls to the spirit *Ruaumoko* in the piano. As the piano falls, its solitary chord punctuates and elucidates the entire film. An aural and physical penetration by an imperialist British culture into the pristine wilderness has occurred.

The colonist's preoccupation with their culture came at the expense of the natural elements of the land that were both ignored and desired. The beauty and ugliness of the sublime landscape introduce romantic influences that add a textual richness to the palette and by association inform an intensity in the audience's readings of the film. The allusion to the romantic period has also been aesthetically significant in the weighted aspect of the film's music.

For its release in 1993, the film previously known, through extensive media coverage, as the *The Piano Lesson*, became *The Piano*.[1] Writers have found many points of departure from which to coax insight from the film's deep interior. What I have found intriguing is the naming of the film. What is the relevance of the title within the plot? Its importance leads me to examine the role of the piano itself. Used as an organising device within the narrative, it cinematically becomes both an expressive cultural element and a mode of communication. The piano, in the context of the film, functions both as a vehicle for the symbolic representation of the close link between women and Victorian domestic culture and as a primary profile for the film about Ada McGrath, Baines and Stewart, or perhaps Ada, Baines and *the piano*.

By changing the title of the film, the narrative emphasis shifts from that of a performative interaction between a student and pupil to the foregrounding of an object around which the story unfolds. There is an explicit difference between a piano lesson and a piano. In questioning this exacting change, I pursue a deeper inquiry into the role of the piano and its symbolic and far from silent meaning.

The instrument, its music and its musician are the agents used to explore the underlying link that posits it as both a body and a cultural object. Endowed with the similarity of several of our bodily characteristics – fingers, legs, voluptuous body – the piano also has an expressive sound. Its organic features are created from natural materials – wood, ivory and metals. It responds through touch to bring to form the unspeakable emotion of the mute Ada. Yet, without Ada's gentle touch, the piano too remains silent. As an instrument of the romantic era, the piano yields an extraordinary amount of referential information, as well as connotation, that enables our interpretation. By examining the social context of pianos and women in the nineteenth century, their roles in the film can be readily interpreted.

THE SOCIAL WORLD OF THE PIANO AND WOMEN

> In my room we got to talking about the 'piano'
> as a piece of furniture that functions in the
> petit-bourgeois interior as the true dynamic centre
> of all the dominant miseries and catastrophes of the household.
> **Walter Benjamin,**
> *Moscow Diary*

Even before Walter Benjamin made this observation, the piano had caused an upset in the European world of music as one of the great implements of German romanticism. "When strings began to be hammered, instead of delicately plucked, a turbulent era found a voice".[2] Its romantic possibilities were exploited in the new philosophy of freedom in Europe which followed on from the French Revolution. Such an independent instrument underpinned the new ideology with its extensive range in octaves and its ability "to peck like one of its tinny ancestors, to blur through the use of the sustaining pedal, to arpeggiate and complement the great speed of scale work with the solemnity of huge sustained chords, to wage war between the black keys and the white."[3] The piano became an expression of the romantic personality. Its range in music benefits several ineffable moments of the film by enabling Ada to extemporise the scope of her emotions by playing music that was equally capable when located anywhere between the extensive range of soft or frenzied tempo. As we find Ada clearly unconfinable in the social order, so too are the possibilities of range in the piano.

In promoting a relationship between Ada and the piano, I must make clear now two points in my argument. I am denoting the piano as being gendered female, firstly by association on a socio-cultural basis, and secondly, through an aural relation to the sensuous aspects of music. Other associations exist – most notably concerning the male gaze – and bodily similarity – but these are not essential to my view. For example, under Queen Victoria's reign, the male gaze was taken seriously. She considered it indecent to display *naked* legs on a piano as the male observer may have been titillated at the sight.

Benjamin observed that the private citizen's living space had become "... phantasmagorias of the interior" and that the citizen's "drawing-room was a box in the world-theatre".[4] The known world had expanded for the middle-class and their home had become a 'microcosm of the universe'. Individualism had come into being. The piano had now assured, in black and white, its acclaimed place in the middle-class. Having the piano as *object* in this space establishes both a sonoric and social importance. It represents one of the more profound experiences of colonisation evident in the nineteenth century. An ironic contrast to its significance in the social space of the British middle-class drawing room is its incorporation as a cultural symbol in the colonising of distant territories. Colonists fervently and successfully transported their entire culture, but it is the piano in particular that held specific connotations for women and their culture. Its status thrived in the British colonies as many diaries, memoirs, novels, art and literature of the colonists that remain in archives confirm.

Memoirs and visual art locate, and also communicate, a sense of the value placed on music and musical sound. Images from the colonies, sent home to family in Britain, show pianos in drawing rooms often with a seated female pianist. Leppert made reference to this by saying "musical imagery could not be used unproblematically....the relation of musical sound to social class, to theological belief and to gender hierarchy, must of social necessity be handled gingerly" as the 'semantic surface' encompassed "potential ruptures and ambiguities".[5] To the colonists, familial bliss was able to be established metaphorically in these images via the association of the harmony of the musical scene with a similar unison of the family. Those frozen images were not simply producing signs of lucid concordance, as music was not valued here for purely aesthetic reasons, but rather the domestic performance of music served as a tool of domination.

The role of the pianist signified the domestic role of those women, while also serving to bond them with cultural hegemony. The images also reveal how cultural icons, such as pianos, were by association a symbolic strength both in the domination of women, and of middle-class oppression of any alternative culture in the colonies. This measure of colonialism was able to reinforce an acknowledgment of their belief in their own power.

One reason for the inclusion of British women in the developing colonies was in order to avoid the prospect of inter-racial marriages and as a result of women's perceived connection to music there was also an influx of piano transportation. Around 700,000 pianos were shipped to Australia alone during the nineteenth century, demonstrating its symbolic importance in preserving a higher social order in colonial culture. The introduction of pianos into Australian colonial life provided entertainment and often, Humphrey McQueen writes, were "the only opportunity that most people had of hearing symphonies and operas, most of which were issued in piano arrangement".[6] The piano was acknowledged as *sine qua non* for the middle-class last century, the "pinnacle of the lower class aspiration" and "... a barometer for class consciousness"[7] in early colonial life. Pianos were similarly transported in vast numbers to the families acquiring wealth and status in nearby New Zealand.

The actions of our forebears seem an extravagance of great magnitude and a derisory imposition on the country's own inhabitants. The English gentry survived colonisation in spite of the fact that they brought their culture with them. They preferred to live as though they were in England, resisting the cultural landscape on which they imposed. Photographs of that period depict colonists in familial settings posed around their piano. Curtained backdrops shielded them, insularising their existence, from what was often described as barbaric, irrational and inferior civilisations.

In *The Piano*, for example, we have a vignetted scene that appears to play a game with this idea. The camera set-up for the wedding photo scene shows Ada against a curtained backdrop depicting scenery of an English countryside. The strange reality of the event is evident to the film viewer. The camera, pulled back in a wide-shot, establishes the reality of that setting – rain, mud, indeed, quite a sight. What the film viewer is privy to here is a more informed sight than will be available to relatives back in the mother country, who will later receive the wedding photo. This evident separation from reality depicts the colonist's blind acceptance of an irrational posturing with no acknowledged reference to the reality of New Zealand's terrain. While British 'norms' are upheld, the colonists resistance of the alien cultural heritage is not in *tune* with New Zealand.

Many of the transported pianos must have spent considerable lengths of time *untuned* in vastly different, often tropical climates of the colonies, their impracticality unheeded. The film introduces a blind piano tuner, brought in by Baines, to tune Ada's piano. A variation between the script and the film left only a small amount of that scene after editing. It held an important moment, in which the viewer is introduced to special sensory knowledge – to the bodily odour of the piano – when we are told it smells of the sea. Many viewers may have missed the tuner's presence altogether as comments made in the press sought to check Campion on an oversight. These comments rested on the idea that a piano left on a beach for a period of time would not remain in tune. However, the tuner is present in the film. What I find interesting here is the acknowledgment of a piano having bodily smells or odours. Later, when Ada attends a piano lesson, Baines smells her dress. It is also appropriately upholding Victorian mores that the tuner who must reach into the interior of the piano's body is blind.

Early scenes in the film divulge information about Ada's middle-class existence. The McGrath family home in Scotland is a large estate with an equally large home, a maid and a piano. The piano, at that time, was a sign of achievement and social belonging to the British middle-class. The women of Ada's social strata did not work although the piano's popularity produced an expectation for these women to learn to play. Further, aspects of domesticity and sensual arousal promoted a strong position for the piano to be signified as a feminine object. This provides a central clue to unravelling its important place in the film, as both Ada and the piano were often found in similar territory and serving similar functions in society. Her piano also becomes a tradeable entity akin to the manner in which Ada herself is traded as a bride, sent or sold to a British man in the colonies; a union of convenience allowing continued respectability for her family.

The problematic social placement of women, the piano and music in that era can also be examined by contrasting the economic and the transcendental natures of music. Richard Leppert writes that music "lacks all concreteness and disappears without a trace (acoustic decay)" that "musical sound is abstract, intangible, and ethereal".[8] Music therefore becomes of greater value as a site of economic resistance resulting from its lack of a tangible value from productive effort – which was, and still is, a focus and philosophy of a modern society. With no economic surplus available, music and musical performance become a site of value, predominantly to the female, where society had forced a repression on the natural female voice. Male attention to the piano was through its use and the ability of their wives to play for company; to enhance the value of their position in society.

In that era, women were socially and economically disadvantaged by divorce and property laws, which in France and England during last century were in a fledgling state. James Laver, in his book on the manners and morals of that era, clarifies women's position:

> "Perhaps there never was another period in history where it would be true to say that the wife was theoretically an angel and was practically a slave. She had no property of her own; anything she possessed before marriage became her husband's property absolutely; anything she earned after marriage, even if she were separated from her husband, was his; even her housekeeping money or the money in her purse when she went shopping was not legally her own."[9]

From this perspective of ownership, Stewart was able to trade Ada's piano for Baines' land via this right of ownership of all his wife's property before marriage. Baines reinforces this aspect of transferred ownership when he closes the lid of the piano while Ada runs her fingers across it after one of their own bargained exchanges. His wider possibilities for possession empowered him in the bargaining process.

LOCATING THE BODY

Artworks depicting British colonists remain as evidence to locate the piano within the cultural heritage of colonisation during that period in Australian and New Zealand history. One of the more interesting aspects in viewing these paintings and photographs, and indeed its portrayal in this film, becomes the *impossibility* of re-*locating* a piano – symbolic of British culture – in the colonies. It seems never a thought was given to the size of objects transported, the focus was to re-establish the same social environment left behind. A strong impression of the *impossibility* of transporting culture is available by reviewing the strange sight of Ada's arrival.

Sailors staggered through the waves with a huge piano shaped box, their longboat lunging in the heavy seas. Ada McGrath, a mute Scottish woman, and her daughter, Flora, stand immobilised on the shore. Ada looks down at her feet sinking deep in the sand which now covers her boots, while the audience becomes enmeshed in the realm of the sublime landscape of the Gothic romance. They have arrived in New Zealand, on the shore of a remote and empty beach. The wretched seamen who carry them ashore, leave them, along with their baggage, on the desolate edge of the land to await the arrival of her new husband while an unrelenting sea moves in to reclaim their boxes. The strange sight of Ada's arrival is quite a surreal vision; of the baggage, the woman and child in those voluminous clothes, and a piano on a beach.

What a strange way to arrive. The image is of flotsam and jetsam – heaved out of the sea. As she stands amongst this debris of her old world, she could be transplanted, in the mind's eye, to an English railway platform. The splendid photography of Ada and Flora with the piano and other possessions standing on a beach produces a rather fantastic proposition, leading to the notion of this scene's impossibility. Standing in the evidence of their cultural roots, transported from a Scottish drawing room, the displaced piano becomes a jarring symbol of this contradictory surface. While the impossibility of this situation is at once also possible as it is visible, it becomes a strategy of the *fantastic*. Vignetted scenes in this film express the contrary nature of the settlement of British colonists in remote landscapes. The narrative result is of transforming the contrary condition from a recognition of what should be the case to acceptance of what is now present. Transportation of the imperial culture, in this sense, to the wilds of the South Pacific, is indeed within the realms of the fantastic.

Through the rainforest that lines the beach, her new husband Stewart approaches the next morning. Unconcerned by the company of Maoris or by the wildness of the forest, he takes out a comb and tidies himself. He arrives on the beach with a group of men and another European man, Baines. Orders are given to the men to take up the baggage. Like a beachcomber collecting driftwood with which to line his hut, Stewart forages amongst the offerings purged from the sea. Ada realises no-one is taking the piano. She insists, but Stewart fails to recognise its importance to her. They leave the black sands and make their way up the mountain. Ada looks back from the verdant mountain track to where her piano stands forlornly, stranded and still encumbered with its boxing. Ada's piano remains boxed for some time until Baines has it taken to his hut. It is seen, we know what it is, but it remains hidden, teasing the viewer to the task of locating the body within.

The sight of the piano stranded on the beach – an unnaturally silent object in unnatural surrounds – provides a strange opening for our *knowing* of the piano. We would expect all pianos to be found in interior spaces. The scope of our seeing it there is broadened from its realist framework into the realms of the fantastic, into a world of impossibilities. It is an object, dislocated from its origins, looming in a strange suspension of temporal and spatial relations. This lone object stands in waiting on a sparse and sullen shore. Our ability to read the piano as a text is disturbed by this sight. The boxed piano on the shore is liberated from a monistic reading by its placement in these supernatural surrounds. This displacement gives voice to the surreal elements of the piano which were unheard, in its previous locatable place in nineteenth century British culture.

The information available in the film's introductory scene to the special world of the colony – of crashing waves and ominous looming cliffs – suggests we are going to brave strange elements. The sublime setting, a romantic vision of the forces of nature, is a theme persisting throughout the film. Art of the romantic period used landscape as "the vehicle of the Sublime" leaving "elements of Nature alone (to) carry the full symbolic meaning."[10] As Caspar David Friedrich, along with Turner and Constable created a landscape genre in painting in the nineteenth century, here the landscape was used cinematically to rekindle the passion of romantic imagery. Black beaches bordered by heavy green cliffs, dense bush and gnarled branches in the landscape were essential ingredients for the representation of a romantic visual fantasy. Sally Sherratt, the location finder, took "four weeks to cast the beaches of black sand and cliff, topped by bush of almost prehistoric density – and mud."[11] Inside this romantic vision, Ada must lay out wooden planks to move around as the mud is always deeper than we expect.

Ada, taut and wiry, as frail as the strings in her piano, traverses the countryside in cumbersome outfits that belonged on English lawns. Bound within a highly strung frame of "corset, huge hoop skirts, petticoats, pantaloons, bodice, and chemise....gracefully manoeuvre(ing) her way through the bush", she needed "strength and stamina as well as grace"[12] to exist in that terrain. The colonists went to impossible lengths to preserve their Englishness. The clothes they wore were just as unlikely as their cultural objects. In a masochistic performance, they retained an unsuitable culture in awkward situations. Ada's body is hidden under these excessive garments which may heighten her erotic appeal of nakedness later.

Brooding dark dresses always cover her body with only the whiteness of her face and hands visible. As she sat at the piano on the beach, upon her initial arrival to New Zealand and on her visit to the piano with Baines later, she invades the blackness of the piano's wooden boxing to play her hands on its white face – the keys. She must push her hands through the boards, through a loose board, to touch its whiteness. Later Baines finds similar enjoyment by locating a hole, a loose thread in her black stockings, as an entry point to her white body. The inquisitiveness of the camera in its scrutiny of objects appeals to Jane Campion and breaks with more 'realist' traditions of film. Elements of the visible and invisible, what is available to be seen and what is hidden, are guarding mechanisms used in this film which lead us to a point of narrative disruption later with character uncovering and laceration.

SOUND AND THE SENSATE BODY

Silence more musical than any song
Christina Rossetti, 1830–1894
Song *'Oh Roses for the Flush'*

Andrew Bowie, in a recent examinaton of aesthetic theory, tells us that "from Romanticism onwards ... music is able more and more to find a language to express what Schopenhauer saw as the 'secret story of the Will': all those aspects of the inner life of human beings which cannot be adequately represented in verbal language."[13] It is the aesthetic value of musical sound that allows Ada the possibility of remaining outside a more formal language; a voice less bounded by social entrapment than her body.

Musical representation in the Romantic period suffered in philosophical argument through the questioning of its being "a sensuous medium which cannot be understood in terms of representation" or whether it was "art devoid of representation."[14] Here we find that piano music, including its decay or silence, is linked to Ada's silence and subjective positioning by her choice of self-imposed muteness. "Music ... only results when there is a self-consciousness which *judges* it to be different from other types of articulation."[15] The music becomes more than just expressive or unspoken dialogue, but conveys the emotive messages of her thoughts and of her feelings toward Baines during the lessons.

Ada, a voluntary mute, has refused the acceptable speaking position. As a child, she made a decision not to talk which has in no way diminished her ability to communicate, but simply changed the manner in which meaning was conveyed. Through her denial of voice, her ability to articulate her identity and her *self* was altered and she learned to produce meaning through her piano. This action provided her with an alternative mode of representation for emotional expression though at the same time, she imprisons her power of autonomy in an object of the culture she rejects. By removing herself from the dominant order of social discourse, she is still defined within much wider social entrapments of definition – those of temporality, spatiality and gender relations.

Her refusal to speak her *self* is an attempt to resist the patriarchal powers of language that construct her as a woman; a language that tells women's experience in a masculine framework, calculated and closed with no attempt to encompass feeling or thought. Her femininity longs to exceed the category which defines her. The piano, with its metred note, gives a form to the music in the film by the element of feeling and a means of communication, especially with the audience.

Although sound is a universal medium, the differentiation of sounds in music is culturally denotative. Meanings in music are of individual significance to different cultures. By the time of the Romantics, many noises of the Middle Ages and Renaissance had been eliminated or increasingly differentiated. Sounds became predominantly informed by culture or social order. Social and philosophical questions about music in the eighteenth century "were defined by and for an elite, in light of a cultural practice".[16] A hierarchy of sounds had developed by embodying a caste system in the social order.

A modern influence is encountered in the ballads played by Ada. Ballad or folk music was not, perhaps, an appropriate form for a young lady of her background to play, considering the orthodoxy of music appreciation in that period. This is not a denigration of the music itself, as it is viewed by a contemporary audience and its temporal appropriateness is not really an issue for mainstream audience acceptance. Michael Nyman used Scottish folk and popular songs as the basis for his compositions which Ada plays. The music had to be 'Ada's repertoire as a pianist'...'as if she had been the composer of it'.[17]

The film's music offers an expressive variance between individual segments. The aural experience of the music Ada first plays on the beach with Baines contrasts with the emotional moments experienced in her anguished moment at the chopping-block. This is in accordance with the possibility of a variant range of piano music. As an element within melodrama, music communicates the characters' perceptions and attitudes by notably punctuating major narrative transitions and underlining such intense passages with a score on the sound-track.

Meanings and affects, in this film, are also dependent upon the sense of sight. The emotional response gauged from the extra diegetic sound of the soundtrack, is still reliant upon what is established by the sight of her playing. In the scene in which Baines takes Ada and Flora to the beach where her abandoned piano stood brooding, there is a long transitionary moment when we see Baines' silent response to the music. Sight renders Baines' experience as concrete and meaningful. He becomes the subject on whom Ada's music takes effect. He hears every note and the lingering camera allows us to view his engagement with the sound and the sight of sound. The effect of sound on the body focuses on the physicality of the music and its making. The unseen qualities of music engender meanings that impact more on the senses and our transcendental nature than a spoken language. To elucidate the relationship of sound to body, Leppert writes that music has a mystical substance and is an '"embodied abstraction" acting "simultaneously in space and in time".'[18]

The film The Piano is unusual as a site of music within the film as music is often just a score on a sound-track. Both social and abstract relations drawn from the sight of the musical performance, locate sound in relation to a wider realm of shared experiences. Ada, who plays the piano, becomes the spectacle of sight. This is a shared experience of the audience and Baines, who chooses not to play the piano. Ada pleads for Baines to take her back to the beach where the piano was left. Relenting, he takes her and Flora. She plays for him and as his reward, Ada ignites his desires through her playing. To Baines, Ada becomes a desirable body, through his own reading and interaction with the music. The experience of watching and listening to her play moves him to arrange a trade of land for the piano with her husband, Stewart.

Baines, having neglected his own culture, was suggested to live very closely with the Maori people, but he is drawn back to British culture through the acoustic effects of a cultural icon. He realises that a way around the moral impediment of obtaining Ada is to get the piano in his house. This opens up a cultural impediment as he cannot have a piano without knowing how to play it. To justify his surreptitious desire to run his hands over her body, he tells Stewart he will need piano lessons. Stewart, in his knowledge that the piano is a functional object, offers the services of his wife to teach Baines to play. By expressing a desire to own the piano, he has secured the opportunity to have Ada in his home, as one necessitates the other.

Baines' desires become enmeshed in her playing. He trades the land for the piano, as Ada's music has colonised his heart. Located within this cultural exchange is the tension between colonial and colonised desire of the two men: Stewart desires ownership of the land; Baines desires Ada. Each man wants what the other man has. The piano, here, embodies the possibility of Baines' ownership of Ada.

As Ada and the piano had became the locus of Baines' desire through the emotive power of the music, another symbiotic relationship exists between Ada and the piano where the act of expression for both Ada and Baines is limited by their requirement of the physical aspect of touch. No instrument can hold up to the human singing voice, tones cannot replace words, but a skilled instrumentalist is, on occasion, acclaimed in their ability to make it *sing* or *talk*. The music will not exist without her playing and, likewise, she is unable to make sound without the piano. It has an unseen quality but more profoundly, it has a sonoric affect. It was Robert Schumann who said, "Music achieved by the fingers alone is sorry work; but music that echoes from within resounds in every heart, and outlives the brittle body."[19] Musical practice "for performers, calls on the sensory perceptions of hearing, touch and sight; for listeners, on hearing and sight alone."[20] Touch is therefore a privilege of the player.

Baines, who had 'gone bush', is a man who lived somewhere between the two cultures of Pakeha (white New Zealander) and Maori. The trappings of an English lifestyle did not seem of great concern at his hut, but the experience of the piano music on his wild, and yet unsettled nature, is a pleasure he sought to repeat. While he has an ocular priority, as he watches but does not play, he is unerringly effected by the aural world presented to him in his passive engagement. A relationship is established between the sound, the sight of music, and the production of music evident here through this view of the physicality of music making and the bodily response of aural reception. As music is felt emotionally, it is therefore a personal experience. Baines' experience of desire is restrained by his visual and aural reception and therefore he is denied the experience of touch. In a hierarchy of desires where touch is paramount, Ada experiences the privilege of all these pleasures through her playing and Baines is left longing for her touch.

To identify an area of deviation and difference from a purely literary interpreta- tion, I find a need to advance here a poetic rationale, as in this film what is implied is to me of greater importance to the depth of the film than what is said. As a "means of communication between souls"[21] musical sound is ethereal. Through the recognition of the mystical quality possible in sound, various meaningful interactions between Ada, Baines and the piano are able to be viewed through a poetics which posits an underlying unity of a romantic force between them.

To realise the ethereal shimmering texture of music, the "shapes that haunt thought's wildernesses"[22] the senses are raised to a condition of insight where sound is given a form. These various associations I have drawn on to interpret the naming of the film provide many glimpses of the role of the piano by connecting its visibility, its social temporality, and its sonoric effect.

Piano music was seen earlier to be more associated with women and as such was seen as a specific threat to masculine identity. 'And worse, when confined to women's practice, its specific relation to physicality and to sexual arousal was perceived as a challenge to [the] husbands' authority'.[23] To the female pianist, the pleasure was bound with the playing, providing a non-verbal, emotive way to establish and preserve identity. As men of the day had interests in science, mathematics, economics and philosophy, women were perceived in their relationship to music, not only through the site of placement, but through the sensuous aspects of the music itself. Campion's use of the piano as a motivation for sensual pleasure for both Baines and Ada is resonant of the way in which music had been approached in the 1800s. Leppert established a defined relationship of sight to the effect of music on the sensate body:

"... music as a sight is "a richly semantic visual phenomenon...an activity subject to the gaze, not least because music, both as social practice and sonority, was thought to possess sensual power. It was understood to act with dangerous immediacy on the sensate body. The 'musical' gaze was supercharged with sexuality, producing an 'interest' simultaneously encoded with pleasure and anxiety."[24]

The semiotic representation of the piano as an object in the film has significance as both a visual metaphor and of socially encoded values. The audience engages with both the sight of the musician and the sound of the music. This contrasts with the pictorial representation of musical activity seen in colonial art. Paintings and photographs can remain only as a visual translation of the three-dimensional and sonoric world into a two-dimensional and silent representation.

When Ada plummets to the silent depths of the sea, she faces only herself. Intertwined with the piano, she undoes the rope binding her to it. The piano, mute now, sinks to the bottom, finding a silent grave. Ada rises up to the surface – destined to find a new voice. By pursuing the theme of Ada's cultural entrapment in her new husband's land, in her mind, and in her body, Campion has developed a film of great depth and meaning through an exploration of Ada's empowering journey. This journey is completed through her final release from both a bodily and a sonoric connection to the piano.

We did not lose the narrative trail of the piano here though. The dénouement played out in the town of Nelson shows Ada with another piano in a drawing room. This fulfils the narrative film tradition of a mythic journey as Ada leaves the *special* world and returns to the *mundane* world. She takes what she has learned and returns to renew her life.[25] We hear her speak another language though even in her 'gesture of surrender' she still dreams 'a weird lullaby'[26] of silence. The Maori had listened for a voice in the piano, as we listened for Ada's, but it was the voice of an imperial culture – symbolically found here in the body of the piano – that pervaded the narrative of the film.

NOTES

1.   The film's name remained *The Piano Lesson* in some European countries. As there was a play performing in Australia with that title, the name change was advised.

2.   Dieter Hildebrandt, *Piano Forte: A Social History of the Piano*, (trans) Harriet Goodman, London: Century Hutchinson Ltd, 1988. p v

3.   Ibid. p viii

4.   Walter Benjamin, *Louis-Philippe or the Interior*, Arcades Project, *Passagenwerk*, (trans) Quintin Hoare, 1938-40. pp167-9

5.   Richard Leppert, *Music as a Sight in the Production of Music's Meaning,, Metaphor – A Musical Dimension*, Jamie C. Kassler,(Ed.), Sydney: Currency Press, 1991. p.77

6.   Humphrey McQueen; *A New Britannia*, Melbourne: Penguin, 1970. p118.

7.   Ibid. p117.

8.   Richard D.Leppert; *The Sight of Sound,* Berkeley: University of California Press, 1993. p xx.

9.   James Laver, *Manners and Morals in the Age of Optimism, 1848-1914*, New York: Harper and Row, 1966. p31.

10.   Rosen, Charles, and Henri Zerner, *Romanticism and Realism: The Mythology of Nineteenth Century Art*, London: Faber and Faber Ltd, 1984. p51.

11.   Jane Campion, *The Piano*, London: Bloomsbury, 1993. p142.

12.   Ibid. p149.

13.   Bowie, Andrew, *Aesthetics and Subjectivity; from Kant to Nietzsche*, Manchester and New York: Manchester University Press, 1990. p261

14.   Ibid. Bowie, 1990. p39.

15.   Ibid. Bowie, 1990. p183.

16.   Op. cit. Leppert, 1993. p63

17.   Op. cit. Campion; '93, Nyman interview. p150

18.   Op. cit. Leppert; '93. p22

19.   Op. cit. Hildebrandt; 1988. Ch. 9 p86.

20.   Op. cit. Leppert 1991. p69.

21.   Proust, Marcel, *The Captive. Remembrance of Things Past*, Vol. 3, Harmondsworth, 1981. p260.

22.   Read, Herbert, *The Origins of Form in Art*, London:Thames and Hudson, 1965. p32

23.   Op. cit. Leppert,1991. p.79.

24.   Ibid. Leppert, 1993. p64.

25.   Seger, Linda, *Making a Good Script Great*, Hollywood:Samuel French Trade, 1987. p98.

26.   Op. cit. Campion, 1993. Scene 151. p122.

CHAPTER 6

TEMPESTUOUS PETTICOATS

COSTUME AND DESIRE IN THE PIANO

STELLA BRUZZI

Clothes in costume films have been used in a multiplicity of ways, most commonly, as in many Merchant-Ivory adaptations, as a decorative patina glossing a precise recreation of a usually literary past. I have previously focused on the distinction between two alternative feminist uses of costume and history: the 'liberal' and the 'sexual'. The liberal method, exemplified by films such as Margarethe von Trotta's *Rosa Luxemburg* (1985) and Gillian Armstrong's *My Brilliant Career* (1979), concentrates on finding a political and ideological affinity between present and past women, whilst the sexual model, exemplified by Jane Campion's *The Piano* (1993), uses the clothes themselves to initiate an examination of women's relationship to their sexual history.[1]

Here, I intend to explore the sensuality as well as the sexuality of clothes in *The Piano*, as both costume and the body appear linked in this film to a complex feminist displacement of the conventionalised objectification of the woman's form dominated by scopophilia and fetishism. Ada's fierce independence is expressed through her repeated refusal to conform to the designated role of the pacified and distanced image of women contained by the voyeuristic male gaze.

In her muteness, her musicality and the expression of her sexual desire through touch, Ada represents the possibility of a radical alternative feminine and feminist mode of discourse, and clothes become this 'language's' most eloquent tools.

Clothing, Renee Baert has noted, "is a compound medium and critical axis of the social (law), the sexual (fantasy), the figural (representation) and the individual (will and desire)."[2] As Baert and historians have noted, such complexity is primarily attributed to women's rather than men's clothes because historically women's social presence has been more closely aligned to, and circumscribed by, their physical appearance. The logical extension of such an observation is, therefore, that gender conventions can be subverted "through clothing itself".[3] A similar subversion tactic is evident in *The Piano*, as Ada's oppressive Victorian clothes are made to function both for and against her, and are both internal and external signifiers of her desire and her social position. But the film further suggests the more radical potential of clothes as part of an oppositional discourse not reliant for signification (even through a positive appropriation of difference) on any such established patriarchal models. Michel Foucault's analysis of the methods by which "modern puritanism imposed its triple edict of taboo, non-existence and silence"[4] on sex and the expression of sexuality (from the eighteenth century onwards), offers a revolutionary thesis for understanding the outcome of such administered censorship. Far from imposing censorship, what was installed was "an apparatus for producing an ever greater quantity of discourse about sex,"[5] so that sex was "driven out of hiding and constrained to lead a discursive existence" which was simultaneously spoken of and exploited as "the secret."[6] The dialectic between intention (to repress sex) and the 'putting into discourse of sex'[7] is given narrative representation in *The Piano* through the conflict between Stewart, the archetypal nineteenth-century colonial husband bound by a burdensome sense of his position within patriarchal history, and Ada, the transgressive wife who creates alternative discursive strategies to counter such intended subjugation. The multiple ways in which such a delineation is manifested is through a series of binary oppositions rooted in a presentation of the primary difference between male and female. The secondary oppositions (masculine/feminine, distance/nearness, looking/touching) are first posited and then subverted, as much by the transgressive male figure, Baines, as by Ada. The complex reworkings of gender stereotypes in *The Piano* are located within costume, the film ultimately advancing a feminist discourse of clothes that neither absents the body nor simply reinforces traditional interpretations of the feminine.

There is an imposed distance between clothes, intended to contain or camouflage, and sexuality; and it is that very conflict or opposition that makes for the 'clothes-language' utilised by Peter Weir in *Picnic At Hanging Rock* (1975) and *Witness* (1985), Jane Campion in *The Piano* or Martin Scorsese in *The Age of Innocence* (1994). A film such as *Picnic At Hanging Rock* creates an adolescent, sexual, mysterious world based on comparable oppositions to *The Piano*, but the differences (like the mystery at the core of the narrative) remain intact. The underpinning reason for this is that the representation of sexuality in *Picnic* is exclusively linked to the act of looking – scopophilia, voyeurism and the fetishisation of clothes – and that look, in a highly conventional way, is masculine: directed from men to women (both from character to character and from spectator to image). This is not unsatisfying, but titillating: playing around with the allure of the prohibited. As Freud writes in the section 'Touching and looking', in *The Sexual Aberrations*: "The progressive concealment of the body which goes along with civilisation keeps sexual curiosity awake. This curiosity seeks to complete the sexual object by revealing its hidden parts."[8] In costume films interested in sexuality (above nostalgia and history telling) the contrast between the obtainable concealed body and the means of enforcing that concealment (namely the clothes) is seen to heighten expectations and arousal. There is, for example, the coincidentally embarrassing and touching portrayal in *The Age of Innocence* of Newland Archer's desire for the Countess Olenska through the action of him stooping to kiss the delicate embroidered shoe that is peeking out from beneath her dress; this scene, though emotionally charged, is reminiscent of Luis Buñuel's comic treatment of shoe fetishism in *Diary of a Chambermaid* (1946). Paul Cox's *The Golden Braid* (1990) dwells on a man's obsessive attachment to a lock of woman's hair, perhaps a more satisfying substitute for the unobtainable object than the scrap of dirty lace Michael clings on to in *Picnic at Hanging Rock*. Important to all these instances of the fetishisation of the woman and of the man's desire is the notion of difference, contrast and, most significantly, distance.

Christian Metz suggests distance rather than proximity is essential to the voyeuristic impulse, that "all desire depends on the infinite pursuit of its absent object."[9] Although perhaps too much has been said about the sequence *in The Age of Innocence* where Newland symbolically unbuttons Olenska's glove and kisses her exposed wrist, such a scene highlights the erotic effect of symbolically suggesting a passion that will never be consummated – where the distance remains intact. Is distance therefore more erotic than closeness? In the poems of the seventeenth-century priest Robert Herrick, the man's desire for the impossible female body is transmuted into a playful, aching longing for his Julia's clothes, reminiscent in its passion and furtive guilt of Foucault's account of the

'meticulous' confessional that shifted the "most important moment of transgression from the act itself to the stirrings – so difficult to perceive and formulate –
of desire."[10] Herrick's verse resonates with a desire for an image of woman so
objectified that the mythic Julia's identity is lost beneath "that liquefaction of
her clothes."[11] Her "erring lace", "tempestuous petticoat" and "careless shoe-
string"[12] are such sufficient substitutes that the poet finds himself doting "less
on nature, than on art"[13]: the artifice, the fabrication is more alluring than the
possible attainment of intimacy itself.

As Freud articulates, fetishism and scopophilia become perversions if, among
other things, "instead of being preparatory to the normal sexual aim, (they)
supplant it."[14] Without entering into the obvious and necessary battle with Freud
over what is 'normal' (although all the films I have cited are emphatically
heterosexual) this misdirection of desire is precisely what occurs in both Herrick's love poetry and Weir's excessive, hysterical sexual fantasy *Picnic At
Hanging Rock*. What Freud terms "unsuitable substitutes for the sexual object"[15]
remain at the core of how fetishistic films such as *Picnic At Hanging Rock*,
Witness, *The Age of Innocence* ,or *Diary of a Chambermaid* represent clothes
and female sexuality: there is an increasing fixation on the clothes, shoes and
hats the women are wearing (the fetishes that remind the male of the "last
moment in which the woman could still be regarded as phallic")[16] and thus a
transferral of desire from them to their conventionally feminine garments. The
act of looking is closely affiliated with men and the expression of masculine
sexuality, and in these costume films a classic heterosexual dynamic has been
constructed whereby the women are defined and confined by their "to-be-looked-
at-ness"[17] whilst the men are positioned as the controlling subjects of the gaze.
If "the simple gesture of directing a camera toward a woman has become
equivalent to a terrorist act",[18] then men are unlikely to desire such disempow-
ering objectification by turning the camera on themselves.[19]

The Piano, enforcing a simple inversion of the normative process, addresses the
question of what happens when the agent of the gaze is female and its object is
the male body. It is necessary, however, to contrast this reversal with the
representation of Stewart as the conventional scopophilic male. Stewart is
isolated in a feminist world by his dependency on voyeurism, being consistently
identified with the detached act of looking: squinting through a camera lens,
spying on Ada and Baines through cracks in the timber and floorboards. Stewart
(whose costume was made intentionally too small for Sam Neill to give him the
air of the repressed, uncomfortable Victorian gentleman) is emasculated rather
than empowered by his possession of (only) the look. There are two scenes in
The Piano which most notably demonstrate female desire of the male body and

the subsequent feminisation of that body as the conventional scopophilic roles are reversed: one which positions Ada as the subject of the gaze and one in which the intermediary figure is dispensed with and Baines is placed "in direct erotic rapport with the (implicitly female) spectator."[20] The latter scene, showing the naked Baines dusting and caressing the piano (which is, by its direct association with her, a fetish substitute for Ada), directly confronts the spectator with an unconventional representation of masculinity: the heterosexual male object of the female gaze.[21] The former scene shows Ada stroking Stewart's body as he is half asleep, emphasising his passivity and her manipulation of him. What characterises both sequences is the use of a luscious golden light and a fluid camera that (ironically in Stewart's case) intensifies the attraction of the male skin. The similarities between these two scenes is indicative of the relative positioning of Stewart and Baines throughout the film as oppositional images of masculinity. Baines, with his Maori markings, hybrid clothes and unkempt hair repeatedly functions to confront Stewart with his own lack. When spying on Baines with Ada, Stewart perceives in Baines his unobtainable and idealised double, whom he then (by trying to rape Ada or by wanting to hear her play the piano) tries to emulate. The active look clearly appropriated by Ada also serves to pacify Stewart, most effectively during his second attempt to rape her as she lies semi-conscious after he has cut off her finger. Her stare of disbelief as she awakes to see Stewart over her unbuttoning his trousers (having been aroused by the flesh exposed through her pantaloons) both interrupts the rape and functions as the mirror to reflect his shame.

In a feminised world in which the distant voyeuristic male look is passive, impotent and unable to intrude, let alone possess, the notion of women connoting "to-be-looked-at-ness" needs to be modified. In The Piano the spectator has become disengaged from the fetishistic male gaze, as our look is most emphatically not aligned with Stewart's. There are two ways in which the spectator's alignment with the feminist perspective is manifested: through an ambivalent treatment of Ada's clothes in relation to her body and sex, and through the prioritisation of other senses (notably touch) to convey the sexuality of the Ada/Baines partnership. In terms of how Ada works in collusion with the signification of her Victorian clothes, she demonstrates the positive or active use of womanliness as masquerade proffered by Mary Ann Doane. Whereas Joan Riviere's analysis of the masquerade finds it to be synonymous with womanliness, in that the excessive presentation of femininity is operating to attract the male gaze and confirm the woman's position as his other,[22] Doane suggests the active, affirmative potential of masquerade which offers women "sexual mobility"[23] by flaunting femininity and thus keeping it at a distance. Although Doane subsequently modifies her views on the feminist potential of masquerade,[24] the performative quality of many of Ada's actions related to clothes implies that an affirmative masquerade is perhaps still possible, that it can indeed "provide a feminine counter to the concept of fetishism."[25]There is, for example, the direct play with the archetypal feminine role as Ada cursorily flings her bridal dress over her day clothes to pose for herself (in front of the mirror), Stewart (looking through the camera) and finally for their commemorative wedding photograph.

This performative potential of costume is most intricately demonstrated in the equivocal meanings attributed to Ada's cumbersome Victorian clothes, the innovation being the discovery of a language capable of articulating a radical opposition to the restrictions often forcibly imposed on the Victorian wife through the very means by which those restrictions are conventionally manifested. It is not simplistically indicated that hooped skirts have suddenly acquired liberating potential: they still hamper progress through interminable mud and prevent Aunt Morag from easily relieving herself when 'caught short'. Rather, the duality of the costumes in *The Piano* is that they function as alternately affirming and undermining forces. At times they conform to expectations of the restrictive mid-Victorian age, giving Ada and Flora the appearance of dwarfish dolls weighed down by the exaggerated hugeness of their multiple skirts, only unshackled when able to take such garments off (as when Flora cartwheels on the beach). Likewise, Stewart is forced into the strict confines of his traditional role via his tight and awkward clothes, in direct contrast to Baines who mixes Maori with European. In Stewart's case, therefore, the clothes maketh the man. Conversely, Ada defies Simone de Beauvoir's pessimism and is not defined or identified by what she wears. The most powerful example of Ada proving that her cumbersome clothes can be protective and fulfil a positive function is during Stewart's first thwarted attempt at raping her in the tangled (sexual) wood. As Ada clings onto the tendril branches of the trees, Stewart tries violently to find a way to the body beneath the layers of skirt, underskirts and hoops, to force the closeness he has seen her enjoy with Baines. The hooped skirt, which (along with Flora calling her) gets in the way here, is a persistent visual indicator throughout the film of Ada's wilful control over her clothes and her life. The hoops, at the outset, offer a protective tent; later, exposed during the sex scene between Ada and Baines, the crouching Baines (unlike Stewart) is permitted under the hoops; and finally as Ada is pulled under the water with the piano her silhouetted hoops almost get in the way of her disentangling her foot.

Ada similarly functions ambivalently in relation to her colour, the whiteness of which is exacerbated by the severity of her dark clothes and formal hair. As Richard Dyer observes, "trying to think about the representation of white-

ness....is difficult, partly because white power secures its dominance by seeming not to be anything in particular."[26] In *The Piano* whiteness is a similarly
inconsistent signifier which in turn represents aggression (the colonial invasion),
the potential sensuality of that colonial male body (the close-ups of Baines and
Stewart), and unaestheticised pallor (Ada). In the first instance, whiteness (like
the colonial master, Stewart) is shown to be ineffective rather than omnipotent:
the Maoris scorn Stewart for offering them buttons rather than money, and they
refuse to exchange their land for his blankets and guns. The most unexpected
uses of whiteness, though, are those linked with sex and sexuality, both of which
serve to accentuate or make strange its presumed signification. The incongruous
eroticisation of Stewart not only conflicts with his persona as European invader,
but draws attention to, rather than takes for granted, his white heterosexual
masculinity: traditionally something which is summarily ignored as the given or
universal category against which others define themselves. Ada's defiance
extends to her skin, the whiteness of which is never fetishised or aestheticised,
so jarring with, rather than complementing, her attractiveness and sensuality; in
the scene in which Stewart pursues her into the woods, the distorting lens and
flat blue light de-eroticise her face completely.

If the masquerade is to be a feminist strategy, then its use should in some way
facilitate the implicit presentation of woman as not merely spectacle: the locus
of the "collective fantasy of phallocentrism."[27] It follows that the reappropriation
of male-designated roles for women is fundamental to the development of Ada's
relationship with Baines. After defining the woman's traditional sexual role as "a
more or less obliging prop for the enactment of men's fantasies", Luce Irigaray
in *This Sex Which Is Not One* suggests that "woman's desire would not be
expected to speak the same language as man's."[28] A woman's (body) language
is described as being related to touch, as "woman takes pleasure more from
touching than from looking, and her entry into the dominant scopic economy
signifies, again, her consignment to passivity."[29] Similarly, *The Piano* suggests
that Ada's progression from passivity to activity is related to her defiance of
objectification and a sexual dialogue reliant on the hierarchical exchange of looks.
In order to win back her piano, Ada agrees to a bizarre striptease relationship
with Baines, bartering black keys for items of clothing. This strip subverts the
norm through the insertion of touching rather than looking as the primary mode
of communication: Baines stroking Ada's arm as she plays the piano, the two of
them lying together naked and finally the two of them having sex. Traditionally,
feminist critics have only been able to perceive a strip as part of a dominant
system that aligns "sexual difference with a subject/object autonomy," that "an
essential attribute of that dominant system is the matching of male subjectivity

with the agency of the look."[30] When, however, the exchanges are defined through touch the relationship defies (or reverses) this binary system, and the dominant discursive strategy is aligned to a female subject. Irigaray talks of a "nearness so pronounced that it makes all discrimination of identity, and thus all forms of property, impossible;"[31] likewise, Ada's 'nearness' decommercialises the strip by changing its (scopophilic) rules, and in so doing defetishises her own clothes and body.[32] Whereas clothes fetishism is dependent on an implied separation of garments from body (and thus of imagination from fulfilment), in Ada's piano-playing scenes with Baines the emphasis is on proximity, as the (touching of) clothes and body are part of the same ritualistic process, leading not to distanciation but sex. To return briefly to Freud's distinction between touching and looking, looking can more easily become a 'perversion' because of the distance it necessarily enforces between subject and object (in *Picnic At Hanging Rock,* for instance, none of the characters who are infatuated with one other touch). Touch, however, in requiring closeness, is an inevitable constituent of 'normal' sex. As clothes in *The Piano* become components of a discourse based on touch, so the difference subsides between the masculine perception of women as (merely) body, whose identity is forged by symbolic interaction, and the feminist redefinition of the woman as (whole) body whose feminine expressiveness is based on that body's reclamation.

The prioritisation of touch over looking is further conveyed, perhaps paradoxically, through the use of the camera, conventionally the tool of mainstream cinema's "inevitably voyeuristic, exploitative and male" gaze.[33] The camera often mimics either the movements or the desire of Ada and Baines, notably during the scene in which Baines is crouched under the piano having got underneath Ada's skirt and is feeling the bit of exposed skin through her worsted stockings with his rough finger. The use of extreme close-up here suggests more than the distance between desire and 'absent object' of the fetishistic films mentioned earlier. The camera's nearness and the contrasting textures convey the pleasure of touch. This alternative sexual discourse which links touch to both clothes and body, and thus suggests a further proximity (in opposition to masculine distance) between clothes and body, is the film's means of articulating Ada's sexual awakening. As her relationship with Baines progresses, so Ada's expressiveness through the sense of touch increases, from running the back of her hand along the piano keys to caressing Stewart's body. Whilst Stewart, for a moment, mistakenly thinks Ada has discovered a desire for him (when he attempts to touch her Ada recoils), this sequence rather suggests that Ada has discovered

a more abstract desire for closeness, confirmed again by the ostensibly anach-
ronistic use of close-up and exaggeratedly warm lighting.[34]

The development of a sexual discourse which foregrounds touch as its dominant
sense, therefore, subverts and supplants its masculine voyeuristic alternative.
Stewart's adherence to that male dependency on the look is what, in this
instance, renders him passive. As the camera often subjectifies Ada's gaze, so
it usually objectifies Stewart's by underlining and looking at his (often physical)
separation from the emotional centre of the film. *The Piano* thus conforms to the
strictures of mainstream cinema, and yet subverts the primary strategy of that
form by distancing the active gaze from the male subject, creating instead an
inter-relationship between an active female subject and the feminine sense of
touch. Of significance to a form of feminine communication foregrounding touch
and the body is Ada's muteness, a further (feminist) rebellion, this time seeking
to marginalise spoken language. Ada's active disengagement from (man-made)
language is necessarily affiliated to her representation as a non-conformist force.
Ada, aged six, stopped speaking, not as the result of a conventional female
trauma as in *Possessed* (Curtis Bernhardt, 1947) or *The Spiral Staircase* (Robert
Siodmak, 1946), but because (more like Christine in *A Question of Silence*
[Marleen Gorris, 1981]) she simply decided to. Her muteness becomes a symbol
for her transgression, control and defiance of patriarchal law. What characterises
most earlier representations of female muteness is the woman's implied desire
to be 'saved' from her vulnerable but threatening position beyond the dominant
(language-based) discourse and to be restored to a traditional role within the
realm of the symbolic by the assistance of a good man. What, conversely,
characterises all of Ada's sensory transgressions is the fierceness with which
she adheres to her non-conformity, the physicality with which she communicates
and defines her personal space. Although functioning in relation to patriarchal
laws Ada is not subsumed by them and, despite all the potential for restriction,
oppression and unhappiness, she is the controlling force of both the narrative
and how the film is to be perceived. The various factors that have appeared
through the film to represent her fierce resolve (her muteness, her clothes, her
piano) converge in the final sequences as Ada decides first to die along with her
piano and then to live. As the voice-over suggests, as an ending death would
have been perfect: quintessentially dramatic, feminine and silent; Ada caught in
the rope half-exposed, half-engulfed in her clothes, eroticised in death. In wanting
to live, however, Ada consigns this image to fantasy, lulling herself to sleep with
it, keeping the 'silence' to herself. Ada's relationship to classic syntax (whether
verbal, scopophilic or narrative) has always been problematic, and to die in the
mode of a tragic heroine would have been to succumb to another masculine

tradition. Instead, Ada defines and communicates herself and her desires differently, unbalancing those traditions and instating female subjectivity.

NOTES

1. Stella Bruzzi, "Jane Campion: costume drama and reclaiming women's past", in Pam Cook and Philip Dodd, (Eds.) *Women and Film: a Sight and Sound Reader*, London: Scarlett Press, 1993. pp232-42.

2. Renee Baert, 'Skirting the issue', *Screen*, vol. 35, no. 4, 1994. p359.

3. Ibid. Baert, '94. p359. It is interesting to note, however, that such categoric distinctions between how women and men relate to clothing are not always valid. In films such as *American Gigolo*, or gangster films such as *Le Samourai*, *Goodfellas* or *Reservoir Dogs*, law, fantasy, representation and will or desire are seen to intersect on the male body and in relation to clothes.

4. Foucault, Michel, *The History of Sexuality Volume 1: An Introduction*, Hammondsworth: Penguin, 1981. pp4-5.

5. Ibid. Foucault, '81. p23.

6. Ibid. Foucault, '81. pp33-5.

7. Ibid. Foucault, '81. p12.

8. Freud, Sigmund, "The sexual aberrations", in *On Sexuality: Three Essays on the Theory of Sexuality and Other Works*, Harmondsworth: Penguin, 1977. p69.

9. Metz, Christian, "The imaginary signifier," *Screen*, vol.16, no. 2, 1975. p60.

10. Op. cit. Foucault, The History of Sexuality, '81. pp19-20.

11. Herrick, Robert, "Upon Julia's clothes," in Alastair Fowler (Ed.) *The New Oxford Book of Seventeenth Century Verse*, Oxford: Oxford University Press, 1991. p275.

12. Ibid. Herrick, '91. "Delight in disorder". pp257-8.

13. Ibid. Herrick, '91. "Art above nature: to Julia." pp273-4.

14. Op. cit. Freud, '77. "The sexual aberrations." p70.

15. Ibid. Freud, '77. p65.

16. Op. cit. Freud, '77. "On Sexuality". pp354-5.

17. Mulvey, Laura, "Visual pleasure and narrative cinema", in Bill Nichols (Ed.), *Movies and Methods II*, Berkeley: University of California Press, 1985. p309.

18. Doane, Mary Ann, "Women's stake: filming the female body", *in Femmes Fatales: Feminism, Film Theory, Psychoanalysis*, New York and London: Routledge, 1991. p165.

19. Dyer, Richard, "Don't look now – the instability of the male pin-up", *Screen*, vol. 23. Nos. 3-4, 1982. pp61-73 for a discussion of some of the strategies posing men adopt to counter the subjugation of being framed.

20. Op. cit. Mulvey, '85. "Visual Pleasure and Narrative Cinema". p311. I have used – but inverted – Mulvey's analysis of direct fetishisation, as she is here talking exclusively of the spectator as male.

21. Baines has been clearly identified as heterosexual, a sexuality not complicated by the implied homosexuality of many other (often narcissistic) male characters like the similarly 'looked at' Julian in *American Gigolo*. See, for instance, Patricia Mellencamp, "The unfashionable male subject", in

Jeanne Ruppert (Ed.), *Gender: Literary and Cinematic Representation*, Gainesville: University Press of Florida, 1994. pp17-24.

22. Riviere, Joan, "Womanliness as masquerade", in Victor Burgin, James Donald and Cora Kaplan (Eds.), *Formations of Fantasy*, London: Methuen, 1986. pp35-44.

23. Doane, Mary Ann, "Film and the masquerade: theorising the female spectator", in *Femmes Fatales*, '91. p25.

24. Doane, Mary Ann, "Masquerade reconsidered: further thoughts on the female spectator", in *Femmes Fatales*, '91. pp33-43.

25. Ibid. Doane, '91. p39.

26. Dyer, Richard, "White", in *The Matter of Images: Essays on Representations*, London and New York: Routledge, 1993. p141.

27. Johnston, Claire, "Women's cinema as counter-cinema", in Nichols (Ed.), *Movies and Methods II*, Berkeley: University of California Press, '85. p211.

28. Irigaray, Luce, "This sex which is not one," in *This Sex Which is Not One*, (trans.) Catherine Porter, New York: Cornell University Press, 1985. p25.

29. Ibid. Irigaray, '85. p26.

30. Op. cit. Doane, '91. p21.

31. Op. cit. Irigaray, "This sex which is not one", '85. p31.

32. It is also significant that Baines gradually takes his clothes off as well.

33. Butler, Alison, quoted in Elizabeth Cowie's untitled entry in *Camera Obscura*, Nov. 20-21. 1989. p128.

34. Usually such identification with Stewart is absent, and scenes that revolve around him are often coloured a much colder blue.

3

POST COLONIAL STUDIES
AND ISSUES OF NATION

CHAPTER 7

THE RETURN OF THE REPRESSED?

WHITENESS, FEMININITY AND COLONIALISM IN THE PIANO

LYNDA DYSON

───

The *Piano* re-presents the story of colonisation in New Zealand as a narrative of reconciliation; in doing so it addresses the concerns of the white majority. It is, in a sense, a textual palliative for postcolonial anxieties generated by the contemporary struggles over the nation's past. During the last decade or so, white New Zealanders have been forced to reassess their colonial history as a result of the demands for justice by the indigenous Maori people which, together with Britain's shift of focus away from the former geo-political alliances of Empire, have brought about a crisis of identity. These have been troubling times for white New Zealanders and it is within this context that I wish to consider *The Piano*.

The critical international acclaim surrounding the film constructed *The Piano* as a feminist exploration of nineteenth century sexuality and tended to ignore the way in which race was embedded in the film. My analysis supplements the existing range of critical commentaries by focusing on the way in which the film reproduces a familiar repertoire of colonial tropes to construct a version of whiteness through a matrix of race, class and gender differences. Whilst the construction of gender and sexuality is obviously a central theme in *The Piano*, the film's representation of a colonial landscape must necessarily be considered within the context of contemporary debates over national belonging in New Zealand – debates which have resonances within the wider field of postcolonial theory.

In the film, Ada McGrath (Holly Hunter) travels to New Zealand for an arranged marriage with the white settler landowner Stewart (Sam Neill). Ada arrives on the coast of New Zealand accompanied by her daughter Flora (Anna Paquin), a grand piano and a clutch of possessions. She is an elective mute and communicates with the world using sign language which her daughter verbalises. The colonial landscape provides the setting for Ada's sexual awakening. Stewart agrees to trade Ada's piano for a block of land belonging to Baines (Harvey Keitel), a white man who speaks Maori and has *moko* (tattoos) on his face. Ada is forced to give Baines piano lessons, but when it transpires that the transaction is an attempt by Baines to get closer to Ada they strike a deal in which the keys of *The Piano* are traded for caresses. An intimate relationship develops which Stewart eventually discovers. In an act of brutal retribution he severs Ada's index finger with an axe. Soon after, he agrees to let her leave to start a new life with Baines and Flora.

The fantasy of colonial reconciliation is played out through the developing sexual relationship between Ada and Baines. At the end of the film Ada chooses 'life' after jumping overboard with her piano. She leaves the instrument (the symbol of bourgeois European culture) at the bottom of the ocean, thus severing her connection with the imperial centre and begins her life anew with her man who has already 'gone native'. They become born-again New Zealanders living in a gleaming white house where the mute Ada refinds her voice.

This romantic melodrama is set in a landscape where 'natives' provide the backdrop for the emotional drama of the principal white characters. The Maori are located on the margins of the film as the repositories of an authentic, unchanging and simple way of life; they play 'nature' to the white characters 'culture'. If we read *The Piano* as Ada McGrath's rite of passage from the twilight gloom of Scotland to the bright, white place in Nelson, New Zealand, then the white settler fantasy of creating a 'New Jerusalem' is represented through the negotiation of the nature/culture divide. This opposition draws on discourses of primitivism which have historically constructed the colonial Other as 'noble savage', inverting (rather than subverting) racialised hierarchies underpinning and legitimating the colonial project in white settler colonies.[1] Indigenous people and their cultures have been privileged as the keepers of spiritual and authentic values. Their perceived mystical attachments to the land and nature are ideal-ised, symbolising all that has been lost through modernity.[2] Primitivism provides the means to deal with the contradictions of white settler colonialism; while the white colonisers saw themselves bringing progress and civilisation to these pre-modern cultures, their project was also energised by the utopian fantasy of building a society free of the political and economic divisions and inequalities of Europe.

In New Zealand, questions of belonging and claims to indigeneity are central to the contemporary crisis of identity. White New Zealanders, who can no longer comfortably call themselves European, are attempting to forge a *pakeha* identity. *Pakeha* is a Maori word, highly contested in translation, referring to those of European ancestry, or more generally 'outsiders'. In recent years the strength of contemporary Maori claims as an 'ethnic' group has engendered new versions of white identity; in particular a renovated *pakeha* identity which claims indi-geneity for the descendants of white settlers. In recent times new versions of whiteness have re-worked the 'sedimented traces' of nineteenth century con-structions, re-presenting early settler myths in relation to nature and the colonial landscape. Jennifer Lawn has argued that post-colonial self-fashioning using the ethnic category *pakeha* also attempts to avoid the connotations of supremacy that the term 'white' has acquired.[3]

In *The Piano,* Ada McGrath and George Baines negotiate, in different ways, the nature/culture split in order to assume an indigenised *pakeha* identity. With her piano at the bottom of the sea and her severed finger sheathed in metal – a symbol perhaps of colonial lack – the film ends with Ada speaking of "the silence where hath been no sound".[4] She has sacrificed her silence in order to take up her place in the new land. The ending suggests an attempt to articulate the perceived cultural emptiness which continues to haunt white New Zealand. It speaks to an 'absent centre' of white identity hovering in an uncomfortable space between coloniser and colonised, no longer European but with no real claim on indigeneity either.

In the following I will firstly consider the contemporary crisis of white identity in New Zealand within the context of political and cultural shifts which have come about through a reassessment of the nation's colonial past. I will then explore the way 'whiteness' is represented in *The Piano* through a matrix of race, gender and class differences.

The trivialising of land purchases in *The Piano*, with the settlers exchanging buttons and blankets for Maori land, reminded me of school history lessons in New Zealand during the 1960s, when we were still being taught the naturalised version of the nation's history; the teleological account of white settlement which largely erased Maori resistance. In fact, land has been the central focus of contestation since the earliest days of settlement. The colonisation of New Zealand involved the installation of a settler majority (through a 'whites only' policy) on territory formerly inhabited by Maori tribal groups. Prospective settler groups – mostly English and Scottish – purchased land from the New Zealand Company having been sold the dream of a 'New Jerusalem' which was to be built on territory 'acquired' from the Maori. In 1840 this land-grab was legitimated by a treaty signed by the British Crown and Maori tribal leaders. In the dominant narrative of New Zealand history, the signing of the Treaty of Waitangi symbolised the formation of the nation and became the pivot for the elaboration of a hegemonic national identity based on the notion 'We are one people'; a construction which attempted to erase divisions of both race and class in New Zealand.[5] The terms of the treaty were never honoured by the colonisers and for more than thirty years following the signing, land wars raged between the Maori and the British Crown. One of the main causes of the wars was attempts by the colonisers to enforce laws concerning the compulsory acquisition of what was deemed to be waste land; land which the colonisers, deploying their ideologies of civilisation and progress, considered not to be cultivated or used in appropriate ways.

During the past decade or so, Maori tribal groups have used the Treaty of Waitangi to successfully contest the legality of these early appropriations in a specially convened Land Court. Controversially large tracts of land and coastal fishing rights have been returned to tribal groupings. These renegotiations (which amount to a re-interpretation of the Treaty) have resulted in profound cultural shifts in New Zealand. The 'Maori Renaissance' has involved a rewriting of the nation's colonial history with the Treaty as the constitutional document around which a bicultural approach is now being constructed. Together with Britain's entry into the European Community (which ended the special economic relationship guaranteeing a market for New Zealand's primary produce) these political, cultural and economic shifts have shattered the national imaginings of white New Zealanders whose power and privilege has been challenged from within and without the nation. Maori culture now possesses an unprecedented degree of prestige although it is debatable to what extent their political and economic power has been enhanced by biculturalism. But despite the historical agency of the Maori people, and despite the fact that this debate has preoccupied the nation for a number of years, they are located on the margins and in the shadows of culture in general,, and this film in particular.

In her discussion of the double articulation of the 'dark continent' as a trope which refers both to the unknowability of the colonial landscape and the enigma of feminine sexuality, Mary Anne Doane explores the way in which representations of white women play a pivotal role in the articulation of race, class and sexuality. She argues that:

> "The nature of white woman's racial identity as it is socially constructed is simultaneously material, economic ... and subject to intense work at the level of representation, mobilising all the psychic reverberations attached to (white) female sexuality in order to safeguard a racial hierarchy."[6]

This analysis is particularly useful in thinking about the way in which racial, sexual and class differences are inscribed on the female body in *The Piano*. Ada, as a symbol of white bourgeois femininity, has access to a spiritual world denied the other female characters in the film. Her emotions are expressed through a powerful fusion between the musical score and the movement of the camera. A recurrent motif in the film is the closeup of Ada's shimmering face, skin bleached out, eyes closed in rapture as she plays her piano. As she plays, the camera circles her, caressing the bared shoulders and delicate stem of neck; her vulnerable spine is exposed and elided with the whiteness of her bodice. While the eroticised image of Ada appears translucent, fragile and free from blemish, the Maori women in the film are physically desexualised through their representation as lank-haired, toothless and devoid of the conventional markers of femininity.

In this film, hair is an important signifier of the nature/culture opposition. Hair which has been worked on, aestheticised and feminised signifies culture; it is also used to symbolise Ada's sexual awakening and liberation. The camera continually fetishises her elaborate coils – at one point the camera literally draws us into the coil at the back of Ada's head, as if giving us access to her complex emotional world. She finally 'let's her hair down' after her first sexual liaison with Baines. We see her and Flora, with their gleaming hair swirling around them as they tumble on the bed, bathed in a golden glow.

Ada's cultural and racial 'purity' – exemplified by her shimmering whiteness and her sublime relationship to her music – is reinforced by the class differences represented within the film. The two plump, white female servants are accorded the status of characters but, like the Maori women, they are desexualised. Morag – with her prominent facial mole and carefully positioned kiss-curl – and Nessie, with her high-pitched mimicry, provide comic relief from the emotional preoccupations of Ada and her men. These women represent the lower orders and, as such, exhibit a lack of 'refinement'. In one scene Morag urinates amongst the trees, her bodily functions serving to reinforce the high/low oppositions which mark out Ada's bourgeois femininity.

Throughout the film the primitivist discourses which construct the nature/culture opposition are expressed through the juxtaposition of the repression of the white characters (in particular Stewart and Ada McGrath) against the authenticity of the Maori. With their bold, sexualised chat, the Maori provide the textual echo for all that has been lost through 'civilisation'. Baines bridges this nature/culture divide. His facial tattoos and his ability to speak Maori signify that he has 'gone native', while his 'self-fashioning' and attachment to the land construct him as a *pakeha*; a 'real New Zealander'. While never relinquishing his whiteness, he is able to arouse Ada's passions because he is closer to nature than Stewart. He too is a member of the lower orders – in an early scene Ada describes him as an 'oaf' because he is illiterate; she insists that he wash his hands before touching the piano. However, his baseness is constructed through the eroticisation of his body. In one scene we see him washing himself in the river while a group of Maori women discuss his sexual needs and, as if to reinforce Baines' desirability, a camp Maori man dressed as a woman watches from a nearby tree. Later Baines strips naked and uses his shirt to stroke clean Ada's piano. His affinity with the land and his easy relationship with the Maori stand in contrast to Stewart. While Baines' hut is surrounded by trees, Stewart's is set in a muddy clearing amongst burnt stumps. He complains to Baines: "What do they (the Maoris) want it (the land) for? They don't cultivate it, burn it back, anything. How do they even know it's theirs."[7] Through this primitivist inversion, Stewart is increasingly shown to represent the 'bad' colonial Other and stands for all that is negative in the white coloniser. He is greedy for land, sexually repressed – the Maori continually refer to him as "Old Dry Balls" – and violent. His relationship to the land is one of brutality and exploitation and this is mirrored in his treatment of Ada. On discovering her relationship with Baines, Stewart severs her finger with an axe and later he attempts to rape her.

While Stewart exploits the bush, Ada and Flora work on and aestheticise the liminal space of the beach. Early on in the film, Ada's hoops are used as a shelter which is surrounded by a wall of gleaming shells, and in another scene they construct an enormous sea-horse from shells while the camera swirls overhead, erasing all traces of labour. The use of aerial shots in this scene is reminiscent of a dominant genre of landscape photography in New Zealand which constructs the landscape as a prelapsarian paradise. It is as if their femininity – played out through their emotions and aestheticised in the realm of culture – separates them from the degradations of colonialism; in this sense they are closer to nature.

Whiteness as purity is a recurring motif in the film. While the Maori are at one with the bush (to the extent that they are even visible) the film continually privileges whiteness through the play of light against dark, emphasising the binary oppositions at work in the text. This whiteness is enhanced by the use of filters, which means that while the darker skin tones of the Maori are barely discernible in the brooding shadows of the bush, the faces of Ada and Flora, framed by their bonnets, take on a luminous quality. The film's photographic director Stuart Dryburgh has described the use of naturalistic lighting as an attempt to capture the authenticity of the landscape:

> "We've tended to use strong colour accents in different parts of the film.
> We tried not to light the bush ourselves but to use natural light wherever
> possible. So we played it murky green and let the skin tones sit down
> amongst it. We tried to represent it honestly and let it be a dark place."[8]

Dryburgh's technicist discourse naturalises the use of photographic technologies and codes which mediate visibility, desire and endow whiteness with what Dyer, in a discussion of representations of 'white', has described as "a glow and radiance that has correspondence with the transcendant rhetoric of popular Christianity."[9] This glow of whiteness and its associations with light, purity and cleanliness recurs throughout the film, for example in an early scene when the Maori approach Ada and Flora on the beach exclaiming, "They look like angels". Later on in the film, Flora, caught rubbing herself in a sexually explicit way against the trunks of trees with a group of Maori children, is forced by the repressed Stewart to scrub gleaming white suds into the treetrunks in the sombre twilight – an act of ritualised cleansing.

The primitivist discourses which construct the Maori as outside culture are exemplified by the way in which the Maori are seemingly unable to distinguish between representations and the real. When the Bluebeard shadow play is performed a group of Maori leap onto the stage to rescue the female performers. In fact, this staged performance foreshadows the moment when Stewart grabs his axe and sets off to sever Ada's finger. But in this later scene the Maori, relegated to the narratival margins, remain mere witnesses to his actions – once more misreading the signs. When Ada and her daughter arrive on the beach in New Zealand, a perplexed Maori character is seen rubbing his finger blindly across the words carved in the side of the wooden crate. Later on in the film a group of Maori men are caught violently thumping the keys of The Piano in 'dumb' incomprehension.

In some scenes however, there is a sense in which the Maori have written themselves back into the script. Early on in the film, when Stewart meets Ada on the beach, he is followed about by a Maori character who stands behind him in a poked straw hat mimicking his action. This character looks straight at the camera and our gaze is temporarily drawn away from Stewart, whose authority is undermined. This is the moment when we begin to perceive Stewart as the 'bad' colonial Other. Such examples, however, are rare, and on the whole the Maori characters remain marginal to the central narrative.

The Piano's critical reception in Britain was, almost without exception, ecstatic.[10] It was hailed as a powerful and evocative exploration of Victorian sexual repression rather than as a representation of colonialism. This aspect of the film was passed over because white settler colonialism remains an invisible or marginalised aspect of the British imperial project. The presence of black people in Britain has brought some parts of the Empire back to the imperial centre and thus foregrounded the colonial relationship with those places. However, with the exception of South Africa, the whiteness of settler colonies such as Australia, New Zealand and Canada continue to be taken for granted. For example, while the anti-monarchist campaign in Australia receives media coverage in Britain because it is perceived to be of direct concern, 'postcolonial' struggles over land rights tend to go unnoticed.

This invisibility also occurs in the field of postcolonial theory where the experiences of the African diaspora and the people of the Indian subcontinent have provided the spatial/historical focus for much important work, largely through the efforts of diasporic intellectuals such as Edward Said, Gayatry Spivak and Homi Bhabha,[11] while the specificities of white settler colonialism and the relationship with 'first peoples' such as Maori, Aborigines, and native American Indians, continue to be peripheral within the field. As the Australian cultural critic, Meaghan Morris argues:

> "Americans and Europeans often assume that we are abstracted like a footnote from their history and devoid of any complicating specificity in intellectual and cultural history."[12]

Representations of New Zealand in Britain, aside from tourist industry constructions of the place as an unspoilt nature park, are confined to media coverage of international sporting events and Royal visits. Coverage of these events often include picturesque snapshots of Maori culture drawn from a limited repertoire of so-called traditional forms such as songs and dances. These representations are contained within a discourse which frames New Zealand as an ex-colony which has achieved racial harmony, a construction which has important resonances given that historically New Zealand has been known as 'the Britain of the South'. For example, much is made of the performance of the Maori war challenge, the *haka*, at the start of rugby internationals, which has been appropriated as a signifier of national identity. Here we have an example of the way in which the culture of the Maori is assimilated into a unifying notion of 'New

Zealandness'. Difference is elided into a mythologised sign of national unity whilst also functioning metonymically to position Maori culture as unchanging and traditional.

The invisibility of white settler colonialism was exemplified by the way in which *The Piano* was marketed in Britain. Publicity material and media coverage constructed the film for its viewing public as an art-house movie about nineteenth century sexual repression. This is not to imply that this entirely determines the way in which the film has been read by cinema audiences but to suggest that the critical reception certainly contributes to the context within which audiences respond. The focus on gender was heightened by media interest in Jane Campion as 'author'. The film's accolades were those conventionally reserved for high cultural texts: Campions work was described in various broadsheet reviews as 'lyrical', 'sensitive', 'original' and 'spiritual'. Her romantic vision was compared to that of nineteenth century writers such as the Bronte sisters and Emily Dickinson. The hyperbole surrounding the film's release reached its peak in the *Independent on Sunday* which ran an extensive feature on Campion's life and work. Having described her looks as pre-Raphaelite (an unthreatening and fragile vision of white European femininity), it went on:

> "*The Piano* feels steeped in literary tradition, entirely original but rich in reverberations. It is Wuthering Heights, a romance of the soul with the wild New Zealand beaches standing in for the stark moors. It's Emily Dickinson, a romance of the soul with its wavering between ecstasy and terror, eroticism and renunciation."[13]

This critical acclaim not only ignored the film's colonial setting but, by focusing on the links between *The Piano* and the English literary canon, Campion and her work were appropriated as distinctly European. While this appropriation can be understood within the context of the relationship between the metropolitan centre and the periphery – historically the privileging norms of the European cultural canon have defined cultural value in the colonial context[14] – it also seemed to consolidate the whiteness of the text. In a sense, the critical reception reinforced the way whiteness is universalised in the film. As Richard Dyer argues: "this property of whiteness to be everything and nothing is the source of its representational power."[15]

The credits at the end of *The Piano* acknowledge the assistance of Maori cultural advisers. The use of cultural advisers to guarantee the authenticity of the Maori reinforces the discourses of primitivism in the film which construct the indigenous people as the repository of unchanging traditional values, in harmony with nature, childlike: the textual echo of all that has been lost.[16] This construction is reiterated in other texts connected with the film, for example, in the production notes published along with the script where the authenticity of the Maori on and off the screen is discussed:

> "In common with his character Baines, Harvey Keitel was struck by the way in which the Maori cast, in role and out of role, tended to have a more profound relationship to the earth and the spirits than the *pakeha* do. Keitel is quoted as saying: 'I was very affected by Tungia, the woman playing Hira in the film. She came down to the beach and the first thing she did was cross to the sea, bend over and sprinkle herself with water. And I said 'What are you doing'... and she said: 'I'm asking the sea to welcome me.'"[17]

The Maori are attributed with a timeless essence in *The Piano*; they are positioned as a collectivity outside of history. This primitive idealisation provides the back-drop for the self-fashioning of Ada McGrath and George Baines. Ada, whose colonial rite of passage enables her to discover her true femininity and Baines, who has undergone 'partial indigenisation', reinvent themselves as born-again *pakeha*. What *The Piano* does, in restaging the colonial encounter, is to indirectly address white New Zealand's crisis of identity; its reworking of the nature/culture trope provides a means of representing and affirming an 'indigenised' identity.

NOTES

1. For a discussion of the way in which 'primitivist inversion' are serving New Age identities in settler colonies see Nicholas Thomas, *Colonialism's Culture: Anthropology, Travel and Government*, Cambridge: Polity, 1994.

2. See Torgovnik, Marianna, *Gone Primitive: Savage Intellects, Modern Lives,* Chicago: University of Chicago Press, 1991.

3. Lawn, Jennifer, "Pakeha Bonding" in *Meanjin*, Vol 53, no 2, 1994. p301.

4. Campion, Jane, *The Piano*, Bloomsbury: London, 1993. p123.

5. After Maori chiefs had signed the Treaty of Waitangi on 6 February, 1840 the British governor William Hobson proclaimed 'He iwi tahi tatou' (We are one people). This affirmation of national unity is celebrated annually by a ceremony on the treaty-signing site at Waitangi; in recent years the event has been disrupted by land protesters.

6. Doane, Mary Anne, *Femmes Fatales: Feminism, Film Theory, Psychoanalysis,* London: Routledge, 1991. p245.

7. Op. cit. Campion; '93. p70.

8. Ibid. Campion; '93. p141.

9. Dyer, Richard, "White", *Screen* Vol, 29, No.4, 1988. p 63.

10. For example, *The Independent*, 17 October, 1993; *The Guardian*, 22 and 29 October 1993; *Sunday Times*, 31 October, 1993; and *Sight and Sound*, November, 1993.

11. Said, Edward, *Orientalism,* London: Routledge and Kegan Paul, 1978; Spivak, Gayatry, *The Post-Co-*

Ionial Critic, London: Routledge, 1990; Bhabha, Homi, *Nation and Narration*, London: Routledge, 1990 and *The Location of Culture*, London: Routledge, 1994.

12.   Morris, Meaghan, "Afterthoughts on Australianism" in *Cultural Studies*, vol 6, no 3, 1992. p71.

13.   *Independent on Sunday*, 17 October, 1993.

14.   For a discussion of these 'privileging norms' see Ashcroft, B, Griffiths, G and Tiffin, H, *The Empire Writes Back: Theory and Practice in Postcolonial Literatures*, London: Routledge, 1989. p3.

15.   Op. cit. Dyer; '88. p45.

16.   Of course, the use of 'cultural advisers' also signals the way in which the politics of race in contemporary New Zealand inflects and problematises all areas of cultural production.

17.   Op. cit. Campion; '93. p143.

CHAPTER 8

FROM LAND ESCAPE TO BODYSCAPE

IMAGES OF THE LAND IN THE PIANO

LAURENCE SIMMONS

Behind our quickness, our shallow occupation of the easier
Landscape, their unprotesting memory
Mildly hovers, surrounding us with perspective,
Offering soil for our rootless behaviour.
Charles Brasch, *Forerunners*

My title moves from a solecism, a somewhat misleading and ungrammatical way of saying landscape, to a neologism used by Jane Campion to describe her film.[1] It is a shift, as we shall see, which, I believe, covers in its fraught confluence the parameters of the uses to which the land has been put in *The Piano*. What I will be considering is how the film weaves a network of textual invocations traversing literary and painting landscape traditions of the European and settler colony. I shall argue that, though it clearly does interrogate colonialism's discursive practices through moments of irony, the fractures and occlusions of its formal syntax, and the psychoanalytic paradigms of its discourses of the body in opposition to a patriarchal order, ultimately *The Piano* re-narrativises the strategies of previous attitudes to the land where only the post-contact European possesses the ability to enunciate and represent the other.

The word 'land escape' also verges on being a malapropism, a confusion of words of not very different sound, a practice which *Fowler's English Usage* felicitously describes as "wordfowling with a blunderbuss." However, I chose 'land and escape,' wisely or unwisely, in the face of grammatical reason, because in its double direction it suggested viewing the land as a means of escape for the filmmaker and the land under view as also somehow escaping her control. One of the small moves my title makes is to change landscape from a noun to a verb, so that we shift from simply viewing landscape as an object to be seen or contemplated, even as a text to be read, and see it instead as interactive, a process that might involve the formation of subjectivities, the scape of our bodies and our sexuality, and ultimately, as I shall argue, of our national identities, rather than simply reflecting these. For it is clear that even attempts to decode the signs of landscapes, to uncover their textual operations as either symbols or allegories, to examine their generic or narrative typologies, to read them rhetorically, that is, as texts, have still treated landscape as a static image, an other to be analysed, rather than, as a recent essay by W.J.T. Mitchell demands, "instruments of cultural power."[2]

I

What has brought about the sort of shift, from noun to verb, that I have outlined here? It has been stimulated, I would argue along with Mitchell, by developments in cinema and more recently television. The more traditional, motionless images of landscape in painting or photography must now be revised to include landscape as a site for appropriation, a medium for exchange, a dynamic of ecological, cultural and economic practices. To employ a term that has been somewhat overworked of late we need now to see landscape as a discourse, and this revision has been engendered by the representation of landscape in film, the medium which itself includes motion from one place and one time to another as its essential characteristic. Such a shift in position involves a process which moves in a double direction: towards what we do to our environment, how we insert or lose ourselves in it, and how our environment as space moves out to envelope and define us. These new representations of landscape in film are not simply mimetic **nor** transparent and their analysis uncovers a complicated process of transformation and exchange. Landscape viewed as a dynamic network of cultural codes contains ambivalences, appropriation, collaboration even exploitation in a process of the formation of national identity. Landscape has helped and helps us write our "imagined community" to use Benedict Anderson's celebrated definition of a nation.[3] Crucial to a full understanding of this double-edged dynamic is an account of how portrayal of landscape effaces its own textuality and the fact that it is always already a representation, the rhetoric of how it seems to present itself as seemingly natural and given, as 'the other' of traditional depictions. The title of Kenneth Clark's classic work on the topic, *Landscape into Art*, innocently belies this issue: there is something called landscape, "things which we have not made and which have a life and structure different from our own: trees, flowers, grasses, rivers, hills, clouds," says Clark, and there is art as "we have recreated them in our imaginations," he continues.[4] But Clark's *into* of his title *Landscape into Art* elides important distinctions between perception of the landscape and representation of the landscape or, at worst, it would wish to collapse them entirely. So Clark ultimately fails to deal with the very potent ambiguity of the word landscape itself, the fact that it denotes either a geographical place or its representation, a painting in his case. As such, landscape partakes of the ambiguity of reference in a term like *history* (as between the events themselves and the narration of them) or *grammar* (the structure of a language versus the description of such structure). As is usual in these cases, the terminological difficulties are neither to be neglected nor to be discussed simply for their own sake, they are portents of significant underlying problems.

II

Let me start with an example from Vincent Ward's 1978 film *State of Siege*. I take it to be emblematic in that it literally involves confrontation of the two media, painting and film. The central character in this film, derived from a novella by Janet Frame, is a painter and art teacher of the old school, Kenneth Clark's sort of painter we might say. A painter of a tradition which we in New Zealand associate with art societies, Sunday painters who on weekend excursions would venture into nature on a sketching trip with portable easel and picnic hamper. Malfred Signal, mistress of such signs, journeys to a wild West Coast location to paint the rocky shore and the Tasman Sea. But representing the landscape is where she frustratingly fails and we see her strain and struggle with her perspective and her palette, her face twisted in a frown as the land escapes her and she finally screws the paper containing her failure into a ball. Yet in a triumph of camera angles, clever editing, and with the perceptual fullness of a soundtrack, this is exactly where Vincent Ward, the film director, succeeds as he masterfully manages to capture with heightened expressiveness the very features which escape poor Malfred: the push and pull of the ebb and flow of the tide, the drama of its escape and also its return.

What Malfred Signal fails to capture is what visual artists since the seventeenth century, but literary writers for a much longer period, have referred to as the sublime: those feelings of awe, excitement, fear or dread that such a view of mountains, torrents, stormy seas might arouse. Such a feeling was captured, or perhaps I should say approached, since the sublime is in essence an effect that ultimately 'escapes' representation, by many New Zealand painters of late nineteenth-century landscapes. For Edmund Burke, its most influential English spokesman, the sublime works our minds to produce "a sort of delightful horror," for the twentieth-century French philosopher Jean-Francois Lyotard, its most recent elucidator, it is still "an intrinsic combination of pleasure and pain" but actualises the avantgarde demand of presenting "the fact that there is an unpresentable" and as such is a model for reflexive thinking in painting.[5]

As the art historian Francis Pound has argued in his influential book *Frames on the Land*, the early European painters of New Zealand's landscape framed the land with a set of European artistic conventions and gestures (the Sublime was one of these along with the Picturesque, the Topographical, and the Ideal). The genres of landscape which these early painters brought with them from Europe offered them various windows onto the land.[6] But it should not be forgotten that the frames of genres are also presuppositions held as much by the spectators of the paintings as by the painters of them. Looking at the land through the frame of genre makes the land able to be perceived, able to be painted and so landscape painting for the early settlers was a way of inventing the land, of modifying it and reconstructing it in pictorial terms, parallel to the physical colonisation of it they actively undertook. Homi Bhabha has argued that "in order to conceive of the colonial subject as the effect of power that is productive – disciplinary and 'pleasurable' – one has to see the *surveillance* of colonial power as functioning in relation to the regime of the *scopic drive*" and, as the writer J.M. Coetzee has noted of South African colonialism, "the politics of expansion has uses for a rhetoric of the sublime."[7] Indeed, the very idea of landscape, Pound argues, is a European import and ultimately there is no such thing as the innocent eye and no possible natural access to a real and pre-existing unmediated New Zealand nature.

Every act of seeing the land is also an act of possession, of colonisation, an attempt to fit the landscape into European habits of mind with the transference of European landscape conventions from the metropolitan centre to the imperial periphery. Such a process of framing the land in painterly conventions and/or imperial gestures can be found in early New Zealand film. We can trace the early moves from one of the first short silent movies, the Australian director Franklin Barrett's *Across the Mountain Passes of New Zealand* (1910–11), through to the many short scenic documentaries of the Government Publicity Office made during the 1920s such as *Queen of the Rivers* (1928), one of the first of many films to extol the landscape of the Whanganui River.

In the early parts of her film Jane Campion remains trapped within these conventions. The liminality of the beachscape, as Leonard Bell has recently noted, was the most frequent site for the represented encounter between coloniser and about-to-be-colonised other in the pre-1840s.[8] For the nineteenth-century urban audiences of increasingly jaded metropolitan centres these colonial landscapes came to be perceived as repositories of romantic subject matter.[9] Campion's images of the land (Karekare Beach, Awakino and Matakana) as charged sites of myth also represent a similar twentieth-century escape for the metropolitan film audiences of New York or Paris and are perhaps even part of a larger "displacement of the country-city dichotomy onto world geography."[10] As the newly arrived Ada McGrath and her daughter Flora are left behind on the beach at the beginning of the film, there is a scene worthy of the nineteenth-century depictions of the sublime where, as the published screenplay tells us, "The two women are but tiny dots on the shore and the view continues back and back over a vast, endless expanse of dense native bush."[11] Similarly, leaving her piano behind the next day when she makes the daunting climb through the unfamiliar bush, Ada turns and pauses at the cliff top and we see her looking out over the coast, the Maori porters moving alongside in a scene almost stolen from Augustus Earle's *Distant View of the Bay of Islands, New Zealand* (ca.1827). But what makes these images in *The Piano* so insistently colonial landscapes, apart from the obvious signs of foreignness of flora, is a sort of systematic over-determination in how a number of devices are employed: a commanding vantage point; the syntax of the sublime; the planar logic of foreground, middle distance with an object of interest, and a light-saturated horizon; its patently staged theatricality.

III

That the process of representing the land was intimately tied to processes of colonisation is repeatedly interrogated in a neglected, but powerful, historical film of the early 1980s: *Pictures* directed by Michael Black. *Pictures* is the story of the Burton Brothers, early colonial photographers, and investigates the tension between their desires to 'document' the actual life of the Maori under colonisation and the colonial authorities' demands for 'safe representations'. *The Piano* explicitly underscores that such a division operates for the settler subject too, when Ada is forced to don a fake, backless wedding dress and pose unwillingly with new husband Stewart in the mud and rain in front of an equally fake painted backdrop of old Europe. Once again in terms of my general argument it is significant that photography here, not painting, is the site of investigation of the ideological implications of representation.[12]

Naturally with film, the conventions of genre drawn upon are not simply those of the tradition of landscape painting or photography. Film, too, by the 1930s and 1940s had articulated a sophisticated range of genre possibilities and ways of framing its diverse subject matter. It is not surprising, then, that John O'Shea's *Broken Barrier*, the only feature film made in New Zealand during the 1950s, frames its presentation of a cattle muster on the Mahia Peninsula with the sounds and iconography of the American Western. Films of the early 1960s such as John O'Shea's next feature *Runaway* draw upon the new road movie and buddy movie genres as do those of the late 1970s and early 1980s such as Geoff Murphy's *Goodbye Pork Pie* and Sam Pillsbury's *Starlight Hotel*. The *Piano*'s indebtedness to the literary genre of the gothic romance has been much commented upon by its director and debated by critics and its preoccupation with mud also creates strong genre links to the film Western.[13] As a revisionist redaction of both these genres *The Piano* once again falls squarely within the ambit of colonialist modes.

In introducing a discussion of the work of pioneer New Zealand filmmaker, John O'Shea, I have already passed from attitudes to the land that mark the period of early colonialism in my diachronic description to the period of cultural national-ism of the 1930s through to the 1960s which so dominates New Zealand painting and literature in the twentieth century and is paralleled by the burst of filmmaking in the 1970s. New Zealand art and literature in the 1930s show a new self-con-sciousness of themselves *as* New Zealand art, they now begin to be constructed not simply as a history, but as a fully self-conscious and unified *tradition,* in which painters and paintings, and poets and poems, both past and present, might openly engage in a nationalistic act of self-definition. In the 1930s, painters and critics and writers began to work with a new and newly declared set of assumptions, and were alive to a new set of concerns, which might then be played up or against. The two major figures of nationalist New Zealand culture, the poet Allen Curnow and the painter Colin McCahon, both talk self-consciously throughout the 1940s and the 1950s of the need to invent New Zealand as a nation.[14] Such self-consciousness is not to be found in the New Zealand film industry until much later for, as I have already suggested, it is only in the decade of the 1970s that we can speak of New Zealand film coming of age.

Just as European artists of the late nineteenth century were making over the image of the land in their own European image, erasing the Maori names of places and things and replacing them with their own in a process of possession and power, so we can discover artists of the period of cultural nationalism now consciously forgetting, rejecting – or rather, *concealing* – the weight of their own debt to Europe. The colonialist landscape was now increasingly the property of the settler subject, the landscape becomes one of their use, but it was still for many of them something other and threatening, a space of alterity in an untamed land. McCahon's *Northland Panels* (1958) are instances of such an attitude to the land and are dedicated to 'a landscape with too few lovers' and, as he writes on the final panel, in such a landscape 'even the manuka in bloom can breed despair'. In McCahon's stark emblematic *The Green Plain* and skeletal *Takaka: Night and Day*, both of 1948, we encounter an image of the land which is pastless and voiceless. This image of the land as an absence, a silence, a solitude, a formlessness empty of meaning and definition that needs filling, means the landscape became what Roland Barthes would call 'an empty sign'. The land is speechless and it is the task of the painter to fill it, which, of course, is one of the reasons why Colin McCahon does that so literally, but surprisingly, with words. New Zealand film, too, is full of these hostile, 'empty' signs of the land: two of many possible examples are Vincent Ward's desolate and wet Taranaki valley in *Vigil* and Geoff Steven's lunar volcanic plateau in *Strata*. In *The Piano* the scree earth scar which Baines traverses with the blind piano tuner, the cabbage tree marsh, the ever oppressive mud, the bush choked with supplejack vines, the sea which encroaches on the beached piano are constant reminders of this hostility.

These are landscapes of estrangement [*dépaysement*] which Lyotard, in another play on the word, calls 'scapelands'.[15] The landscape as our psychological scapegoat. This emptiness and alienation was felt, too, in earlier nineteenth-century painting with its sparsely-populated landscapes and many illustrations of the *terra nullius* of the South Island. Depictions of the Pakeha belief that the Maori had long ago abandoned an island now up for grabs were, naturally, to aid colonial appropriation of land.[16] But for the cultural nationalists there was also talk of the need for a new imaginative or psychological colonisation as opposed to the material colonisation of the nineteenth century. Bill Pearson in his influential essay, *Fretful Sleepers* written in the early 1950s argued that hostility does not reside per se in the landscape but that "it is we who are hostile. We haven't made friends with the land."[17]

IV

Nationalism drove painters to use repeatedly such icons of New Zealandness as the burnt-out native tree stump painted repeatedly by John Holmwood and Eric Lee-Johnson among others. The tree stump icon, which has been examined in an essay by Michael Dunn, was both a sign of the creation of a new landscape and a trace of its colonisation.[18] The tree stump tells of the destruction and burning off of bush and its conversion into farmland, and charred tree stumps literally mark our paddocks even today. So they are both a sign of change and of new materialism and, at the same time, an agonised sign of loss of the pre-existing native bush, an environment we have all but destroyed. In film we find their numerous examples in the Westland of John O'Shea's *Runaway*, the Taranaki valley of Vincent Ward's *Vigil*, and Jane Campion's *The Piano*. Ada arrives to find her prospective home "bleakly set amidst smoking stumps"[18a] and later we see the Maori porters manipulating the piano through these stumps from Baines' to Stewart's hut. There is a significant scene of Stewart at his woodchop cutting firewood and displaying his virtuosity as an axeman. Later when he displays that virtuosity all too graphically Ada, perhaps understandably, but also symbolically, walks blindly into a tree stump after her finger has been excised. Caught up in this dynamic there is a double bind for the artist and filmmaker: to be pure the landscape must formulate itself as the antithesis of the land as real estate, yet for us to say that the landscape is not real estate is to erase the very signs of our own constructive activity in its formation and to conceal the use value of its representations.[19]

The geographer Jay Appleton has recently generalised psychological explanations for the recurrence of landscape forms and their aesthetic gratifications. He has proposed what he calls a 'prospect-refuge theory' which postulates that "because the ability to see without being seen is an intermediate step in the satisfaction of many ... [biological] needs, the capacity of the environment to ensure the achievement of *this* becomes a more immediate source of aesthetic satisfaction."[20] Appleton asserts that the aesthetic values of landscape are not found in a philosophy of aesthetics, nor in a culturally bound artistic symbolism, but in the biological and behavioural needs that we share with other animals. Appleton believes that we should consider the possibility of a symbolism representing elements that are crucial to survival in the habitat of living creatures since, he argues, a "landscape which affords both a good opportunity to see and a good opportunity to hide is aesthetically more satisfying than one which affords neither." His ideal spectator of the landscape, albeit in a distant biological past, is grounded in a visual field of violence, exposed as unwilling prey to all types of natural threat. Appleton proposes a terminology of abstract terms for describing the aesthetic elements in landscape, terms indicating features that increase the likelihood of survival: *prospect*, which allows an animal to see and control from an elevated place; *refuge*, which allows it to hide; and *hazard,* which stirs a feeling of being threatened and of wanting to escape. The perception of these elements in a represented landscape, such as a painting or in film, both verifies the spectator's ability to survive and elicits an emotional response similar to that felt when they are encountered in a natural environment. The standard picturesque landscape, for example, is pleasing to the eye because it places the spectator in a protected, shaded spot (a 'refuge'), with screens on either side to dart behind or to entice curiosity. In such an attempt to valorise the body as an agent of cognition we are moving close to Jane Campion's understanding of the reflective role of a 'bodyscape'. But, of course, the problem with Appleton's insistent biologism is that it ignores both the political functioning of landscape *topoi* and the settler subject's desire to write his or her symbolic presence over the traces of previous inhabitants.

V

In another but related twist, according to Roland Barthes, reading a landscape is "firstly perceived according to one's body".[21] Landscape is probably the most powerfully cathected of objects, recalling the originary areas of the female body and re-enacting a sexual-psychological text of desire that is shaped towards the recovery of primary scenes. Or equally one might readily think of landscape representation as Freudian dreamwork, since its primary process thinking which characterises the unconscious, and is marked by condensation, displacement and representation, tends to be pictorial in nature. So it is no surprise that almost naturally, or at least it is presented to us as natural and transparent, we find a series of bodily and sexual metaphors for our transactions with the landscape in the literature, painting and film of cultural nationalism. The first of these is 'the land as woman' both lover and mother: "Man must lie with the gaunt hills like a lover,/Earning their intimacy in the calm sigh" Charles Brasch wrote in his poem 'The Silent Land' from the collection *The Land and the People*. "Rock pudenda thrust into the sea...the bones of rock, the body of my lover" as James K. Baxter writes of his sexual encounter with the land in his poem on Makara Beach.[22] The land is also delivered up naked, unclothed in the raw and stripped bare, an unruly outrage to culture.[23] As Colin McCahon said of his painting of Takaka Valley: "The actual valley as I saw it was like a geological diagram, only overlaid with trees and farms. In my painting all of this has been swept away in order to uncover the structure of the land."[24]

In short, a land of depths to be plumbed and penetrated, where the overtones of possession and desecration of the landscape lead ultimately to phallocratic metaphors of rape and we have seen how the colonial landscape provides special voyeuristic opportunities for the male explorer. For the male settler subject the state of being rooted to the land is also, as Francis Pound has wittily suggested, to use the land in its New Zealand vernacular sexual sense, to 'root it'.[25] On the one hand, *The Piano* continues this metonymic tradition when, for example, the puritan Alisdair Stewart disapproves of the sensual masturbatory game of making love to trees which his new stepdaughter Flora plays with fellow Maori children while his new wife literally makes love for a wooden piano key carved, of course, from a tree. On the other, with its notion of 'bodyscape' it defines new territory. If for the early male cultural nationalists the land was woman, later feminists have deconstructed that notion to explore other directions of the equation. One of which is 'woman as land'. *The Piano*'s windswept beach, but also its oozing mud, clinging wet foliage and clammy vines, mark the landscape as a state of mind, a sexual and psychological terrain. The land like Ada, as I have already noted, is treated as a sexual/emotional commodity and, as Ann Hardy has suggested, "there is enough buying and selling in the film (the piano for land, the land for buttons, the piano for Ada's sexual compliance) to make it plain that neither she, the land, nor the Maori are expected to have self-sover-eignty".[26] The caged hoops of Ada McGrath's skirts are echoed in the snaking, black supplejack vines which both entangle her and Stewart as he frantically chases her and must be finally discarded to the mud, but they also give Ada and Flora shelter and protection during their first night on the beach. This mud, too, acquires a persistent force in the film through its relationship to and counterplay with the human body, but it is the filming of the bodies (bodyscapes) of Ada and Baines, their slow, erotic fulfilment framed through the dual gazes of Flora's primal scene and Stewart's frozen voyeurism and sensually, almost viscerally, enhanced by the dog that licks his dangling hand, that is the most subversive. However, what undercuts the power of opposition of these contending images is the tension that exists between the striving after a discourse of the pre-symbolic and the very language of the symbolic in which this is articulated, such as the obviousness of the castration scenario of Ada's finger, or the maternal underwater landscape where Ada chooses life, her body attached by an umbilical cord to the canoe above or, more simply, Flora's miniature landscape of moss and twigs recreated on a dinner plate along, as she says, with Adam's tree and the serpent with a very long tongue.

VI

One of the complaints of the paternalistic Stewart in *The Piano* when they refuse to sell him their *tapu* ground is that the Maoris don't do anything with their land: "What do they want it for? They don't cultivate it, burn it back, anything. How do they even know it's theirs...?" he intones.[27a] But the land has always been central to Maori culture and, although the Maori had no genre of landscape in the Western pictorial or scenic sense, they did represent the land by images of primary ancestor figures, as well as making marks upon the land with many figurative rock drawings and carved wooden poles delimiting tribal territories, food plots and *tapu* zones. While engaged in a systematic programme of alienating Maori from their tribal territories since contact, Pakeha have at the same time consistently represented the relationship of Maori people to the land as one of more intimate and natural belonging than their own. In this portrayal of the pre-contact Maori as the last refuge of a pre-civilised people living in an innocent state of nature, as "islands of history" to use Marshall Sahlin's memorable phrase, there is a fetishisation of the past with touches of the nostalgic primitivism that Levi-Strauss expresses for his ethnographic subjects.[27] But, if one consults Maori attitudes to the land, there is a story to be told very different to this relegation to nature. Pakeha have positioned Maori in a natural bond with nature and therefore viewed them as less acculturated, their nature to our culture, but from a Maori point of view the nature/culture opposition does not work.[28] The differences are rather ones between cultures, for like the Pakeha representation of the land, the Maori one is also constructed through complex but different beliefs, myths and metaphors. It is another form of geography which as its etymology suggests is a 'writing of the land' (*geo*, earth; *graphien*, to write).

Campion's settler landscape, as we have seen, is a liminal zone of beaches of encounter and boundary fences between self and savagery, and she re-employs the compositional habit that relegated the farm labourer or the native to the shadowy margins of the nineteenth-century canvas with its metaphors of the eclipse, the silencing, the occultation of the other. At the same time, by attributing an authentic native essence, and possibly sexualising its content, she runs the risk of reinviting the violences which characterise the very ideology of colonialism itself. For it is not a question of simply identifying stereotypes, as Homi Bhabha has argued, "the point of intervention should shift from the ready recognition of images as positive or negative, to an understanding of the *processes of subjectification* made possible (and plausible) through stereotypical discourse."[29]

I began with a scene where a frustrated painter, Malfred Signal, failed to capture the landscape but where the filmmaker concerned triumphs in his encounter. Let me end with a similar anaclisis by propping one landscape representation against another having the same site of articulation. There is an early scene in *The Piano* of Alisdair Stewart emerging from the bush accompanied by his Maori guides hovering ever-present in the background. He stops to look at the small framed photograph of the wife he has ordered, has been married to, but has not yet seen, but in a movement which discloses both the self-interest of his desires and the hand of the filmmaker, he tilts the photograph so it reflects first the bush behind him and then his own face as he uses it for a mirror to comb his hair. Ada as an image and a person is blanked out by the land and, in turn, subsumed under Stewart's own image.[30] There is here a logic and trajectory of strategies which reprise the exclusionary colonialist gestures which the film and the director's comments on it would want to negate. Let me insist: despite the disruptions of colonialist modes of viewing the land on which its overt rhetoric relies and which at moments it achieves, *The Piano* is grounded in cognitive systems which perpetuate those modes and so ultimately institutes a practice that diverts and disperses the engagement with the political conditions it also describes. Into such a position are enfolded the ironies of the difference of landscape, both the thing represented and the form of representation, the picturing of power and the power of picturing, the land as a form of escape but also ultimately escaping control.

NOTES

1.   The phrase 'Land Escapes' has also been used by the sculptor Neil Dawson as a generic title for a series of works on metal mesh that he completed in 1982. These works knowingly play with received representations of landscape in the tourist snapshot and postcard exposing them as part of the grid that culture imposes on nature. Jane Campion uses the expression 'bodyscape' when talking to Mary Colbert about her film's affinity with the genre of gothic romance: "My exploration can be a lot more sexual, a lot more investigative of the power of eroticism. Then you get involved in actual bodyscape as well, because the body has certain effects – like a drug almost – certain desires for erotic satisfaction which are very strong forces," *Sight and Sound*, Volume 3, Issue 10, October 1993, p6; and reprinted in the notes to the screenplay *The Piano* (London: Bloomsbury, 1993), p140. The term is also used by Mary-Louise Pratt when describing John Mandeville's accounts of the inhabitants of distant isles which "begin with the body as seen/scene. Such portraits conventionally do so, commonly with the genitals as the crucial site/sight in the 'bodyscape'," "Scratches on the Face of the Country; or What Mr. Barrow Saw in the Land of the Bushmen," *Critical Inquiry*, 12 (Autumn 1985), p120.

2.   Influential for my thinking on 'the politics of landscape' has been the collection of essays *Landscape and Power,* edited by W.J.T. Mitchell, Chicago: University of Chicago Press, 1994, in particular Mitchell's opening essay 'Imperial Landscape' where he deals briefly with nineteenth-century New Zealand painting.

3.   Benedict Anderson, *Imagined Communities: Reflections on the Origin and Spread of Nationalism.* London: Verso, 1983.

4.   Kenneth Clark, *Landscape into Art*, 1st published 1949; reprinted Boston Mass.: Beacon Press, 1963.

5.   Edmund Burke, *A Philosophical Enquiry into the Origins of our Ideas of the Sublime and the Beautiful*, 1st edition 1757; Menston: Scholar Press, 1970; Jean-Francois Lyotard, "The Sublime and the Avant-Garde," in Andrew Bennington (Ed.), *The Lyotard Reader*, Oxford: Basil Blackwell, 1989.

Roland Barthes in an essay on travel guides writes of what he calls the helvetico-protestant morality that promotes an aesthetic of mountains, gorges and torrents and maintains that this ideology is a 'hybrid compound of the cult of nature and of puritanism': "The Blue Guide" in *Mythologies*, trans A. Lavers, New York: Hill & Wang, 1986, pp74-7. Laleen Jayamanne in a paper entitled "Post-Co-lonial Gothic; the Narcissistic Wound of Jane Campion's *The Piano*," given at the Under Capricorn Conference *Is Art a Western Idea?*, Wellington, March 4-7, 1994, gave a detailed discussion of two forms of the sublime, melancholy and gothic, in *The Piano*. Jayamanne suggested that Campion actively inverts Burke's gendering of the concepts of the beautiful (woman) and the sublime (man as capable of experiencing terror, the limits of reason).

6.   Francis Pound, *Frames on the Land: Early Landscape Painting in New Zealand*, Auckland: Collins, 1983.

7.   Homi K. Bhabha, "The Other Question: Stereotype, Discrimination and the Discourse of Colonialism" in his *The Location of Culture*, London and New York: Routledge, 1994, p76; and J.M. Coetzee, *White Writing: On the Culture of Letters in South Africa*, New Haven: Yale University Press, 1988. p61.

8.   Leonard Bell, "Augustus Earle's *The Meeting of the Artist and the Wounded Chief, Hongi, Bay of Islands, New Zealand 1827*," an illustrated lecture given at the Auckland City Art Gallery, August, 1994.

9.   Bernard Smith discusses how New Zealand became identified with the romantic landscape in his *European Vision in the South Pacific*, 2nd Edn., New Haven: Yale University Press, 1984. p69.

10.   David Bunn, "'Our Wattled Cot' Mercantile and Domestic Space in Thomas Pringle's African Landscapes," in W.J.T. Mitchell (Ed.), *Landscape and Power*, Chicago: University of Chicago Press, 1994, p129. Lydia Wevers in "A Story of Land: Narrating Landscape in some Early New Zealand Writers or: Not the Story of a New Zealand River," *Australian & New Zealand Studies in Canada* 11, 1994. pp1-11, notes "In Europe at least the scale and unexpectedness of the landscape presented in *The Piano* made it much more than a background for the film's suggested narrative, and for any viewer the film's accreted images of topographic wildness and difficulty stand in meaningful opposition to everything represented by the belongings and activities of the characters. As it was for nineteenth century travellers and settlers in New Zealand, the landscape of *The Piano* is the initial scene of authentication, the register of difference which is at the same time a sign of reality, a sign always complex, multiple and emotionally charged." (p1)

11.   Jane Campion, *The Piano*, London: Bloomsbury, 1993. p16.

12.   On the importance of photography in *The Piano* see Pam Goode, "Foundational Romance, History and the Photograph in *The Piano* and *Far and Away*," *Span* 42/43 (1996): 52-64.

13.   For the gothic romance see Laleen Jayamanne, op. cit.

14.   Allen Curnow said in the *First Yearbook of the Arts in New Zealand* (1945) that "strictly speaking New Zealand does not exist yet, though some possible New Zealand's glimmer in some poems and some canvases. It remains to be created – should I say invented – by writers, musicians, artists, architects ..." and Colin McCahon remarked in 1966, in his *Landfall* essay, 'Beginnings', that he wished to convey to New Zealanders something "belonging to the land and not yet to its people. Not yet understood or communicated, not even really yet invented." Quoted in Francis Pound, "Silence, Solitude, Suffering, and the Invention of New Zealand (A Fictitious Story)," *Interstices. A Journal of Architecture and Related Arts*, no. 1, 1991. p63.

15.   Jean-Francois Lyotard, "Scapeland" in his *The Inhuman: Reflections on Time*, translated by Geoffrey Bennington and Rachel Bowlby, Stanford: Stanford University Press, 1991. pp182-190.

16.   For the Marxist critic, John Barrell, this dark side of the landscape is also found in the English

landscape movement and is to be read in the context of the dispossession of the English peasantry from their land holdings. See his influential *The Dark Side of the Landscape: The Rural Poor in English Painting, 1730-1840*, Cambridge: Cambridge University Press, 1980.

17.   Bill Pearson, "Fretful Sleepers: A Sketch of New Zealand Behaviour and its Implications for the Artist," *Landfall,* vol. 6, no. 3, September 1952, p226.

18a. Op. cit. Campion, 1993. p29.

18.   Michael Dunn, "Frozen Flame and Slain Tree: The Dead Tree Theme in New Zealand Art of the Thirties and Forties," *Art New Zealand*, no. 13, 1979. pp40-45.

19.   More recently there have been suggestions that *The Piano* takes poetic licence with the New Zealand landscape: "That *The Piano* could scramble our landscape, mixing various vegetations even birdsongs with impunity, was remarked upon frequently." Annie Goldson, "Piano Recital," *Screen* 38, 1997. pp275-281; 277.

20.   Jay Appleton, *The Experience of Landscape*, London and New York: Wiley, 1975. p83. See also his later and more popularising *The Symbolism of Habitat. An Interpretation of Landscape in the Arts*, Seattle and London: University of Washington Press, 1990.

21.   Roland Barthes, "La lumière du sud-ouest," in his *Incidents*, Paris: Editions du Seuil, 1977. p20. (My translation).

22.   See Trudie McNaughton (Ed.), *Countless Signs. The New Zealand Landscape in Literature*, Auckland: Reed, 1986, for these and other examples of the *topos*.

23.   See Wystan Curnow, "Landscape and the Body," *Antic*, no 3, November 1987, p145: 'nakedness in this context marks not so much the presence of nature as the absence of culture'.

24.   Quoted in Gordon Brown, *Colin McCahon, Artist*, Auckland: Reed, 1984. p24.

25.   Francis Pound, *Interstices*, op. cit. p69.

26.   Ann Hardy, "The Last Patriarch," *Illusions*, no. 23, Winter 1994, p11.

27.   Marshall Sahlins, *Islands of History*, Chicago: Chicago University Press, 1985 and Claude Levi-Strauss, *Tristes Tropiques*, Harmondsworth: Penguin, 1992.

27a. Op. cit. Campion, 1993. p70.

28.   See Priscilla Pitts, "The Unquiet Earth. Reading Landscape and the Land in New Zealand Art," in Mary Barr (Ed.), *Headlands: Thinking through New Zealand Art*, Sydney: Museum of Contemporary Art, 1990. pp87-98, for a further elaboration of these issues.

29.   Homi K. Bhabha, op. cit. p67.

30.   The quote and the identification of the importance of this sequence belong to Ann Hardy, op. cit. p.8.

CHAPTER 9

A LAND WITHOUT A PAST

DREAMTIME AND NATION IN THE PIANO

ANNA NEILL

In the act of bringing New Zealand history and landscape to the appreciative attention of international cinema-going audiences, *The Piano* gestures at an important historical interface between questions of sovereignty that troubled the colony in the 1850s and representations of national and cultural identity that characterise the globalising spirit of the 1990s. A highly modernist and post-colonial text, the film tells stories about the loss of colonial authority, about the tensions in settler consciousness between notions of home and exile, and ultimately about the violent history behind the emergence of a distinctly Euro-New Zealand identity. Yet less intentionally, *The Piano* also speaks to another, more contemporary history – that of the late capitalist, transnational era in which the voices of the colonised are once again silenced.[1]

As New Zealand governments continue to act out their economic obligations to neoliberal institutions like APEC and OECD by guaranteeing multinationals open access to land and resources, these governments must clear national culture of claims for Maori sovereignty. Indigenous struggles for land and other resources and for cultural self-determination threaten the neoliberalism that depends on the state's uncontested capacity to cede sovereignty in multilateral trade agreements. For all its worthy feminist, anti-colonial and environmentalist politics, I shall argue here, *The Piano* flattens out race history in New Zealand and in so doing gives voice to a national identity which is not troubled by Maori claims for sovereignty. It does so, I will suggest, by way of a modernist aesthetics that relegates colonial and patriarchal violence to a kind of dreamtime – before the beginning of national history – and by situating Maori grievances in that dreamtime. In this sense the film seems to articulate a national commitment to Asia-Pacific in the 1990s even as it can boast the Palm d'Or as the proof that New Zealand holds a place in the canon of European high-art cinema.

As soon as it was released, *The Piano* was hailed as radical feminist cinema. Reviewers described it as a "Bronte in the bush;"[2] a story of the "outsider woman, the renegade from convention;"[3] a text which along with *Howard's End* and *The Age of Innocence* documents "the end of civilisation as we know it [as it reverses] the basic assumptions of Western culture from the garden of Eden."[4] Less romantically, Carol Jacobs identified in Campion's self-conscious cinematography and witty preoccupation with the metaphor of the screen, and in her refusal to provide satisfying narrative coherence in the triple ending of the film, a radical and ultimately political form of aesthetics that narrates history according to the trajectory of a woman's "undisciplined will."[5] *The Piano*, like Campion's other films, is actively trying to create an alternative libidinal economy in which the woman becomes the subject of the gaze. I will say more about this below, as well as about the way the film's cinematic challenge to the law of the father also presents itself as an anti-colonial tale of national origins. Before I do so, I want to suggest that each of these commentaries *takes history out of the landscape,* either by investing this landscape with Romantic and/or mythical properties, or else by arguing that a historiographical revolution takes place through the visual and narrative texture of the film, and while apparently forgetting that every luxurious shot – including an overhead that travels across miles of virgin bush and a close-up of weary mud soaked feet trudging along barely marked paths – sensuously packages the location of the film for an international audience. Despite, or more precisely, because of the way the film's luscious footage of remote bush trades in the exotic, it brings New Zealand right into the global economic arena, offering its hardly touched landscape up to the tourist's (or foreign investor's) eye.

I say hardly touched instead of untouched because, as Jacobs has pointed out, neither the land nor the people who have lived on it the longest are simply associated with nature in this film. The relationship of the Maori to the land is "never unmarked by culture"[6]. Even the land itself is shown to be 'encultured', bearing a kind of value to the European a world apart from that which it holds for the Maori. The Maoris' deep connection with this land, contrasted repeatedly with the enclosing appetite of the coloniser (who is always looking for land that he may buy reasonably), is expressed in their respect for the *tipuna* who are buried in it, and their marking out of particular areas as *tapu*. Maori culture is identified with what is sacred – a sacredness about which Stewart, the English coloniser, is shown to be brutally ignorant – and is conspicuously juxtaposed with the fragile icons of European culture and civilisation like tea cups, hooped skirts and petticoats.

Yet while the Maori may not exactly be relegated to nature, they do not inhabit anything like a contemporary historical space within the colonising culture. They alternate between childlike fascination with and terror of the mysterious objects that the Europeans fetishise (a fascination and a terror which are shared to some extent by the childish, scatter-brained Scots character Nessie); they make Rabelaisian mockery of the sexual inhibitions of the settlers and they refuse to sell land that is *tapu*. Scenes of contact are limited to these moments of cultural inscrutability, stripped of any sense of political conflict, as if by the 1850s the Maori had no political strategies at all for challenging the radical alienation of their land which had been going on for at least twenty years, and as if questions of land ownership had not already been articulated in New Zealand at the level of political sovereignty in 1840. Instead questions of culture are de-politicised and the Maori become frozen in sacred time.

My contention here is that this fetishisation of Maori tradition provides the occasion for an articulation of a white settler identity that is something other than British – an identity whose indigeneity is marked in contemporary New Zealand by the term Pakeha. *The Piano*'s often infantilising scenes of encounter in which the Maori peer at a hooped petticoat, fondle a scarf, or playfully bang on the piano deliberately defamiliarise these objects of curiosity and, in so doing, seem to highlight the perilous condition of British colonial culture. A vertiginous shot down into Stewart's tea cup draws us semiotically into this feeling of peril. Drinking tea out of fine bone china scarcely enables the settlers to forget that civilisation ends at the drawing room door. With their shifty, anxiously exchanged looks and frantic waving of fans in the damp winter weather they appear to be constantly afraid – afraid not so much of Maori retaliation as of things not being, as Morag puts it, "quite right"; afraid of the possibility, perhaps, that New Zealand cannot be culturally remade as Britain. The fragile colonial society will have to refashion itself as something more enduring if it is to transform this wilderness into a habitable country. As it dramatises this fragility and the trouble that it engenders, *The Piano* uncovers another, more authentic, more indigenous cultural option for those settler characters who themselves have indirectly been victimised by imperial violence. Baines, the illiterate Scotsman whose lack of education and manners alienate him from the other settlers and send him "in too deep with the natives,"[7] is indigenised in the film by his tattoo and by his liminal position as translator and cultural interpreter for Stewart. Ada, the mute bride who is punished for her infidelity by a husband who twice attempts to rape her and who slices off her finger, inhabits a private realm of sign language into which only her daughter has admittance, and the way in which Stewart feels so excluded from this women's world is clearly paralleled with his ignorance of Maori. He is baffled and clumsy in the company of both his wife and his Maori subjects. This confusion points to the alienation and ultimately the humiliation of the colonial settler class and at the same time to the triumph of the new settler culture which becomes indigenised by its association with the Maori victims of colonial oppression.[8]

In part, this requires that colonial and patriarchal abuse become identified with one another. When Stewart loses his wife to Baines he identifies the latter as native other, saying to him: "...you have your mark, you look at me through your eyes, yes, you are even scared of me..."[9] In an earlier scene when the chiefs, who had presumably hitherto cheerfully traded land for blankets and guns, refused to negotiate a sale of land which is *tapu,* Stewart complained to Baines that the Maoris are ignorant and that they do nothing with the land, and suggested that the two of them go ahead and survey it anyway. Not only are these episodes tied together by the theme of lost property, but Campion uses the connection between them to link the trope of colonial blindness to cinematic voyeurism and in so doing visually highlights the colonised status of Ada. It is hard not to associate the shots of impenetrable bush through which Baines and Stewart clamber with Stewart's frustrated peering through the cracks in Baines' hut to see his wife undressing. Moreover, the Victorian patriarch is also a settler farmer who cuts off his wife's finger with the same swing of his arm that he uses to beat in a fence post. Colonial and patriarchal rule are inseparably linked. What one reviewer has aptly described as the "terra incognita of female emotions"[10] proves unenclosable, too willful to be the fenced property of the coloniser.

In another episode an archaic Maori valor becomes the palimpsest for a perform-ance of bravery by the newer generation of settlers. Shortly after Ada and Flora arrive at the settlement, the community stages a performance of *Bluebeard*. Maori 'naivety' about the theater fuses with 'warrior instincts' when several young Maori in the audience leap to the defense of Nessie who is playing the last of Bluebeard's wives and, in so doing, bring the performance to a chaotic close. Yet in another sense these men do not so much disrupt the play as participate in it, since the avenging and defending warriors who leap on stage assume the part of the brothers who in the original tale arrive in the nick of time to kill Bluebeard and release their sister. This role of avenger then gets played by Baines later in the film when he promises to crush Stewart's skull for having done what he has to Ada. Maori resistance is contained here by its comic role in the pantomime, but it nonetheless provides the theatrical anticipation of the 'true' event of rebellion and escape which will take place later in the film.

Although a variety of colonised subjects are being conflated in these scenes, eventually Maori culture gives voice to a distinctly white post-colonial subject. When Ada and Baines go off to start a new life in Nelson at the end of the film, their newer and less socially constrained settler lifestyle is marked by the freakishness of Ada's metal finger and her stumbling efforts to begin speaking. These are the signs of both colonial/patriarchal wounding and symbolic recovery. As Ada moves into the world of language, she becomes, as it were, post-colonial. Her guttural sounds are those of the new, barely encultured voice of the post-coloniser. Where the alternative ending of the film leaves Ada in "a silence where hath been no sound....In the cold grave, under the deep deep sea",[11] cut off forever from life, sound and land, the scene in Nelson releases her from the threatening imagery of a watery flight (the shot of Flora's angel wings dipping in the stream) and places her for the first time firmly on shore, speaking. At night she thinks of herself floating silently above her piano in the ocean grave. This thought seems to mark the place of prehistory; the death and loss out of which only a will to life and to a new beginning can uncover itself.

In this way *The Piano* maps out New Zealand's future in a gesture of mourning. Ada's loss and her surprising discovery that despite it her "will has chosen life"[12] at the end of the story mark her transition into a new place in which she may have given up the sadistic strength of silence but in which her will can express itself symbolically. Since Ada's oppression has already been linked to that of the Maori, it is also the colonised who are being mourned here. The film's attitude to colonial history, one might say at this point, takes the form of a modernist fascination with the primitive. This is to say that it asserts the nobility of its object of study in an implicit reminder of the corrupting force of civilisation. For Lévi-Strauss the ethnographic subject is always just out of reach, like the Amazonian tribes whose disappearance *Tristes Tropiques*[13] unhappily records. The ethnographer/traveler is caught between the fantastic spectacle of the other which is entirely inaccessible (he can only look on in awe) and the vanishing reality of a culture corrupted by Western contact in which he is inevitably implicated.[14] Campion is to some extent a Lévi-Straussean ethnographer, drawn to the figure of the vanishing primitive. Yet hers is a gesture of mourning rather than melancholy since such loss will end in symbolic recovery as the film discovers a post-colonial and post-patriarchal identity for the Pakeha subject. Her own account of being Pakeha is a description of cultural and historical emptiness:

> "I think that it's a strange heritage that I have as a Pakeha New Zealander, and I want to be in a position to touch and explore that. In contrast to the original people in New Zealand, the Maori people ... we seem to have no history, or ... tradition. This makes you ask 'Well, who are my ancestors?' My ancestors are the English colonisers ..."[15]

Ethnic identity, Campion reminds us, must be attached to some kind of history, some kind of tradition. Yet being a Pakeha New Zealander, she seems to suggest, is not quite the same thing as being the descendent of an English coloniser. Something has happened to transform this genealogy, and that event is readable in Campion's syntax: the Maori are the first people in New Zealand; the Pakeha is a white New Zealander. For the latter, history and identity in fact depend on nationhood, not on European blood, and not on the transmission of European traditions. It is the rupture with the colonial past which begins the history of the Pakeha.

Ernest Renan was the first to write difference – of race, language or religion – out of the constitution of the modern nation and to replace it with the notion of a shared relationship to the past. "A nation," he claimed:

> "is a soul [and] two things constitute this soul or spiritual principle....One is the possession in common of a rich legacy of memories; the other is ... the will to perpetuate the value of the heritage that one has received in an undivided form ... A heroic past ... this is the social capital upon which one bases a national idea."[16]

In a post-settler colony like New Zealand, this notion of the development of soul is peculiarly troubled. The settler's identity has been secured by his fencing out of the wilderness; civilisation is located in the domestic space which must be protected from savage invasion. (This is a trope of settlement which is thoroughly debunked in *The Piano* when Aunt Morag points out to Stewart that in imprisoning Ada he has bolted the door on the wrong side, the Maoris will lock him in!) Yet for the Pakeha, the marking out and fencing off of colonial soil only reminds her that she is an interloper with no authentic cultural relationship to the land. She needs the stuff of myth, a heroic past, at the very least a collection of memories to secure her to the land. But without a war of independence to remember, Pakeha national consciousness is rather dry of myth and memories.

Instead, the Pakeha Nation tries to create soul by attaching itself to the idea of the new. Katherine Mansfield, the best known of New Zealand's modernist poets, writes:

"From the other side of the world
From a little island cradled in the giant sea bosom
From a little land with no history,
(Making its own history, slowly and clumsily
Piecing together this and that, finding the pattern, solving the problem
Like a child with a box of bricks.)"[17]

The infancy of the nation is here metonymically translated into the youthfulness of the island. Geological evolution is collapsed into the history of human cultivation, and it seems as though culture, history, rock and soil are all the products of a single, fantastic volcanic eruption. The idea that history is very young in New Zealand appears everywhere in the literature of settlement. New Zealand, for Blanche Baughn is "[h]ere at the end of the earth, in the first of the future,"[18] for Edward Treagear it is "a songless land",[19] the New Zealander, in Arthur Adam's words is a "poet of a newer land/Confident, aggressive, lonely/Product of the present only/Thinking nothing of the past."[20] Literary nationalism gives voice to what Arthur Adams calls in a title to one of his poems "The Brave Days to Be." The poem begins:

I looked far in the future; ...
And through the cold grey haze of Time I saw
The fair fulfilment of my spacious dream.
My Maoriland! She sat a new crowned queen."[21]

The crowning of Maoriland is what enables the recovery of national time. Maoriland invokes the pre-history or dreamtime of New Zealand before the arrival of the European. Literary nationalism strategically straddles both dreamtime and history so as to dissociate the new New Zealanders from the dubious glories of British national memory ("No tribute lands that she had trampled on/ With pitiless foot of triumph")[22] as they identify instead with the innocence of pre-contact Maori, and at the same time to imagine themselves as New Zealand's first people.

This national figure of Dreamtime was particularly powerful in the early part of this century when there was a dramatic decline in the Maori population. In 1910 the government commissioned bronze busts of prominent Maori figures to serve as a national memorial of the brave race that would soon disappear.[23] It is at such moments that national consciousness most conspicuously intersects with the concerns of modernist ethnography, as a melancholic sense of contact fatally impacting on primitive life becomes an occasion for the erection of national monuments. New Zealand's transformation from a colony to a nation, formally completed with the adoption of the Statute of Westminster in 1947, has its origins in the creation of monuments and museum pieces. The New Zealand and South Seas Exhibition in 1889, picking up on the late nineteenth century museum fashion for ethnographic curiosities, displayed relics of Maori culture among the geological exhibits and memorabilia of settler life.[24] In implicit competition with the Melbourne exhibition of 1888, and taking place a year before the jubilee of the colony, the exhibition was clearly intended to be a nationalist event, expressing resistance to the idea of an Australasian federation.[25] The modernist trope of the vanishing primitive thus helps to articulate a nationalism that looks back regretfully at a culture destroyed by the impact of settlement and looks forward with hope to the creation of a distinctly New Zealand identity.

Such nationalist mourning for an unrecoverable, pre-historical past is manifest in cultural texts like *The Piano* which offer a very selective representation of post-contact history. Since, as we have seen, the experience of contact in this film is reduced to a moment of cultural unreadability, it is no surprise that the Treaty of Waitangi, the single most significant political event in nineteenth century New Zealand, gets no mention. In 1840 the tribes who signed the treaty were granted the rights of citizens, the protection of the Crown, and "full, exclusive and undisturbed possession of their lands and estates, forests, fisheries and other properties"[26] in return (according to the English text) for the surrender of the sovereignty which they exercised over their territories. The Colonial Office saw the Treaty as necessary to restrain the New Zealand Company which, in the 1830s, was seeking a charter from the British Government to privately develop the colony.[27] Between 1840 and 1862 (apart from the brief period between 1844 and 1846 when the Government lacked the funds to buy enough land to satisfy British immigrants) the crown maintained pre-emption on all purchases of Maori land. Yet in *The Piano*, oddly enough, all land purchases are made privately. It seems strange, on the face of it, that a story which relies so heavily on the history of Maori land purchases in the middle of the nineteenth century should be interested only in the moment of miscommunication between the primitive, who has invested the land with mystical meaning and the capitalist landowner who is committed to enclosure and profit. Maori struggles to reclaim stolen land in the wars and to establish a nationalist movement for the protection of their remaining lands in the 1850s get no mention here. The aestheticisation of Maori relationships to the land leaves them outside national time, even as the brutal colonial disregard for these relationships makes them the object of national mourning.

If the Pakeha subject is sutured to the nation by mourning, she is also attached to it by shame. The affect of shame, as Beth Povinelli has observed, is the vehicle by which the state expresses its regret over material abuses committed against indigenous peoples and in so doing brings the traumatic memory of these abuses into the fold of a national hegemonic project:

> "On the one hand, the court and state deploy an abstract language of law, citizenship, and rights – a principled, universalising, pedantic language. On the other hand, they deploy a language of love and shame, of haunted dreams, of traumatic and reparative memory, of sensuality and desire....As they do so, the court and state make shame and reconciliation – a public, collective, purging of the past – an index and requirement of a new abstracted national membership."[28]

In *The Piano,* colonial violence, or the patriarchal violence which stands in for it, is overcome by shame. The brilliance of the film is that the moment of most intense intimacy takes place, not between Baines and Ada, whose desires simply continue to surprise one another, but between Ada and Stewart when the latter hears his wife's voice "there in my head...[although] her lips, they did not make the words."[29] This pure form of communication (for which no translator would ever be necessary) had hitherto taken place only between Ada and Flora's father, who at some point "stopped listening."[30] Stewart hears Ada just as he is about to rape her, aroused by his own guilt and renewed compassion as she lies in a fever-induced sleep brought on by his attack on her with the axe. When he hears her, not only is he shamed out of the rape, but he decides almost there and then to release her and allow her to leave with Baines.

If we can truly see the final scene in Nelson as the founding moment of the nation, then that nation is predicated on a moment of intense intimacy, shame-provoking but also utterly utopian, between oppressor and oppressed. Stewart has never understood his subjects. Now suddenly his most enigmatic, most elusive, most aggravating subject has laid her thoughts out for him 'in his head' in the process of asserting her will and warning him of its strength. The struggle between coloniser and colonised is transformed into a democratic utopia in which desire, loss and shame will be part of the collective memory but will also signify the emancipation of the nation from British colonialism. No wonder Aunt Morag complains that Ada's piano playing is strange, "like a mood that passes into you ...To have a sound creep inside you is not all pleasant ..."[31] Such intimacy breaks down the linguistic and cultural boundaries between self and savage that have enabled Europeans to remain civilised in the wilderness. It helps to forge a newly indigenised Pakeha identity.

This impossible closeness is represented cinematically in the non-naturalistic, often claustrophobic shots that have become the signature of Campion's filmmaking. At one point the camera finds itself inside Stewart's pocket when he reaches into it for the portrait of Ada; at another moment we look up through the water at the underside of the canoe which is bringing Ada and Flora to shore; in the opening shot of the film, the camera appears to have found its way between Ada's eyes and the fingers she has pressed over them, an image whose echo is to be found in the shots of bush where the viewer has to peer past the trunks of *ponga* to make visual sense of the human action in the middle distance. These defamiliarising strategies may have the effect of de-suturing us from the naturalistic aspects of the narrative, but they draw us in to the politics of the film in a much more profound way. We experience the landscape, not as foreigners, but as radically intimate interlopers; the dark spaces of the bush are like those taboo or extraordinarily intimate parts of the clothed body, in the pocket or under the skirt, where the camera goes when Ada and Flora are camping on the beach. The shameful intimacy of these shots at once makes us feel complicit in the constant threat of colonial/patriarchal violation (we, after all, have been able to hear Ada's mind's voice too at times) and yet to see this violence as part of the nation's pre-history, it's pre-symbolic. This time of invasion and violation is the time before national language. Remembering this violation and lamenting the brutal effects of it is part of a collective purging of national guilt.

J.G.A. Pocock has recently warned that Maori land claims based on the Treaty of Waitangi which challenge the Pakeha understanding of property in terms of appropriation and alienation, and which in so doing undermine the very foundations of liberal jurisprudence (but which only offer in their place a language of dreamtime, a description of sacred relationships), are barred from becoming effective actors in history. History, rather needs to be "subverted and partly rewritten so as to give [legal] voice to the tangata whenua and substantiate their claims."[32] A text like *The Piano* uses the figure of dreamtime to express what I have described here as a post-colonial national consciousness. In a gesture of post-imperialist self-accusation and an attempt to construct a future for the nation out of the relics of Maori culture, it expels the Maori out of history even as it claims to be re-narrating the nation from the side of the oppressed. Ada's recovery of language at the end of the film offers a critical narration of the colonial past even as it preserves the colonised as the truly muted subjects of that history.

I am not the first to argue that *The Piano* is historically blind to the way that representations of white women's bodies are so pivotal in the articulation of raced identities in colonial and post-colonial/nationalist texts.[33] What I have also suggested here, however, is that the exclusion of the tangata whenua from history in this film – an exclusion which takes place at the interface of traumatic memory and symbolic recovery – has everything to do with sovereignty. When the shame of the coloniser and sacred relationships with the land fuse to become part of national pre-history, the question of Maori title gets lost somewhere in mythic hyperspace. On the other hand, it is difficult for New Zealand and all its luscious scenery to become the object of an international gaze as long as the sale of state owned enterprises to foreign investors can be challenged by a prior claim to ownership. Commodification of the nation depends on the production of a cultural hegemony in which self-determination comes to signify cultural independence from Britain (and hence Pakeha identity) rather than anything as globally unnegotiable as divided Pakeha/Maori sovereignty.

In an aestheticised bi-culturalism where a sense of place is generated through a series of modernist metaphors, the identities of both Maori and Pakeha are radically dehistoricised. As a national narrative of Dreamtime, *The Piano* demonstrates that the further away white New Zealand manages to move from Britain the more globally integrated it becomes, selling itself as best it can to the rest of the world as "the little land with no history."[34]

NOTES

1. On a related topic see Pihama, Leonie, "Are Films Dangerous? A Maori Woman's Perspective on *The Piano*," *Hecate* 20:2, October, 1994. pp240-241.

2. *Chicago Sun-Times*, November 30, 1993.

3. *Time*, November 22, 1993.

4. *The Washington Post*, November 21, 1993.

5. Jacobs, Carol, "Playing Jane Campion's *Piano*: Politically," *MLN*, 109, 1994. pp757-785.

6. Ibid. Jacobs, '94. p760.

7. Ibid. Campion; '93. p90.

8. Lynda Dyson has put this succinctly: "[In *The Piano*] Maoriness becomes available to fill the absent center of white identity which hovers in the uncomfortable place between coloniser and colonised." She argues that the film articulates a response to the cultural emptiness which haunts white New Zealanders, and that it invigorates the trope of nature vs. culture "to provide the means to represent and affirm a newly 'indigenised' national identity." See Dyson, "The Return of the Repressed? Whiteness, Femininity and Colonialism in *The Piano*," *Screen*, 36: 3, Autumn 1995. pp267-276.

9. Op.cit. Campion; '93. p114.

10. *The Daily Telegraph*, October 29, 1993.

11. Op.cit. Campion; '93. p123.

12. Ibid. Campion; '93. p121.

13. Strauss, Levi, *Tristes Tropiques*, (trans) Doreen Weightman and John Weightman, Harmondsworth: Penguin, 1992.

14. Ibid. Strauss; '92. p 43.

15. Op.cit. Campion; '93. p135.

16. Renan, Ernest, "What is a Nation?" (trans.) Martin Thom, in *Nation and Narration,* (Ed.) Bhabba, Homi K, London: Routledge, 1990. p19.

17. Mansfield, Katherine, "To Stanislaw Wyspiansky," *An Anthology of Twentieth Century New Zealand Poetry*, (Ed.) Vincent O'Sullivan, 3rd edn., London: Oxford University Press, 1987. p18.

18. Baughn, Blanche, "Maui's Fish," *The New Place: The Poetry of Settlement in New Zealand 1852-1914,* (Ed.) Harvey Mcqueen, Wellington:Victoria University Press, 1993. p211. For an account of the instability of the figure of landscape in colonial and postcolonial New Zealand literature see Lydia Wevers, "A Story of Land: Narrating Landscape in some Early New Zealand Writers" or "Not the Story of A New Zealand River," *Australian and New Zealand Studies in Canada*, June 11, 1994. pp1-11.

19. Treagear, Edward, "Te Whetu Plains," *The New Place*. p186.

20. Adams, Arthur, "The Dwellings of our Dead," *Maoriland and Other Verses*, Sydney: The Bulletin Newspaper Company, 1889. p189.

21. Adams, Arthur, "The Brave Days to Be," *The New Place*, Wellington: Victoria University Press. p121.

22. Ibid. Adams; p121.

23. Sinclair, Keith, *A Destiny Apart: New Zealand's Search for National Identity,* Wellington: Oxford University Press, 1986. p203.

24. See Dark, Philip J.C., "Developments in the Teaching of the Arts of the Pacific,"*The Development of the Arts in the Pacific,* Wellington: Pacific Arts Association, 1984. p96.

25. Op. cit. Sinclair; '86., p111.

26. I am using the text of the treaty reproduced in Jane Kelsey's "Legal Imperialism and the Colonization of Aotearoa," in *Tauiwi: Racism and Ethnicity in New Zealand*, (Ed.) P.Spoonley et al, Palmerston North: 1984. pp28-29.

27. See especially Hugh Kawharu (Ed.), *Waitangi: Maori and Pakeha Perspectives on the Treaty of Waitangi,* Auckland: Oxford University Press, 1989; Claudia Orange, *The Treaty of Waitangi,* Wellington: Allen & Unwin, 1987; Jane Kelsey, "Legal Imperialism and the Colonization of Aotearoa," in *Tauiwi: Racism and Ethnicity in New Zealand*, (Ed.) P. Spoonley, et al, Palmerston North: Dunmore Press, 1984. pp20-43.

28. Povinelli, Elizabeth A., "The State of Shame: Australian Multiculturalism and the Crisis of Indigenous Citizenship," *Critical Inquiry* 24:2, Winter 1998. p580. My comments on intimacy and national belonging are also indebted to those of Lauren Berlant. See Berlant, *The Queen of America Goes to Washington City: Essays on Sex and Citizenship,* Durham: Duke University Press, 1997.

29. Op. cit. Campion; '93. p114.

30. We learn this from a bed-time story Ada tells Flora, when they sleep on the beach after their arrival. It is not in the published script.

31. Ibid. Campion; '93. p92.

32. Pocock, J.G.A., "Tangata Whenua and Enlightenment Anthropology," *Journal of New Zealand History* 26: 1, April 1992. p45.

33. Op. cit. Dyson; '95. p270.

34. Op. cit. Mansfield; '87. p18.

CHAPTER 10

BIRTH OF A NATION? FROM UTU TO THE PIANO

BRIDGET ORR

In 'The national longing for form'[1] Timothy Brennan argues that "Nations ... are imaginary constructs that depend for their existence on an apparatus of cultural fictions in which imaginative literature plays a decisive role," and that chief among these literary forms is the novel, whose "objectifying of the 'one, yet many' of national life ... allowed people to imagine the special community that was the nation."[2] For the last thirty years at least, however, film critics have been inclined to see the cinema as the pre-eminent medium for the production and circulation of myths of national identity; a process which is peculiarly marked, it can be argued, in settler societies such as the United States, Australia and New Zealand/Aotearoa. The genres of choice in these three countries for the European film-makers engaged in the process of narrating the nation are the Western and the romance.

In the American case, the period repeatedly returned to for such originary myths is not, as one might imagine, the founding moment of the Republic, the Revolutionary War, but the decades between 1860 and 1890, the period in which 'the West was won'. The Australian film industry focuses on a later three decades, those between 1890 and 1920, during which the 'native type' of the bushman emerges, the Federation is established and settler manhood is proved on the bloody stages of the Great War. In Aotearoa, the equivalent period is emerging as the 1850s and 60s, the first decades of substantial Pakeha settlement and time of the New Zealand Wars.

My discussion of *The Piano* will focus on the film's simultaneous imbrication in, and subversion of, these dominant modes of cinematic settler discourse. Jane Campion's citation of Victorian Gothic fiction by women as her primary inspiration,[3] returns us to the Western, which was a form that developed directly out of nineteenth century romances and adventure stories.[4] The cinematic Western drew on the feminocentric romance, as well as the sketch of Indian or pioneer life and tales of settler hardship on the prairie and in the desert, the Outback or the bush, to produce a genre which celebrated both rugged masculinity and domestic order. At the same time, colonial New Zealand women writers such as Katherine Mansfield and Jane Mander along with Australians like Miles Franklin, used romance forms to contest the emergent mythicisation of the masculine pioneer subject, whether gunslinger, bushman, larrikin or digger. But their fiction was still caught up, however ambivalently, in the settler project they criticised and Campion's film, playing off romance and Western, displays a similar kind of alienation from, and involvement in, the process of textualising colonial settlement.

The Piano's counter-narrative to the dominant representations of settlement as a process involving the imposition of European law, the appropriation of land from its indigenous owners and its subsequent commodification and improvement, along with the establishment of bourgeois domesticity, situates the heroine's accession to agency in a context in which her constitution as a desiring subject is mediated by a Pakeha-Maori. As Ada becomes ardent – and eventually, happily domesticated in the civil environs of Nelson – Baines, whose moko signifies his in-between status racially, is reclaimed from the indigenous community. Ada's achievement of a 'speaking subjectivity' is enacted through a successful escape from an oppressive patriarchal familial structure in which she is to serve as a maternal subject only, but the film's critique of that maternal role and familial structure begs the question of the relation between settler domesticity and colonisation. The film's final wish-fulfilling retreat from the 'frontier', the back-blocks site of pioneer endeavour, to the gentility of Nelson, concludes a process by which Baines is transformed into the sentimental hero of female desire, while Stewart is left alone in the bush. Thus, arguably, *The Piano*'s feminocentric narrative seeks to recentre its female protagonist by writing her out of history into romance; to absolve her from settler guilt by linking her through an erotic metonymy to Maori, and to focus colonial culpability on the male pioneer's sexual and territorial possessiveness.

WHY THE WESTERN?

Commentators on the Western have consistently noted its foundational role in the construction of American national myth and identity.[5] Its theme is colonial settlement and the genre forms and celebrates a specifically masculine and imperial subject, focusing, as Andrew Ross suggests, upon a period of territorial aggrandisement to justify genocide and wild misogyny through the codes of "manifest destiny", "lawlessness" and "maverick male autonomy."[6] Less frequently remarked is the fact that the earliest successful 'story films' and the most technically innovative, in American cinema, were Westerns.[7] After Edward Porter's groundbreaking work, the Western flourished as the most popular of all the incipient genres, among which films taking as their subject the 'new woman' and America's minority groups were also prominent.[8] The next most significant breakthrough in cinematic technique, after Porter's introduction of editing, was provided by D.W. Griffith's *The Birth of a Nation* (1915).[9]

The Birth of a Nation, initially titled *The Clansmen* was not only technically revolutionary but deeply racist, figuring the Ku Klux Klan as the saviours not just of the South but the American nation as a whole.[10] The film's release prompted widespread protests, including riots, and the country became for the first time aware of the "social import of moving pictures."[11] It seems a curious, if predictable aporia in film theory and criticism, that while the oppressive sexual implications of the classic Hollywood style have been meticulously analysed, the imbrication of racism in the first great example of this cinematic practice is unremarked except as a thematic. But as Merata Mita has commented in regard to early film-making in Aotearoa/New Zealand: "It is clear that as early as 1930, the screen was already colonised and had itself become a powerful colonising influence, as Western perspectives and stereotypes were imposed on indigenous people."[12]

The Birth of a Nation was not itself a Western, but it haunted the genre ever after. This was partly owing to its provision of a range of new techniques and topoi and partly its success in fixing the Reconstruction – which figures in this imaginary history as an alibi for expansion Westwards – as the imaginary origin for the twentieth century American nation.[13] Both the success of, and the resistance to, the film's vision of recent history are also important indices of the role cinema would play in the national imaginary of other settler states. Movies became, as Graeme Turner puts it in a discussion of Australian film and identity, the quintessential twentieth-century story-teller, by providing 'the model through which we articulate the world'.[14] And certainly, Griffiths' influence is no more striking than in the work of Rudall Hayward, New Zealand's first expositor of the pioneer myth in *Rewi's Last Stand* (1925), *The Last Stand* (1940), and *The Te Kooti Trail* (1927), films which not only incorporated Griffiths' techniques and themes but established the 1860s as the period in which 'New Zealand' emerged.

THE BIG COUNTRY

In the renascent Australian film industry of the seventies and eighties, the Federation period emerges as a favoured scene of nationalist narration.[15] *Picnic at Hanging Rock* (1975), *My Brilliant Career* (1978), *Breaker Morant* (1980) and *Gallipoli* (1980) are all set in the period beginning in the 1890s and ending after World War One. While none of these films can be described as a straight Western, they share certain concerns and topoi with the form: not least their combined production of an imaginary national origin and identity.[16] In the case of *Gallipoli* and *Breaker Morant*, the films' staging of anti-colonial insurgency sets specifically Australian masculine types – bushmen, hard-cases and larrikins – against brutal but effete Englishmen, in military conflicts in distant climes which nonetheless provide occasions for the display of mateship and improvisational valour. For white – or perhaps, more specifically, Anglo-Celt Australians – these imperial scenes of battle are their own West. Disavowing implication in the process of colonisation, white Australian nation-building is coded not in terms of the territorial expropriation of Aboriginal land or genocide, but as the struggle of rugged 'Ocker' individualists against the imperial British. In these films, the Outback and the bush have already been appropriated, and stand as guarantors of uniquely Australian male identities which can be heroically mobilised against an antagonist whose imperial oppressiveness is specifically metropolitan.

Ironically perhaps, two romances which provide female counterparts to these masculine myths set in the same Federation period figure the Outback much more overtly. *My Brilliant Career*, based on Miles Franklin's feminist revision of the masculinist myth of the bush most famously associated with Henry Lawson, acts as an interesting counter-point to *The Piano* by reversing the relations of romance and 'the real'; unlike Ada, who travels to the bush and back again, Sybylla Melvyn is transported from the backbreaking labour of a marginal farm to a pastoral idyll but chooses to return to the 'frontier'. This refusal of the role of romance heroine, often read as an allegorisation of the process by which pioneer life opened up new possibilities for female agency, maturity and autonomy seems truer to the inevitability of entrapment within an ideology of domestic responsibility in settler families for whom women's labour was vital. As Pauline Kael has acidly remarked, the heroine's motivation for refusing her lover seems, psychologically speaking, inexplicable: only a knowledge of the novel's suggestion of her lesbianism can make supplementary sense of her actions.[17] In Peter Weir's *Picnic at Hanging Rock* there is no such attempt at a feminist revision of either the original fictional romance or the myth of the bush; the film plays out a logic of isomorphic identification of the female body and the Australian landscape (although it should be noted that some commentators see 'the rocks' as phallic).[18] For one recent commentator, the film stages a confrontation between Man and Environment, in which the specifically English values of the girls' college are tested against the power of an alien continent, and fail. This is a kind of castrated Western, for while it is common in the genre to see the effeminate values of genteel refinement defeated by the harsh Nature of the frontier, it is precisely the rugged masculine qualities of cowboys and bushmen which usually supplement such weakness. It is tempting to speculate that *Picnic at Hanging Rock*'s failures of human agency are in fact symbolic of specifically European difficulties not just in coming to terms with the Australian landscape but with its indigenous peoples. The invisible agency of the rocks, their silent and inexplicable 'motiveless malignity', figures perhaps the unconscious settler guilt and anxiety in relation to Aboriginal peoples, whose representation, *The Chant of Jimmy Blacksmith* aside, is marginal in the Australian national cinema.[19]

AOTEAROA/NEW ZEALAND

The trio of New Zealand films that serve as a kind of uneasy counterpart to the Australian movies discussed above are *Pictures* (1983), *Utu* (1983) and *The Piano* (1993). All three are set in 'the dying days of the Anglo-Maori Wars',[20] as is also, perhaps, *Desperate Remedies* (1993) and all thematise, with varying degrees of directness, the process of colonisation. David Blythe, whose recent study is organised around the representation of Maori in local film, has argued that since the early eighties and the definitive dissolution of a New Zealand nationalism based on racial 'integration', cinema practice in Aotearoa has been marked by irony, parody, pastiche and allegory, all quintessentially post-modern modes whose use for Blythe figures Pakeha dis-ease with the ideological freight of conventional genres.[21] It is certainly suggestive that the first released of the historical films, *Pictures* – however ambiguous one might judge its success as a critique – takes as its subject, quite specifically, the photographic representation of Maori towards the end of the New Zealand Wars. Jane Campion has said that seeing nineteenth century photographs of Maori in the Turnbull Library provided the initial inspiration for *The Piano*.[22]

Thus, while the use of the Western and the romance should, I think, seem over-determined, well-nigh inevitable in the context of Pakeha representations of the early and apparently decisive stages of colonial conflict and settlement, Blythe's emphasis on the pervasive irony of recent settler film practice helps explain these movies' frequently irreverent reworkings of generic codes.[23] Nicholas Reid's complaint that *Utu*'s "dramatic intensity" is seriously damaged by "the film's mimicry of Westerns"[24] misses the point; Westerns are precisely what Westerners – or here Pakeha – have to represent such processes and no amount of nostalgia for a realist aesthetic will generate full, accurate and impartial narratives of our histories. *Utu*'s modification of Western conventions provides, in fact, the measure of its cultural specificity as well as the means by which audiences both in Aotearoa and abroad can identify parallels with colonial conflicts elsewhere.

Perhaps the most obvious revision of the form is suggested by the film's title. *Utu* means the settlement of a wrong or payback and its use as the title establishes a Maori category as the primary frame for understanding the action which follows. But Te Wheke's invocation of *MacBeth* as another heuristic device for making sense of his actions, complicates an interpretation which tries to reduce the theme to revenge. *MacBeth* is not a revenge tragedy, strictly speaking, but a tragedy of usurpation and wrongful ambition. Viewing the action of *Utu* in the latter terms indicts the Pakeha who have wrongfully assumed sovereignty in Aotearoa and caused dreadful individual hurt to Maori. *Utu* shifts the focus to the kind of familial losses experienced in the Shakespearian text by MacDuff and in the film, by Te Whetu. The kind of sheer, untrammelled lust for power embodied by MacBeth himself in the play is represented in the film as the destructive lust for domination which is shown to characterise Pakeha culture as a whole. The analogy Te Wheke draws thus appropriates and revises one of the great texts of the Pakeha tradition, (an act of utu in itself) as well as making a joking and subversive allusion to the late nineteenth century predilection for drawing analogies between Maori and Highlanders.

Utu rings a remarkable number of changes on the Western. Although, as Reid points out, the film's prologue, which reveals the massacre of Te Wheke's family by Pakeha, recalls 'pro-Indian' films of the seventies, the film's characterisation and structure, as well as its tonal shifts are highly original." There is, for example, no single protagonist; the closest is Te Wheke himself, but Lieutenant Scott, the settler Williamson and, eventually, Wiremu Te Wheke are all also of central importance. As the title suggests, in fact, the film is concerned with the processes of human conflict as much as particular agents; processes which can be understood in terms of utu and of tragedy, but also as historical developments involving colonial ambition and indigenous resistance. It is notable, however, that the characters who have the widest range of cultural referents – and the

broadest, as well as the only specifically *political* understanding of events, are
the two Te Whekes. The Pakeha characters are governed solely by personal
motivation, whether love or ambition, with the only possibility for Scott's
awakening to a broader set of values appearing to stem from his New Zealand
birth. However, *Utu*'s scapegoating of Colonel Elliot as the arrogant, ignorant,
self-indulgent imperial who sets the 'colonials' off to some advantage, recalls
the Australian use of a similar displacement of settler guilt in *Gallipoli* and *Breaker
Morant* and the love affair between a Maori woman, Kura and Scott, which serves
to humanise the latter is conducted ultimately at the expense of Kura's life. With
the significant exception of Matu, in fact, and their considerable verve notwithstanding, both the main Maori and Pakeha female characters in *Utu* serve
primarily to give substance to the confused or crazed Pakeha men. The film's
originality is not particularly legible in its treatment of gender.

But *Utu*'s complex local modification of Western codes in the service of national
myth is strikingly apparent in the trial scene, with which in contrast to the usual
shootout, the film concludes.[25] The establishment of law is a primary theme of
the Western and *Utu* is centrally concerned with interrogating British justice in
its local operations, as a system and as an instrument and justification of colonial
domination. The final scene, in which Scott attempts to try Te Wheke in a military
court, suggests that the alternative Maori code of utu provided the main means
by which characters both Maori and Pakeha in New Zealand sought to redress
wrongs in this period. In an extraordinary speech, however, Wiremu Te Wheke,
who has served as an often reviled member of the colonial militia, but reveals
himself at this point to be Te Wheke's brother, deconstructs and relegitimates
the court and assumes the judicial function of which Scott, motivated by personal
revenge and without mana in the place, is manifestly unworthy. Citing his
membership of the militia and his mana as tangata whenua as the grounds of
his authority, questioning the sovereign power (of 'a fat German lady in a distant
land') by which the colonial court assumes its legitimacy, Wiremu Te Wheke
reconstitutes the court along bicultural lines and himself administers justice.[26]
It is tempting to read in this conclusion – particularly in the version of the film
released abroad that was actually structured around the final trial scene – an
allegory of the way the contemporaneous Maori 'Renaissance', a many-faceted
movement of political, social and cultural regeneration and self-assertion, was
contesting the legitimacy of Pakeha sovereignty, and bringing forth what has
become known as a Treaty discourse. Flowing from this process, Aotearoa has
seen policies of bi-culturalism which see the relationship of Maori and Pakeha
as partnership, as well as the establishment of a new institution for the adjudi-
cation of Maori grievances in the form of the Waitangi Tribunal. The Tribunal,

like Wiremu Te Wheke, belongs to two worlds, Maori and Pakeha; and the film certainly implies that justice or utu can only be established by a judicial process (or individual) that is also bicultural.

HERSTORY

There is a piano in *Utu* but like Williamson's wife, it gets short shrift. Emily retreats from the imminent threat of Te Wheke's attack to tinkle the ivories in her upstairs parlour before being persuaded by her husband to help him secure the house. After a spirited defence in which she dies, the homestead is looted by Te Wheke's warriors and the piano, after a second, cacophonous parody of performance, is toppled ignominiously from the second storey. Emily and her instrument, coded as the metonymic embodiments of a metropolitan polish that proves surprisingly robust, both lie broken in the Taranaki earth.

The Piano takes the conventional identification of settler femininity with polite cultural production figured by Emily's musicianship and exorbitates the self-expressive and defiant possibilities offered by this classic trope of female refinement. Where *Utu's* narrative marginalises the female characters, establishing Emily's cultural value primarily in order to motivate Williamson when she is killed, Campion's film uses Ada's attachment to the piano as the central organising device for action and characterisation. This feminocentric revaluation of a Western trope is typical of the film's reinscription of Western codes and topoi in terms of a female counter-narrative which in generic terms, refigures the process of settlement in terms of romance.

The Piano's structure depends on but substantially reworks the classic Western pattern of action, whereby a stranger arrives in a settlement, provoking or becoming embroiled in social disruption before order is re-established. Although recent feminist Westerns – such as *The Ballad of Little Jo* – pick up on a late nineteenth century tradition of Amazonian heroines, a female protagonist is unusual and Ada is certainly no woman warrior miming the codes of masculine conduct. Her disruption of Stewart's pioneer project turns on her refusal of the proper role of settler wife and mother (exemplified in the film by Aunt Morag and Nessie) and her ability to transcode the narcissistic pleasure she identifies with her musicianship, into erotic love.

Ada's refusal to serve as Stewart's sexual and domestic partner, her continued close attachment to her daughter and the piano and finally her involvement with Baines, all disrupt the structure of masculine exchange on which the Pakeha world of the film, from Scotland to the West Coast of the South Island, is predicated. It is, of course, the liminality of the frontier context which allows

Ada's resistance – figured in Scotland in the passive form of silence – to become active and turn her into a speaking subject. In her relation with Baines, a Pakeha-Maori and thus a figure already implicated in improper inter-racial commerce, Ada begins an adulterous traffic with her one asset – her body – only to have her male 'partner' refuse to continue in a structure of exchange: wanting instead, it seems, to rewrite the sexual contract along equitable and unexploitive lines. Liberated sexually and emotionally by this relationship, Ada is able finally to remove herself from oppressive male power and begin a new affective, passionate and expressive existence. To this extent, the film is in the tradition of settler feminism, which saw new possibilities for women in 'new lands'.

But *The Piano*'s feminism is an ambiguous affair, clearly unconcerned with the production of a public role for women. In obvious contrast to *Utu*, which focuses on the way in which masculine identities both Maori and Pakeha are constructed around public, political and historical issues of law, justice, sovereignty, utu and mana, *The Piano* quite deliberately addresses the private sphere of sexuality. The Law which is contested here is the law of the father, and colonial society, which desperately required the participation of Pakeha women to render settlement viable, exists as a marginal and sketchy frame for an action which invokes the mythic in a register of melodramatic romance.

The mythic dimension of the text is most evident in Campion's invocation of the Ovidian legend of Philomel, whose tongue was cut out to prevent her complaining of her rape. A feminist reading of Philomel might see that double castration as symptomatic of the way male violence re-enforces women's powerlessness as erotic and sexual subjects. *The Piano* goes further however, suggesting that the deliberate adoption of silence might be a subversive strategy in a discursive universe dominated by men; certainly Ada's mutism keeps Stewart at a greater distance. And the other instances of European female speech in the film are not alluring; the most discursively aggressive is Aunt Morag, a New Zealand version of 'God's police'. A woman who has internalised the values of the dominant masculine settler order, Morag speaks entirely from within and in support of that culture, suggesting that pioneer women at their strongest can only be mimes of men.

But the film goes further than suggesting silence can be subversive. The two acts of masculine violence enacted against Ada – Baines' suborning of her body and Stewart's axing of her finger – serve paradoxically as the means by which she takes up a full subject position. In the relation with Baines she functions as an agent in the exchange, trading in her own commodity, and eventually the exchange is transmuted into erotic and affective partnership. The loss of her finger is the mark of her loss of self-sufficiency, of the narcissistic pleasure in self-expression associated with her piano-playing and its replacement by an erotic other-directed investment. Campion's treatment of sacrifice here suggests that as is the case for men, women's experience of castration may be understood as social process rather than biological fact. The anthropological *idee recue* that the entry to sociality is universally predicated on sacrifice is here recapitulated to provide Ada with an access to a subjectivity that is not the fragmentary or psychotic feminine identity her sexual difference prescribed in Europe. The connection between sacrifice and subjectivity is accepted here as necessary but mutable. The colonial setting is crucial to this fantasy because it provides a context which for the European characters appears pre-social; in a new world, Ada is able to fall into sociality in a new way.[27]

Baines' tattoo is another suggestive index of the connection between European fantasies of re-invention and the supposedly primal space of the colony. For Aunt Morag, Baines, like Ada, is an irritatingly weak link in the fragile carapace of settler society, a good marital prospect lost to the community through his predilection for the company of the natives. Baines' status as a Pakeha-Maori also looks suspicious to contemporary New Zealand viewers, to whom the idea that the repressed sexuality of the European heroine is best released by a figure associated with the purportedly uninhibited Maori, seems like an ill-considered recycling of a very familiar racist trope. In terms of Campion's exploration of sacrifice, however, the inscription of Baines' face can be read as proclaiming a desire for self-refashioning through a painful entry into another social order. (One of the key markers of Te Wheke's turn from the British is his assumption of a tattoo). The problem is, of course, that just as Ada is not living in a pre-social, mythic space but a thoroughly inhabited and encultured one, construed as primal only through a refusal to recognise Maori society, Baines' attempt to refashion his identity depends on an act of appropriation. However understandable his alienation from the settler society presented in the film, his relation to Maori seems in the end parasitic, as he abandons his hybrid identity and re-enters a fully Pakeha world.

If *The Piano* exploits the relative social fluidity of its colonial setting in order to explore the subject-constitution of European women in a way that seems at best clumsy in its representation of the relation between the imperial female subject and the colonised, it is by no means, as Gayatri Chakravorty Spivak points out, the first feminist text to display such difficulties.[28] The end of the movie sees Ada and Baines removed from the bush, from the site of settlement in its raw and most overtly pioneering form, to the genteel town of Nelson. Part of what seems unsatisfactory about this conclusion is its apparently unironic relation to the codes of romance which provide one of the most powerful conventional symbolisations of the feminine; it seems curious that Ada's resistance, first figured by her initial excoriation of the idea that she get back on the boat and sail on to the town, should be rewarded by her establishment in white picket contentment. The effect, however, is to confirm Stewart, marginalised and indeed castrated by the amatory narrative, as the pioneer subject of history whose continued habitation of the frontier, where masculine and Pakeha identity both are continually challenged, keeps open the possibility of change. For while Stewart figures for much of the film as a compendium of conventionally deplorable colonial attitudes, he too exhibits a remarkable capacity for self-fashioning. Whitford suggests that the symbolic castration men have yet to effect consists in cutting the umbilical cord which links them to the mother, as a result of their being finally able to distinguish between the mother and the woman.[29] Stewart's release of Ada can, perhaps, be understood as just such a gesture of renunciation.

The Piano's action is framed by a prologue and epilogue voiced by Ada. The use of a female voice-over is highly unusual in a medium in which, as Kaja Silverman and others have argued, women function within the soundtrack in a manner comparable to their appearance on screen, as mirrors which help secure a rather shaky masculinity.[30] The determined feminocentricity signalled by these gestures does shape and inform the film as a whole and is doubtless an important factor in its limited success as a myth of national identity, when one considers the continuing importance of masculinist discourses in such constructions. It is not just a matter of predictable resistance to a Western which turns into a romance, however, or antagonism to a feminine attempt to reconstrue our historical imaginary through audacious mimicry which is responsible for the ambivalence with which the film is regarded in Aotearoa. Gender is not available as an alibi for participation in colonial history.

NOTES

1. Brennan, Timothy, "The national longing for form", *Nation and Narration* (Ed.) Homi K. Bhabha, Routledge: London and New York, 1990. pp44-70.

2. Ibid. Brennan; '90. p49.

3. Campion, Jane, Interview in *Cinema Papers* No.93, May 1993. pp6-7.

4. See Kitses, Jim, *Horizons West: Anthony Mann, Budd Boetticher, Sam Peckinpah: Studies of Authorship within the Western*, London: Thames and Hudson, 1969. p14.

5. Ibid. Kitses; '69, p12: "What we are dealing with here...is no less than a national world-view: underlying the whole complex is the grave problem of identity which has special meaning for Americans."

6. Ross, Andrew, "Cowboys, Cadillacs and Cosmonauts: Families, Film Genres, and Technocultures",

Engendering Men: The Question of Male Feminist Criticism, (Ed.) Joseph A. Boone & Michael Cadden New York and London: Routledge:,1990. p88.

7.   Jacobs, Lewis, *The Rise of the American Film: A Critical History*, New York: Teachers College Press: Columbia University, reprinted 1978. p42.

8.   Ibid. Jacobs; '78. pp72-73.

9.   Ibid. Jacobs; '78. pp178-79.

10. Ibid. Jacobs; '78. p177.

11. Ibid. Jacobs; '78. p178.

12. Mita, Merata, "The Soul and the Image", *Film in Aotearoa New Zealand*, (Ed.) Jonathan Dennis & Jan Bieringa, Victoria University Press: Wellington, 1992. p42.

13. See Tuska, Jon, *The Filming of the West*, New York: Doubleday & Co, 1976. p47.

14. Turner, Graeme, *National Fictions: Literature, Film and the Construction of Australian Narrative*, Sydney: Allen & Unwin, 1986. p9.

15. See McFarlane, Brian, *Australian Cinema*, New York: Columbia University Press, 1988, for a discussion of the reasons for the cinematic preference for this period in historical film-making.

16. Brian McFarlane, Brian & Meyer, Geoff, *New Australian Cinema: Sources and Parallels in American and British Films,* Cambridge: Cambridge University Press, 1992: the authors argue, rather more generally, that it is the unmatched power of the classical Hollywood style in presenting melodramatic narrative which has led to its adoption within other national film industries.

17. Pauline Kael interviewed in Peter Hamilton & Sue Mathews, *American Dreams: Australian Movies* Currency Press: Sydney, 1986. p26. Kael also comments suggestively on the parallels between Australia and the USA: 'What we see here is a culture that in some ways is plagued by problems similar to our own, although you have your Aboriginals so tucked away in some films that they're not very visible. In some films, they're not visible at all. You also have a huge, rough country that was settled by people who are not exactly nobility. The people who went to Australia were very much like the people who went to the U.S. We are people who are outcasts, exiles or bums, people with the excitement of going to a new place'. (p26).

18. Op. cit. McFarlane; '88. pp72-3.

19. This is a fact generally noted but not really explained in Australian film history and criticism. For example, see Ibid. McFarlane, '88. pp69-70.

20. Reid, Nicholas, *A Decade of New Zealand Film: Sleeping Dogs to Came A Hot Friday,* Dunedin: John McIndoe, 1986. p79.

21. Blythe, David, *Naming the Other: Images of the Maori in New Zealand Film and Television,* New Jersey & London: The Scarecrow Press/Methuen, 1994. p231.

22. Op. cit. Campion; '93. p6.

23. It's also important to note here the active participation of Maori actors and advisers in a range of recent films, including *Utu*, participation which must have modified Pakeha directorial practice.

24. Op. cit. Reid; '86. p86.

25. Nicholas Reid points out that the version of *Utu* released internationally structured the film as a series of flash-backs centring on Te Wheke's eventual 'trial' (Ibid. Reid; '86. p83). My own comments are based on viewing of the version released in New Zealand.

26. 'Mana' is often translated as 'prestige'; it also implies power and authority. The 'tangata whenua'

are the people of the land, the first inhabitants and the term is used to distinguish Maori from other, later arrivals in Aotearoa/New Zealand. Tangata whenua derive authority from their status as such.

27.   See also Kristeva, Julia, *Strangers to Ourselves*, Harvester Wheatsheaf: London and N.Y., 1991, in which Kristeva argues for the necessity of replacing socially imposed and oppressive forms of sacrifice (such as castration) with highly specific modes which would allow individuation and socialisation to occur without producing the violence in individual subjects and collectivities currently observable.

28.   See Spivak, Gayatri Chakravorty, "Three Women's Texts and a Critique of Imperialism" in *"Race", Writing and Difference*, (Ed.) Henry Louis Gates Jr., Chicago: University of Chicago Press, 1985. pp262-280.

29.   See Whitford, Margaret, "Rereading Irigaray" in *Between Psychoanalysis and Feminism*, (Ed.) Teresa Brennan, London and New York: Routledge, 1989. pp106-126.

30.   See Lawrence, Amy, *Echo and Narcissus: Women's Voices in Classical Hollywood Cinema*, Berkeley, Los Angeles and Oxford: University of California Press, 1991.

4

DIARY

CHAPTER 11

CUTTING IT FINE

NOTES ON THE PIANO IN THE EDITING ROOM

CLAIRE CORBETT

PRELUDE: AUTUMN 1992

Veronika rang me at work today and offered me the job of second assistant editor on The Piano. The wages are low but every assistant editor in the world wants this job. I'm elated but anxious. I can't consciously remember all the skills I need. The knowledge is in my hands. As soon as I touch the machines I will know what to do.

My father was a television director and though I didn't grow up with him, I spent some time around his film crews. I especially liked being with crews when they were shooting on location. There we were part of a self-contained world that operated by its own rules, irresistible for a child. In this sealed but transparent world of the location, control and chaos battled constantly for the upper hand. The film production itself introduced dangerous elements (most memorably, a mountain lion) and then attempted to control the results.

Although I had worked as an extra, my first leap into film crew work took place in my second year of university, when I was hired as an assistant film editor on Jane Campion's first feature, *Sweetie*. My film apprenticeship took place in that cutting room. This (mostly) calm, intimate world was very different to the controlled anarchy of the location set. The period that followed was one of the best in my life. Most people on the film were new to features, including Jane and her editor, Veronika, and incredibly excited about working on this film. Jane and Veronika and Jane Cole, the first assistant editor, were the sweetest, funniest and wisest teachers, each in her own way, that anyone could have had. One night I stayed back synchronising film rushes alone until one or two in the morning, crying with frustration as I pitted my newly acquired synchronising skills against the unslated rushes. When I came into the cutting room the next morning, a bouquet of white roses was sitting on my bench from the director.

As the cut entered its final phase, we lived fourteen-hour days in the cutting room. We ate all our meals there. We had no other life. At one point we worked fourteen days straight. Once I lay on the floor, feeling a motor, an engine of will, grind to a halt inside me. I wasn't sure how I would get up again. On the fourteenth day, when we were almost delirious, our producer, John Maynard, came in and cut up a banquet of fresh melons and berries for us.

The director gave Jane Cole and I sequences of her film to cut under her direction. This was exciting and nerve-wracking but we knew Jane wouldn't let us go wrong. Jane set me the task of writing my own versions of the opening voice-over. I have never met a creative person more supportive of the creativity of those she worked with or more pleased by the talents of those around her. It is one of the best qualities a film director can have but that doesn't mean it is common.

WINTER 1992: THE FINE CUT – MONTH ONE

I began work on *The Piano* in the first month of the fine cut in Sydney after the film and crew returned from the shoot in New Zealand. At that stage the film was still called *The Piano Lesson*.

In the Roxy, Film Australia's screening theatre carpeted in vivid purple, we saw a film today that will never be seen again by anyone. It was my first viewing of the two and a half hour rough-cut of *The Piano Lesson*. It will evolve further as the weeks go by but it is already powerful. At the end of the screening we were emotionally exhausted but happy. It is these screenings that make post-production exciting, that bring the process to life. There is a wonderful intimacy to the cutting room and it is magical to see the film evolve from screening to screening.

The Roxy is *icy*. We asked them to turn up the heat but they don't seem to be able to do anything about it. After nearly three hours in there we felt frozen, especially after watching the final underwater shots. Heidi, the first assistant editor, and I have to leap up at the end and carry the silver cans of film and sound back to her car. There are about thirty of them. Each big film can holds about ten minutes worth of film. Working as an assistant editor is the only time I develop biceps; weight lifting is not nearly as effective. "You girls are so strong" Veronika marvels when she sees the great stacks of cans we carry.

When I come into the cutting room for the first time, I am nervous. I don't belong. I am joining a team already forged under the pressure of the location shoot. Sound editors must have to deal with this feeling on every single picture because they always start so long after the shoot is over. It is the privilege of film editors to start work on the first day of the shoot.

Photographs from the shoot in New Zealand line the walls of the cutting rooms: photos of the actors in costume, of the crew, of Harvey Keitel in a dress. Jane Campion always has a dress day at least once during her shoots; all cast and crew have to wear dresses. The men love it. The most macho change their dresses several times a day. Often the women find it more traumatic. Jane says she feels much closer to her male crew members once she's seen them in a dress.

At the Spectrum cutting rooms there is always a hierarchy of films at any one time, based on the prestige of the project. *The Piano Lesson* is in the happy position of occupying the apex, literally and figuratively. Our rooms are at the top of the building and have dormer windows that open out onto the rooftops. It reminds me of Paris except for the unmistakable winter gold of the Australian sun. Here there is an outer room at the top of the stairs. It is the domain of Heidi and I, the two assistants. We have our benches where we wind and rewind film, usually by hand, as we search for the exact pieces of film that Veronika and Jane want to look at next. A complete breakdown of the film by scene numbers and shot numbers is written on cards and tacked to the wall. Each card identifies the physical reel of film where the scene numbers can be found. This is how we keep track of the film. Here the reels and reels of film rushes are stored in square white pizza boxes on racks. There are over a hundred each of sound and image, the image labelled in blue, the sound in red. We follow this convention rigidly.

While the film is in the editing stage the sound and image are always kept separate. The sound and image are "married" when the film is finished. The release print, the final version of the film released to cinemas, has the soundtrack transferred onto a magnetic stripe on the print itself. It is vital that sound and image be separate during the edit, however, or no creative work with the soundtrack would be possible. For example, sound from a scene is often laid over the beginning of the next scene for a particular effect, to provide a smooth transition or increase a sense of foreboding. The sound editors work with the sound intensively and separately to the image, redoing lines of dialogue, adding sound effects, and so on.

Here in our outer room we all eat together. Heidi and I make coffee, bring in breakfast and make elaborate lunches for the four of us. Film crews are like armies; their state of mind is directly related to the quality of their food. Two more rooms open off the outer room. One is a small office for Jane where she keeps a desk, typewriter, books and ring-binders filled with research and preparation for the film. A list of possible titles for *The Piano Lesson* is stuck to the wall. We are urged to think of others. *The Piano Lesson* is the name of a play and the copyright holders have advised they will sue if the film is released with that title.

The other room is the inner sanctum. This is the cutting room proper, where the two massive Steenbecks whirr and roar as they wind reels of film back and forth on their horizontal metal plates and where the sun is never allowed to shine. The cutting room must be kept dark so that we can see the small image of the film on the Steenbeck screen. Although this is where the *picture* is cut, the world of the cutting room is a world of sound. You can see the images only if you are actually sitting at the Steenbeck but you can hear bits of sound from the film all over the rooms, sometimes all over the building. Sometimes the sound from several different films floats up the stairs to us from other cutting rooms.

Sound is such an emotional medium that I find my feelings suddenly prodded by bursts of music, snatches of dialogue played over and over at high volume, speeded up, slowed down, reversed. Peter Weir has said that there is nothing that can compensate for the emotional cost of making films you don't really care about and the truth of this is very clear in post-production. To be subjected to the sounds and music of a film you disliked for months on end would be a refined form of torture. We are especially lucky on *The Piano*, a film so interwoven with music, to have Michael Nyman's music flowing through the cutting rooms for hours every day. Working to this is grand. There is no other word. The most mundane work becomes uplifting.

Looking at the cutting rooms for *The Piano*, it strikes me that there is hardly a machine or procedure carried out there that would not have been much the same a hundred years ago. Film is a nineteenth century art form. Unlike video, it is a physical and chemical medium, not an electronic one. A film camera is a simple mechanism that works along the same lines as a sewing machine or a machine gun and was invented at about the same time. These machines all work on the principle of grabbing a strip of perforated material (a sewing machine makes its own perforations), advancing it by a fixed length, holding it, grabbing the next frame and so on. The perforations at the top and bottom of film stock are called sprocket holes and they enable the film to be wound back and forth onto a number of different machines.

The technology of the cutting room has therefore traditionally been simple. Film is handled and stored on 1000 to 2000 foot reels, so each machine in the cutting room must accommodate feed reels and take-up reels and be able to wind from one to the other. Handling these reels can be tricky. Film is glossy, slippery stuff, intolerant of moisture or grit. The assistant editor's nightmare is for the plastic core at the heart of a 2000-foot reel of film to slip suddenly out of a loosely wound reel. You are left with a mass of film and no way to unwind it except by hand. This can take hours of time you don't have. Sometimes you just have to cut your way out of the mess.

There are other films in post-production sharing the building with us, however, and the technology they're using seems to be a sign that the traditional method of editing films is coming to an end. Veronika and Heidi and I are all concerned that the changes might be destructive to the craft of editing. It is easy to see, given the constant winding of large reels of film necessary to find particular shots, that film editing is a time-consuming process. The advance of computer technology promises to change that. Shots will be stored on computer and called up instantly by the editing program. The film will be essentially edited on video. The negative cutter will then cut the negative of the original film according to the editor's final cut, as happens now.

Just because a film can be cut in a month, however, instead of three or four, does not mean that it ought to be. Once it is possible to edit a film in radically less time than it now takes, the pressure on editors to do so will become irresistible. This could be disastrous because editing is not just a logical process. There is an alchemical process at work as a film evolves and this alchemy is crucial in the editing room. Ordinary logic cannot cope with the decisions necessary to carve 100,000, 200,000 or even a million feet of film into ninety minutes worth of footage (about 8000 feet of 35mm film). Editors and directors rely on time spent in the cutting room to give them a feel for their film. The often tedious time spend looking at sequences over and over and over again is necessary for directors and editors to make the intuitive leaps that pull form and meaning out of chaos. Editors and directors need time to think. I doubt that four weeks is enough on a feature film.

Heidi and I talk as we work, sorting and filing trim bins full of film and working from lists of shots that Veronika has given us to find for her. We put the film away by running the reels through the gang synchronisers on our editing benches to put the sound and image back in sync. Sometimes we sit with Jane at the second Steenbeck in the inner sanctum and run through reels of film with her while Veronika cuts a sequence she and Jane have already discussed. We pull shots out of the rushes under Jane's direction.

Heidi runs the cutting room from our outer room, booking facilities, ordering supplies. We need a sound-mixing theatre in a few months but another director has booked everything in town for months ahead. He cannot possibly need all the facilities. We are exasperated with his selfishness and lack of professional confidence but though he is just down the hall we say nothing. We know when the time comes that we'll get what we need. We buy white grease pencil to write on the film, white cotton gloves to keep the film free of oil from our hands, squares of cotton velvet and a big bottle of fast-drying liquid Freon (to clean the film before screenings – also good for cleaning clothes) and rolls of splicing tape for our splicers. Editors are particular about the quality of splicing tape they use. Bad tape is hard to peel off and leaves streaks of glue on the film. We wait for shipments of our tape from Japan.

THE FINE CUT – MONTH TWO

One of my favourite times in the cutting room is early in the morning before anyone else comes in. Heidi and I take turns to come early or stay late. Early is 6:30 or 7am, late is anywhere between 7 and 10pm. It's the depth of winter, so the first thing I do every morning is switch on all the heaters. Veronika's Steenbeck is temperamental and needs to be warmed up for almost an hour before use. I turn it on and set all the plates spinning. The machine flashes HELLO in red LED letters. I turn my Prince tape up loud or sometimes the music Michael Nyman has already composed for the film and bop around the cutting rooms as I clean the Steenbecks and get everything else ready for the day's work.

The rooms are filled with flowers. Jan Chapman, our producer, sent a magnificent bouquet of Australian wildflowers and a card after a particularly good screening. The card thanked everyone for their work on "this wild beauty of a film". A gorgeous Maori carving of a woman with shell eyes, holding a boat with another figure at the prow, arrived from the Maori cast and crew this week from New Zealand. It was made for Jane and has now taken up residence in our outer room. It adds a richness and mystery to the room. We fill the boat with flowers and fruit.

The post-production schedule is tacked to the wall in the inner sanctum: there is a screening next week, there are so many weeks until Michael Nyman comes, so many weeks until the sound editors start, so many weeks until the end of the fine cut, so many weeks until the recording of the music, until the final sound mix. Michael Nyman has already booked the orchestra in Munich.

Heidi and I have talked to Benita, who is assistant editing on the TV series *Police Rescue* downstairs. They are using the new computer programs for editing and Benita confirms that there is another problem with the new method of editing, one we had suspected already. It is much more exhausting to work from a computer or video screen than to cut and tape film with your hands. This is because cutting film is a more active task. The body has a chance to move and you are not subject to the emanations from a video screen.

There is a lot of hard physical labour in most phases of film-making; this is part of its archaic charm. The body is very much part of film-making. Even in the fairly sedate world of the cutting room, assistant editors must be strong and have real endurance and it has long been known that one of the major qualities needed by an aspiring film director is the stamina of a horse. Film-making also preserves a few of the last resonances in modern culture of some of the values and attitudes, frustrations and satisfactions of working in a medieval craft guild, in spite of its recent origins. While film technology retains some of the beauty, durability and charm of other nineteenth century technology, the echoes of older ways of working are there. For example, some of the most highly skilled film technicians literally belong to craft guilds. Entry to the American Society of Cinematographers or the British Society of Editors cannot be begged, bought or commanded. It is by invitation from peers only, and only when they feel there is a body of work good enough to merit inclusion. Until recently almost all technicians worked their way up from unskilled positions, relying on their mentors to teach them their trade. These apprenticeships were unofficial but essential for the lore of film-making to be enriched and passed on.

The hierarchy within any given film is rigid and deserves comment. While the director and producer, depending on contractual obligations, have final say on almost every aspect of a film, the rest of the film crew is not lined up on a single ladder of rank. A film consists of a set of hierarchies, each one ruled by a head of department. These heads of departments include the picture editor, the sound editor, the director of photography (DOP), the production designer and the composer. Each head of department has absolute power to hire personnel and run his or her department as he or she sees fit. Rank within a department is not transferable to another department. The DOP has no authority in the cutting room. A production designer, though much more senior, has no power over an assistant editor. Strictly speaking, even the director should not tell assistant editors what to do but in practice, working so closely in the cutting rooms, we oblige each other. Sensitivity to the nuances of the hierarchy is never lost though. If Heidi and I ask Jane if we can go home early she says "I'm not your boss!" and we ask Veronika. Prerogatives of rank are jealously guarded from above and below. A director who so much as touches the camera on set commits a serious breach of propriety. We were even jokingly reluctant to let Jane touch the Steenbecks or loop the film onto their plates.

The most important aspect of film-making, by far, in which it resembles its older cousins in the other arts and crafts is that it is not only *process* but *product*. You are making something. This is why artists are envied by professionals in secure jobs with high salaries. When all is said and done, few jobs in the late twentieth century involve *making* anything. A great deal of lower echelon film work is tedious: difficult, repetitive and painstaking, with much attendant anxiety. What matters though is that no matter how dull the process, it is regularly transformed through screenings into meaning, into sound and images that have the power to enchant no matter how many times you see them. When the work and exhaustion are forgotten, the film remains.

THE FINE CUT – MONTH THREE

I have been offered work as first assistant editor on a documentary after *The Piano* finishes but I have decided, after talking to Jane and Veronika, that *The Piano* will be my last film as an assistant editor. It is the best experience a crew person could have and I want to leave it at that. Assistant editors aren't hired to be creative. We are hired for our skills and to create a pleasant working environment for the editor and director. I also realise I have no desire to climb the crew ladder to become an editor.

Working with Jane should be intimidating; she is so incredibly successful. In fact it is inspiring. I've absorbed a lot from working around her, especially about the kind of creative risks you can, and must, take. I was especially impressed when she decided on the spur of the moment (or so it seemed to us in the cutting room) that she wanted a brief animation in the scene where Flora is describing her fantasy of the death of her father. Jane got Heidi to make a brief scratch animation to put there to give us a feel of how that might work. Scratch animations are the way we distract child visitors to our cutting rooms. We give them some clear film or black film leader and let them draw and scratch pictures on it. When they've done a strip of film long enough we lace it onto the Steenbeck and let them see the results. There is always surprise at how quickly what looks like a long piece of film spools through the machine.

This week is intense, getting ready for the screening. Veronika doesn't think I am careful enough double splicing the work print (putting the tape on both sides of each cut so that the film won't come apart in the projector) for the screening. I am double splicing very quickly because we have so little time but I accept her criticism and slow down. I think it is the first time she has been cross with me since we've worked together. Veronika is rightly concerned about how the work print looks during a screening. Every hair, streak and dustmote is agony to her.

The rest of the week is a horror because of lack of sleep. Both Veronika and I are too wound up to sleep easily and by Friday I am operating on less than seven hours sleep in two days. I fall asleep during the screening. The Roxy is freezing – again. The more important it is that we sleep the more our anxiety prevents us. I have to get up at 5am and am awake at 3am. This can't go on. Jane staggers her hours, comes in later and sometimes spends whole days away from the cutting room when Veronika has enough work to go on with. She is drawn with fatigue. She has been working non-stop for well over a year. Jan Chapman gave us a good bottle of champagne after a screening but we can never find time to drink it.

These final exhausting weeks of the cut are the real test of our characters. These are weeks composed of six or seven ten-to-twelve hour days as Jane and Veronika struggle to use their last chance to make the film perfect and ready to face the world. Whole scenes are taken out. A long sequence where Baines gets some schoolgirls to read Ada's message on the piano key to him is dropped. After the film is released reviewers will quibble over why Ada sent a written message to a man who can't read. This seems utterly irrelevant to us. There is no doubt Baines gets Ada's message just by receiving the piano key.

We have another screening. A scene is put back in. It is modified. Undone. Taken out again. Jan Chapman says "But that is one of my favourite scenes". At some point in this process each one of us loses her sense of humour. Temporarily, of course. It is easy to see that, all other things being equal, film personnel are often hired on the basis of personality, given that there are lots of people in the lower ranks of the industry who have the technical skills needed. The relationships that *must* work in the cutting room are those between the director and editor, between the editor and first assistant and between the first assistant and the second assistant. All other combinations of people can avoid each other if they wish. I don't know whether our intimacy is easier because we are all women but it seems that way.

Jane is grey with exhaustion. Veronika is drawn and even Heidi is suffering intermittent losses of her sense of humour. On Monday Veronika was in a foul mood; it was her eighth straight day of work and now Jane didn't agree with her about the cutting of the underwater scene. Veronika couldn't hide her frustration over the loss of one shot Jane wanted to take out. I could see both points of view. The shot of Holly Hunter underwater, hair and clothes swirling, is stunningly beautiful. It also slows the scene down. Veronika is a disciplined and objective editor, totally supportive of the director's control of the project. She complies but she is unhappy. "I'll get over it," she says.

The cutting room is used to rehearse a few lines of voice-over. Veronika is so stressed by being forced to stop work for a few minutes that she paces in our outer room. The Roxy screenings, icy though they are, are vital. The doctrine of frequent screenings of the cut on the big screen was taught to us by producer John Maynard on *Sweetie*. He knew it was essential to see the film on the cinema screen to judge whether the cut is working. As Veronika explained it to us, the eye physically takes longer to roam over an image on a big screen than it does to look at an image on a Steenbeck or television screen. I think this is why movies are often so disappointing on video. The rhythm of the cut is wrong for the small screen.

Sorting trims of shots cut by the editor and reconstituting them into rolls of synchronised sound and image is a painstaking task and one of our main jobs as assistant editors at this stage in the cut. The trims must be reconstituted so that they are instantly available when needed. It is our job to keep track of and be able to quickly lay our hands on any and every frame of over a hundred rolls of sound and over a hundred rolls of picture, each roll up to 2000 feet long. One of Heidi's most important skills as first assistant editor is to devise a logical system that helps us to do this. Written on the rolls of image and sound in blue for image and red for sound is the following information: the scene number and then the numbers of the shots and the takes that comprise these shots and then any other necessary information, eg. whether it is silent ("mute"), at a different camera speed, shot on more than one camera, or special effects from the lab. Assistant editors also rely heavily on the documentation of each shot provided by the camera assistant, sound recordist and continuity person and keep these in separate binders. A coded description of the action in one shot might read: "HA GS. Camera pans LR end on MCU Jack. JACK xs CL." Translated, this means: "High angle group shot. Camera pans from left to right and finishes on a medium close up of Jack. Jack exits to the camera's left." Actors are always referred to by their character's name.

Our greatest moments of stress occur when it takes us too long to find something, when it seems that a piece of film may have been lost. Of course a copy of the shot could be struck from the film's negative at the lab but we don't have the time to wait for that and besides, *it is our job*. Every film technician wants to appear fast, competent and enthusiastic at all times. It is a freelance industry, after all.

Something that becomes increasingly clear to the editing team as the weeks of the cut spin past is the calibre of the performances in a film. Some actors need all the help the editor can give them. It becomes funny, dreary and then painful to watch them over and over. Sometimes you feel angry with the actors for not being good and putting you through such tedium. Such pain is rewarded, with interest, by the joy of watching inspired actors. Holly Hunter and Anna Paquin are so good I never tire of watching their performances. Sam Neill is so strong as Stewart I can't help wondering whether audiences might hate him.

The magic of the performances gets stronger as the editor and director cut and polish. If I am making it sound as if the editor merely tinkers with the film, setting this and that to rights, then that is the wrong impression. An editor can almost rewrite a film if necessary. Even in a film with a fairly definite plot line it's surprising how many scenes can be rearranged, dropped, added to, or otherwise doctored. Few people understand just how much is possible. There are stories of directors in the Hollywood studio system who shot their films in such a way that the editors had no choice but to cut it in the way the director wanted. This tactic may have worked partly because both director and editor were working within an understood pattern of storytelling in film.

The fine cut of the film is drawing to a close. We all have mixed feelings about this. Jane has been depressed. From now on she loses her real intimacy with the film, from now on other people mostly take over and do what they have to do. The sound editors will do their work, Michael Nyman will compose the rest of the music and it seems as if the film moves beyond her grasp. Last Monday we met Lee Smith, the sound designer, and had a screening for him and the other sound people: the dialogue editors, the FX editors, the ADR editors and Gethin Creagh, the sound mixer. Over three or four hours in the freezing Crystal Palace theatre Veronika mixed the several soundtracks we're already using down onto one soundtrack while Heidi and I relaxed under the gum trees in the sun. We froze in the Roxy during the screening again.

The sound men and women love the film; they've brought a whole new energy to our world, opened us up again, intruded on our insularity. Although they work downstairs and we don't see that much of them, they are up and down the stairs frequently and always have something interesting to tell us. They say that one of the actors mouths a line silently before delivering it. This was confusing at first to the sound editors as they juggled dialogue and worked out where to lay tracks. This is such a subtle habit no audience will ever see it and in all the months of picture editing none of us had noticed it.

THE FINE CUT – MONTH FOUR

Everyone's thoughts are moving ahead. Jan and Jane are thinking about the recording of the music in Munich. The dramatic fall of the British pound means that it would be cheaper to record the music in England but the musicians and facilities are already booked. Artists have come into the cutting room to discuss the main credits and the animation sequence. Jan and Jane discuss putting the film into the Cannes Film Festival. Last minute agonies over the title are thrashed out. Jane has thought of many titles but finally settles on *The Piano*. We thought The Black Keys was a contender for a while but *The Piano* sums it all up.

Our last screenings of the film are exhilarating. The fine cut is more or less complete. There are technical rough points to be smoothed out. The soundtrack is yet to be mixed and half the music is missing. Some dialogue has to be re-recorded. The film itself needs to be colour graded in the striking of the release prints, so that the colour tones within each scene are appropriate and harmonious. Audiences care much less than technicians about technical perfection. In fact, film technicians work mainly for the approval of their peers, not for that of the audience. A sound editor is judged by other sound editors, a cinematographer by other cinematographers.

Though *The Piano* is not finished, it excites us each time we see it. We have a small champagne party on my last day and finally get to drink the bottle that Jan gave us. Jane promises to take the cutting crew out to dinner, just the four of us, and she does. Jane gives each of us gifts, including a still from the film of Flora and Ada on the beach. We sit in Jane's flat before we go out to dinner, leafing through stills from the film. We covet them all.

WINTER – ONE YEAR LATER: PREMIERE SYDNEY SCREENING OF THE PIANO AT GREATER UNION CINEMAS, PITT STREET

This film has nothing to do with the technicians who worked on it anymore. We don't belong at the premiere screening with all the well-known faces. What possible involvement can this famous writer or that celebrity have with this film? None of them could feel as impatient as I do to see the finished version of it. Since the fine cut it's travelled the world and won the Palme d'Or at Cannes. There is not an empty seat in the theatre. This is the most electric screening of any film I've ever seen. All the way through I am as moved, horrified and thrilled as the rest of the audience though I've seen the film many times. Or that's what I thought. Of course, in reality, like that first time at the Roxy, this is a film I've never seen before.

The party afterwards was one of the best I've ever been to because I've never seen adults so giddy with happiness. Gethin Creagh, probably the best sound-mixer in the Southern Hemisphere, was elated. "Come along and watch me mix anytime," he urged and told me that more than any other director he's worked with, Jane knows what she wants. As we left the party that night the image that stayed with me, the image from the film that has always haunted me as the symbol of joy, was the slow-motion snowfall of Flora's white petticoats as she cartwheels in the blue garden. Some people say the film's happy ending lessens its wildness but for me those slow-turning cartwheels arcing through and over the music are the essence of disciplined creative joy – the state we were lucky enough to reach while working on *The Piano*.

CODA – SUMMER 1994

While finishing work on this article I hear that Veronika is among the eight Academy Award nominees for The Piano. She is the first Australian editor to be so honoured.